CHRISTIANITY
AND THE MARKET

CHRISTIANITY AND THE MARKET

Christian Social Thought for Our Times

John Atherton

First published in Great Britain 1992
SPCK
Holy Trinity Church
Marylebone Road
London NW1 4DU

British Library Cataloguing-in-Publication Data
CIP data for this book is available from the British Library

ISBN 0–281–04603–4

Typeset by Falcon Typographic Art Ltd, Fife, Scotland
Printed in Great Britain by
Mackays of Chatham plc, Chatham, Kent

Contents

Acknowledgements

Writing a book of this kind is as much about the author's journey as the subject matter. It certainly represents a personal intellectual voyage, but only through a variety of involvements in the affairs of Church and nation. These stimulated and resourced that pilgrimage, and were in turn helped by it.

My gratitude is therefore to the organizations and individuals who are fellow-travellers on a similar road. Indeed, I cannot envisage how such an enterprise could be entered upon and so much enjoyed without this collaboration. With regard to this project, the organizations and individuals are worth setting out in some detail because of the perspectives they bring to the task.

The supportive organizations include a two-year dialogue between Conservatives and leaders of the Church of England, consummately organized by Michael Alison MP and David Edwards, and resulting in *Christianity and Conservatism* (Hodder & Stoughton 1990); a one-day seminar convened by the Methodist Division of Social Responsibility in 1991 to respond to a fine report on *The Ethics of Wealth Creation* drafted by Owen Nankivell of the Hinksey Centre, Oxford; the management committee and staff of the national Linking-Up Project working with local churches on the economic regeneration of urban priority areas; the Industrial and Economic Affairs Committee of the Church of England – in particular its secretary, Chris Beales, and its residential meeting on social market economies in 1986 (where I first engaged in dialogue with Lord Harris of the Institute of Economic Affairs); the William Temple Foundation and its connections with grassroots European church groups, and particularly for the contact with Ulrich Duchrow; the Faculty of Theology of the University of Manchester and the students on the courses entitled 'Sources of Christian Ethics in Contemporary Perspective' and 'Theology and Contemporary Society.'

It is difficult to single out individuals who have made important contributions to this project, but they include: John Hughes, retired Principal of Ruskin College, Oxford, for his years of friendship and ethical understanding of economics and Labour movement matters; Donald Hay, Fellow of Jesus College, Oxford, for his correspondence on theological method and his splendid book *Economics Today*, partnered by John Pickering, both fine representatives of the evangelical tradition; Jonathan Clark, Fellow of All Souls College, Oxford, for his rewarding suggestions on the reinterpretation of late eighteenth- and early nineteenth-century history; Alan Waterman, Professor of Economics in the University of Manitoba, for sight of his manuscript on *Revolution, Economics and Religion: Christian Political Economy*, 1798–1833; Lords Ralph Harris and Brian Griffiths for their support and contacts, especially on social markets; Duncan Forrester and his Centre for Theology and Public Issues, for providing links with Scottish economists; Peter Sedgwick, Hastings Fellow on Wealth Creation, for his friendship and industrial and civil service contacts in his support group; Kenneth Strachan, a retired priest in Scotland who trained me as a young curate and has continued to ensure that I treat liberation theology with the seriousness it deserves; and finally, to Ronald Preston and David Jenkins for their inimitable conversations and friendship.

Without the active support of the Chapter of Manchester Cathedral, which I serve as Canon Theologian, I would not have been able to take a three-month study-leave to write this book, and without the encouragement of Philip Law, Senior Editor at SPCK, I would not have begun this task three years ago. Finally, I have to thank Mrs Kathleen Petch, secretary to the dean and canons of Manchester Cathedral, for typing this manuscript, and my family for living with chaos for four months.

John Atherton
November 1991

Part One

Challenging Contexts

*No man I think will ever be of much use to his generation
who does not apply himself mainly to the questions which
are occupying those who belong to it* (F.D. Maurice, *The
Kingdom of Christ*, London 1842; dedication to Derwent
Coleridge).

Facing the great questions of today's world with realism and hope
is particularly difficult, not least for Christians. It is difficult
because it is an increasingly complex world. One reason why the
Soviet economy collapsed is because its central planners could not
cope with the 'vast scale and innumerable interdependencies of
the modern industrial economy'.[1] Human bureaucracies cannot
co-ordinate such intricacies with adequate efficiency. It is difficult
because it is an increasingly changing world. Thus we are told
that '50% of all the natural scientists who ever lived are alive
now'[2] – such is the acceleration of technological and scientific
development. It is difficult because we are increasingly aware of
the international nature of our society, and how dependent we are
on those seemingly remote interconnections. Almost every day
we are told what the Stock Exchange movements are in Hong
Kong, Tokyo, New York and London. Sophisticated electronic
communication systems now connect them in seconds, and touch
all our lives. Finally, it is difficult because making sense of
our world increasingly involves understanding economics, which
intrudes into every area of life in every place. Unfortunately, facing
that central determining reality of modern life is an 'economic
illiteracy' affecting all levels of society.[3]

Given its commanding relationship to complexity, change,
the international dimension of life and economics, the market
economy is an appropriate choice for helping us to engage
in this contemporary context. Yet any attempt to develop a
systematic understanding of the encounter cannot afford to
suggest a static capture of such a phenomenon. It has to reflect

I

its interconnections and dynamism. It has to range across systems, nations, disciplines and histories. It is the kind of encounter that affects the style as well as content of an argument. Yet through the flow and counterflow of the argument, the market economy offers a way of understanding this context. It offers one of the greatest challenges to Christianity, just as Christianity in its turn challenges that context by its refusal to be integrated fully into it.

All the principal ingredients of this rich mixture will be introduced in these opening chapters. Chapter 1 will take us straight into actual contemporary and related historical contexts. This should help us to understand the nature and significance of context for Christian thought and practice today. Chapters 2 and 3 take one of these signs, the market economy, and discuss it in detail. The plan of the book is placed deliberately at the end of Chapter 1 as an articulation and reflection on the themes and style of the project introduced in the earlier part of the chapter and developed through the rest of the book.

Notes

1 A. Nove, *The Economics of Feasible Socialism* (Allen & Unwin 1983), p. 33.
2 R.H. Preston, *Religion and the Persistence of Capitalism* (SCM Press 1979), p. 138.
3 P. Donaldson, *Economics of the Real World* (BBC and Penguin 1973), p. 9.

One

A Year of Marvels:
Reading the Signs of the Times

On 16 June 1989 a great national ceremony took place in Heroes' Square in the Hungarian capital of Budapest. To outsiders it was a strange, almost eccentric, event: the public funeral of Imre Nagy, thirty-one years after his death. In 1956 Nagy had led the 'Hungarian revolution', only to see it ruthlessly suppressed by Russian tanks and troops. He was later hung after being lured from the Yugoslavian embassy by a solemn undertaking from Janos Kadar guaranteeing his safety. He had then lain secretly in an unmarked grave in plot 301, in the same way that Lajos Kossuth, leader of the Hungarian revolution of 1848, had also been buried by a regime he abhorred. Now, a generation later, Nagy was to be formally put to rest by the Hungarian people, through the agency of the Committee for Historical Justice. The Communist Party and government remained aloof. Suddenly, in the midst of all the great ceremonies, a survivor of 1956 invited the enormous crowd to join hands and recite the words of Sandor Petofi, the poet of the Hungarian revolution of 1848: 'No more shall we be slaves.'[1]

So the second, and this time successful, revolution in Hungary began, following the Polish one, and was succeeded by those in East Germany, Czechoslovakia and Romania. The year 1989 was truly a year of marvels, an *annus mirabilis*, when regime after regime in Eastern Europe was overthrown by popular uprisings and whole nations seeking the political and economic freedoms of liberal democracy and market economies.

It is instructive to note that at the heart of the Hungarian revolution of 1989 there occurred the vivid recalling of the events of the great upheavals of 1848, 'the springtime of nations',[2] when country after country in Europe rose in revolt against authoritarian regimes. There are, indeed, some remarkable resonances between the two years of marvels which stimulate the flow of understandings and inspirations between them. They combine to contribute

3

to our understanding of the importance of contexts in general, and of our own in particular. For both sets of revolutions occurred after 'forty years of peace and stability',[3] however much it was built on what Lewis Namier, describing the 1848 outbreaks, called 'a consciously counter-revolutionary basis'.[4] Each, too, reflected the emergence of ideas whose time had come, and ideas whose time had gone. They expressed hopes as much as discontents,[5] but, in the case of 1848, the icy forces of suppression killed off the early spring of liberation. Finally, in both, intellectuals played an important part, whether it was F.D. Maurice in the England of 1848, or Vaclav Havel in the Czechoslovakia of 1989. It is not surprising that they could be described as 'moral insurrections' (*une insurrection morale*), using the words of the hapless King Louis Philippe, deposed from the throne of France in 1848.[6] No wonder King Wilhelm of Wurttemberg, another monarch greatly embarrassed by the events of 1848, could excuse himself to the Russian minister Gorchakov with the words, 'I cannot mount on horseback against ideas' (*Je ne puis pas monter à cheval contre les idées*).[7] Truly a springtime of nations and peoples fully realized 150 years later in 1989.

Of course, moving between one period of history to another has its dangers. It can contrive and so suggest the 'relentless unfolding of a grand plan'[8] rather than the random nature of history. Yet despite this warning there is much illumination to be gained for the contemporary task by recalling seemingly equivalent events, particularly when today's actors use such connections as explicit parts of their involvements in society. The importance of 'communities of memory',[9] including powerful traditions, occupies a prominent place in resourcing responses to contemporary contexts, not least for Christians facing up to the market economy.

The year 1848: annus mirabilis – the year Christian socialism was born

If we are asked what is our equivalent of the historical events surrounding the Hungarian demonstrations on 16 June 1989, the arguments are heavily in favour of 10 April 1848. For British Christians it is a date surrounded by matters of seminal importance for their communities of memory. As they seek to engage a changing context dominated by an international market economy, it raises major themes that need to be addressed in this project because they recur in the 1989 context.

The 1840s in Britain were rightly described as 'the hungry forties'. A series of harvest failures and economic crises had depressed even further an already immiserated working class in both urban and rural areas. As a country parson, Charles Kingsley witnessed these conditions at first hand and was converted by them. The experience highlighted the continuing influence of the disturbing social consequences of economic change on the formation of Christian social thinkers, from Gore and Tawney in Britain to Rauschenbusch and Reinhold Niebuhr in the USA. For example, Gore's conversionary encounter occurred when Joseph Arch, Methodist leader of the newly formed agricultural labourers' union, took him round the homes of rural workers in the 1880s; Tawney's was in the first decade of this century through his involvement with textile, mining and pottery workers in Rochdale and Longton; Rauschenbusch's was as a young pastor in the late 1880s ministering on the edge of the notorious Hell's Kitchen in New York; and Reinhold Niebuhr's was as a newly ordained minister towards the end of the First World War in the mushrooming city of Detroit, home of the ruthless Ford Motor Company.

Kingsley's experience was typical of them all. As a result, he wrote his influential polemical novel *Yeast* in 1848, in which he described the plight of the rural poor. His vivid portrait resonates with much of our understanding of Third World poverty today, and is not unfamiliar to those who work with many of the poor in contemporary Britain. He writes of

> the oppression that goes on all the year round; and the want that goes on all the year round; and the filth and the lying . . . and the sickening weight of debt, and the miserable grinding anxiety, from rent day to rent day, and Saturday night to Saturday night, that crushes a man's soul down, and drives away every thought out of his head but how he is to fill his stomach.[10]

Thus there began to emerge an influential social tradition of Christian conscientization through novels and tracts for the times.

5

Out of the misery of the 1840s, the Chartist movement sought to promote a political programme with the intention of introducing reforms, including universal adult suffrage and secret ballots, that we now regard as integral to our understanding of political democracy. On 10 April 1848 a great demonstration set out from Kennington Common in London to present the Chartist petition to Parliament. Violence was anticipated by the authorities, but a downpour of rain dispersed the crowds for them.

On that same evening, three friends – John Ludlow, Charles Kingsley and F.D. Maurice – met in the latter's house in Queen's Square. Their general intention was to respond to the events of the day as symptomatic of a wider social, economic and political disturbance. Their particular concern was to try to persuade the Chartists to reject the way of violence and to recognize the connection between their nobler aspirations and the liberating message of the Christian Church. By 4 a.m. on the following morning they had completed a placard addressed to the 'Workmen of England', signed by a 'Working-Parson'. Through it, they sought to assure the workers that 'almost all men who [have] heads and hearts' know their great wrongs, and to challenge them and society by declaring: 'Who would dare refuse you freedom? For the Almighty God, and Jesus Christ, the poor Man, who died for poor men, will bring it about for you . . .'[11]

Charles Raven, in rather grandiloquent language, described it as 'the first manifesto of the Church of England, her first public act of atonement for a half-century of apostasy, of class-prejudice and political sycophancy', irrespective of its content.[12] With benefit of hindsight, he was more accurate to describe the event as 'epoch-making', in the sense that it can be seen as disclosing major elements in Christian responses to market-dominated contexts, including our own. Thus encounters with the Chartists in 1848 and subsequent meetings with some of their leaders established a link, albeit with some reluctance in Maurice's case, with the struggles for political democracy and civil liberties. Indeed, so stirring were the occasions that contemporaries talked of the Cranbourne Tavern gatherings as infused with 'the apocalyptic feelings of the times'.[13] Sixty years later, another great Christian socialist, the young R.H. Tawney, had a similar experience (expressed in the same eschatological language) at meetings of the Independent Labour Party in Longsight, Manchester. He talked of 'an apocalyptic fervour rejoicing that the axe was laid to the root of the capitalist tree'.[14] Contemporary theologians of hope, led by Jürgen Moltmann, have transformed such insights into a theological system and style. The eschatological and apocalyptic sense continues to be a key ingredient in the Christian response to the signs of the times.

Occupying a more central place in that early Christian social involvement was the recognition of the predominantly economic character of urban-industrial change. Indeed, for F.D. Maurice and so much subsequent Christian criticism of market economies, its central organizing principle of competition was morally unacceptable. The very heart of *laissez-faire* capitalism was rejected as 'a lie';[15] it was regarded as contradicting the divine constitution of life in which people were ordained to live in community with each other, and so with God. The early Christian socialists therefore again began a tradition that continues into the present: of preferring the way of co-operation to that of competition. Their early endeavours helped to inaugurate a number of producer co-operatives, and a central support organization called the Society for Promoting Working Men's Associations. Along with their Working Men's College of 1854, a pioneering organization for adult working-class education (again, a tradition continued in later generations by Tawney and Temple), they developed practical strategies to implement their aim of Christianizing socialism. The other side of the coin, equally important and far more successful, was their aim of socializing Christianity. This 'logical' relationship between Christian beliefs, practice and the form of the Church continues to be an important part of the contemporary Christian agenda – and of this book.

Alongside the involvement in politics and economics, there emerged an incipient but largely undeveloped international dimension in the Christian social response. Through John Ludlow, one of the triumvirate who met at Maurice's house on 10 April, there was created a formative link with the French socialists and co-operators, some of whom were involved in the French Revolution of 1848. They included Saint-Simon, Proudhon, Buchez and Blanc, with the latter's associative workshops in Paris being direct inspirations of the producer co-operatives in London.[16] Maurice himself preached a provocative sermon on 2 December 1848, in which he reflected on the convulsions affecting Europe in that

7

remarkable year: 'Do you really think', he demanded of his startled congregation, 'the invasion of Palestine by Sennacherib was a more wonderful event than the overthrowing of nearly all the greatest powers, civil and ecclesiastical, in Christendom?'[17] A few months later he was continuing to argue for the need to hope that a new society would emerge out of the ruins of the old.[18]

It was this recurring theme of the Christian obligation to address contemporary change that lay behind the growing Christian concern with industrialization and urbanization in general, and with their harmful effects in particular. The latter especially was part of a wider agenda which led to the emergence of the great countermovements to industrial capitalism.

Again, the 1840s played a decisive role in our understanding of these responses. Perhaps no one has described the significance of these productive forces and countermovements more vividly than Frederick Engels in his *The Condition of the Working Class in England*. Written in 1844 (possibly in Chetham's Library – now part of the Chetham's School of Music – adjacent to Manchester Cathedral, presumably unbeknown to the good dean and canons), Engels recounts how he crossed the Pennines into Lancashire, over Blackstone Edge, over which now runs the Pennine Way. Sprawled out before him lay the great conurbation of South East Lancashire, with Manchester at its heart. So proceeding down the Roman road 'we enter upon that classic soil on which English manufacture has achieved its masterwork and from which all labour movements emanate'.[19]

It was that manufacture in which he engaged in Manchester, and that labour movement which, with his friend and colleague Karl Marx, he came to so inspire. Their task was how to dismantle the economic base of industrial capitalism which so oppressed ordinary men and women and their communities, and how to replace it with a more just and humane industrialization. Thus they came together in 1848 to write *The Communist Manifesto*, the final part of the linkage between the events of 1848 and 1989.

In this great tract for the times it is made abundantly clear that communist ends 'can only be attained by the forcible overthrow of all existing social conditions. Let the ruling classes tremble at a Communistic revolution. The proletarians have nothing to lose but their chains. They have a world to win.'[20]

And so it turned out to be, from 1917 in Russia to Eastern

Europe in 1989. Yet the gradual construction from 1848 of what was to be essentially a radical political and economic alternative to industrial capitalism is important to our Christian task today for more than these obvious reasons. For Marx was clear in his condemnation not only of the forces of capitalism, but equally of radical Christian responses to it: 'Christian Socialism is but the holy water with which the priest consecrates the heart-burnings of the aristocrat.'[21] What is interesting for our investigation is that it was Charles Kingsley, writing at the same time as Engels and Marx in 1848, who pre-empted the communists' classic denigration of the Christian misuse of the Bible and religion: 'We have used the Bible as if it was a mere special constables' handbook – an opium-dose for keeping beasts of burden patient while they were being overloaded – a mere book to keep the poor in order . . .'[22] In the same way that Christianity predated much in communist criticism of the Church, there is now every indication that Christianity has outlived communism in Europe. That difference in achievement may be accounted for by the multi-faceted and, despite Christian socialism, essentially accommodationist relationship to market systems, complemented by an increasing and long-standing commitment to political democracy. But that is to take us forward to 1989. Such are the continued interconnections between histories, themes, movements and individuals for those who seek to address the contemporary context through the market economy.

The year 1989: annus mirabilis – *'the year communism in Eastern Europe died'*[23]

Throughout Eastern Europe in 1989 the most astonishing events occurred, signalling the end of one empire's oppression of smaller nations. Dramatic events followed one after another as ordinary people rose up and overthrew well-established dictatorships. They were people's uprisings in which participants grasped 'the historical dimensions of the event',[24] as did F.D. Maurice of those of 1848. It was a year of refolutions in Poland and Hungary, and revolutions in East Germany and Czechoslovakia, with the former guided by 'a strong and essential element of change "from above"', supported by popular pressure 'from below'.[25] The chronology of

9

these changes is worth recounting since it illustrates their dramatic and cumulative impact on world events.

Poland, with a decade of Solidarity campaigning behind it, held its first free elections on 4 June 1989, and began a process that led to the election of the first non-communist Prime Minister within what was, for most people, living memory. Given the chance, the people voted out of office a party and a system that, as one worker bluntly exclaimed, 'had not yet given them toilet paper even after two generations in power'.

June also saw the reburial of Imre Nagy in Budapest.

Most dramatic of all, because it took place in the most hardline communist regime, was the breaching of the notorious Berlin Wall in November 1989; for over a generation it had cruelly divided West and East Germany, and had witnessed the shooting of a refugee in no man's land as recently as February 1989. For the first time, again in almost living memory, East Germans could walk into the West – so astonishing for them and yet in another way a journey as mundane as a bus ride from Hackney to Oxford Circus: 'What could be more normal? And yet, what could be more fantastic?'[26]

The final event occurred in Prague, from 17 November to the end of December, and was the most colourful and personal of all. Led by the playwright Vaclav Havel, who shortly afterwards became the President of Czechoslovakia, it learned much from the economic and political mistakes of the Poles. As a result, demonstrations were timed for out-of-work periods, to preserve continuity of production!

Despite the distinctive character of each revolution, they shared much in common. They all occurred in countries that had suffered for years from increasingly depressed economies. Yet they all required a breakthrough in the political sphere before the economic crises could be addressed. Constitutional change appeared as an essential prerequisite for the development of the civil, political and economic liberties of an open society.[27] The cumulative effect of such apparently routine change was the wholesale transformation of societies. Balint Magyar, a Hungarian sociologist, certainly realized this when he declared: 'Our programme is to change the system, not to reform it.'[28]

The order of change was certainly that. It represented a movement from neo-Stalinist dictatorships to multi-party democracies, and from planned economies to market economies based on private ownership. It was a process of popular protest and elite negotiations, with prisoners becoming prime ministers, and prime ministers becoming prisoners, often within a matter of weeks. The result was the sudden end of the *ancien régime* of Eastern Europe – and it was a change heightened by the massacre of peacefully demonstrating students in Tiananmen Square in China. Writing from the midst of the revolution in Poland, the political commentator Timothy Ash was able to capture the irony of the situation in vivid language:

> It was an uncanny experience to watch, with a group of Polish opposition journalists, on the very afternoon of the election, the television pictures from Peking. Martial law. The tanks. The tear-gas. Corpses carried shoulder-high. We had been here before: in Gdansk, in Warsaw.[29]

Tiananmen Square was the other side of the coin of 1989: a constant reminder of actual alternatives.

So by the end of 1989, in virtually the whole of Eastern Europe, governments had begun to try to govern in the way Western Europe had experienced for generations. Yet that meant engaging in real politics with all their compromises and evasions, the bread and butter of operating liberal democracies and market economies. Ash, observing his Solidarity friends entering into the practice of politics, experienced almost a nostalgia for the

> moral clarities of the martial law period. One might passionately wish Poland to have 'normal politics'. But it was quite another thing to watch your own friends starting to behave like normal politicians. Yet what is the alternative? Came the answer: 'Tiananmen Square'.[30]

The *Methodist Recorder*[31] captured this new mood of sombre realism when it referred to a Hungarian editor's admission that 'it is easier to destroy than to build'. This led commentators like Jürgen Habermas to regard the revolutions, particularly the German one, as exercises in 'Deutschmark (DM) nationalism'. It is that cynicism that has been reiterated by more radical

German Christians like Christa Springe.[32] Yet Ash may well be more perceptive in his judgement that, 'first the DM of course, but not just the DM, also the free press, the rule of law, local self-government, and federal democracy'.[33] Life in West European-type societies is certainly always about DMs, but it is always about more than economics.

Out of these growing self-doubts, certain issues began to emerge; these issues followed each other in a consequential way and related to the 1848 themes of politics, economics, internationalism and church life. The first continues the arguments begun by Marx and Engels in *The Communist Manifesto*, but only in the sense of bringing them to an abrupt end. When discussing 'What is socialism?' with Alexander Dubček, the leader of the abortive Czech uprising in 1968, Havel was clear that it had lost all meaning 'in the Czech linguistic context'[34] over the previous fifteen years. The future would be concerned with plural forms of ownership. Even Dubček's arguments for 'socialism with a human face', for a reformed communism, were rejected as an idea whose time had gone. The way forward was not even to be a form of democratic socialism, but rather a social-market system. This was despite the grave warnings from many Western commentators who emphasized the defects of market systems as well as their advantages, and their variety, stretching from the West German social market to the 'casino capitalism' of Thatcherism and Reaganomics.[35] Communism was rejected because of the scale of its political and economic failures, but in the end (and more damagingly) it was rejected by Havel because of its fundamental moral failures: 'We are all morally sick, because we all got used to saying one thing and thinking another.'[36]

Yet the revolutions of 1989 were not just about the decisive rejection of communism and socialism. They were equally about the decisive movement to liberal democracies and market economies, with the latter in the end being of greater long-term importance.[37] It was this development that presented the sharpest challenge to one hundred and fifty years of history, and to much political and theological opinion – 'and for the left this is perhaps the most important statement: there is no socialist economics, there is only economics. And economics means not a socialist market economy but a social market economy.'[38] Some, like the historian François Furet, regarded all this as 'old hat': 'not a single new idea has come out of Eastern Europe in 1989'.[39] Yet that is to miss the point. The year 1989 was not about new ideas, but about a return to the normality that we in the West foolishly take for granted. It was essentially the 'restatement of the value of what we already have, of old truths and tested models'.[40] The most famous of all Polish poems, Adam Mickiewicz's 'Pan Tadeusz', captures this wisdom:

> Lithuania, my fatherland, thou art like health;
> How much we should value thee, he alone learns,
> Who has lost thee.[41]

The most dramatic effect of 1989 lay in the international field. With the dismantling of the Iron Curtain, the reunification of Europe became a real possibility, following on the heels of Germany's. The implications for our political language are enormous, with the irretrievable decline of the 'Second World' and the 'cold war'. Besides offering real progress towards new collaborations in Europe and beyond, these changes also bring the First and Third Worlds into a much starker and unmediated relationship. Now 'there is only one world left with serious claims to development and hegemony (as Fidel Castro and one or two other relics of the past have discovered to their dismay)'.[42]

Such change has affected the churches, and their more reformist individuals and organizations. The decisive rejection of the communist – socialist alternative left church progressives in Eastern bloc countries and the World Council of Churches in a vulnerable position. Like pastor Edelbert Richter, and the group called Democracy Awakening in the GDR in 1989, they continued to argue that, 'Not only the word socialist but certain social principles of socialism still sound good to us.'[43] Yet the indignant voices from below were uttering a different sound. Church leaders had failed to read the signs of the times. Like so many progressive intellectuals, they had failed to listen to enough people. Like so many political leaders in the USA and Western Europe, they had failed to reject the long-emerging political, economic and moral disasters of Eastern Europe. Even in 1989, Karoly Grosz was still in power in Hungary and had been hailed by Mrs Thatcher only a year previously as a man in her own image.[44]

Only a decade ago, the American and British governments fêted Ceauşescu as a visiting hero. The politics of deceit was a disease affecting Western political conservatives as much as ecclesiastical progressives.

The growing and sometimes reluctant recognition that the changes in Eastern Europe were dominated by the rejection of communism and the advocacy of liberal democracies and market economies leads inexorably to the increasing influence of the European Community (EC) on West European affairs. Indeed, 1989 should be seen as the complement to 1992 and the implementation of the Single European Act, with its four freedoms of movement of goods, services, capital and people. Beyond this, there stretches the even more important likelihood of European monetary and political union.

At the heart of all these historic and monumental changes lies the concern for liberal democracy and the market economy conjoined into various forms of the social market economy. David Edwards, in his book *Christians in a New Europe*, rightly focuses on these developments, acknowledging the central importance for the EC, alongside the free market, of the Social Charter, the Social Fund, and the protection of consumers and the environment. 'Nothing less than a high estimate of human rights (reinforced by electoral considerations) lies behind the aim to make the Community as attractive to workers as it is to enterprising businessmen.'[45] It is these concerns for social justice in the EC, and particularly for the growing ranks of the poor and unemployed, that has generated a Churches' European Network to advocate the rights of the marginalized.[46]

Because these changes are so complementary to developments in Eastern Europe, there is an increasing relationship between them, not simply through agencies like the new Development Bank (to assist the capital reconstruction of Eastern Europe), but also in the wider economic and political field. For what the EC has done for Ireland's prosperity it could surely do for Poland's, and what it has done for Spain's growth to democracy it could do for Romania's. 'There is one thing stronger than armies, an idea whose hour has come.'[47]

In all these ways, the ebb and flow between historical periods like 1848 and 1989–92 are so striking as to confirm even further the dominant features in the contexts within which we operate. They compel us to address the questions that so concern our generation, as F.D. Maurice tried to do with his.

Reading the context: discerning the signs of our times

> Away then with that cowardly language which some of us are apt to indulge in when we speak of one period as more dangerous than another; when we wish we were not born into the age of revolutions. . . . In this time we are to live and wrestle, and in no other. Let us humbly, tremblingly, manfully look to it (F.D. Maurice).[48]

For most contributors to Christian social thought – from Maurice in 1850 to Moltmann in 1990 – their context or situation has been of instrumental importance in the development of their contributions to Church and society. It has been an influence acknowledged across national, denominational and political boundaries. Thus it stretches from the American Roman Catholic conservative Michael Novak to the German Lutheran liberationist Ulrich Duchrow; from the American Methodist and democratic socialist J.P. Wogaman to the British Anglican conservative Brian Griffiths.

Many economists too have accepted the effect of the social and political situation on the formation of economic thought. Thus the great economist J.K. Galbraith observed that 'economic ideas are always and intimately a product of their own time and place'.[49]

It is the convergence of that recognition by theologians and economists that confirms the need to take our context seriously, with particular reference to its economic dimension. That decision has been suggested by the recurring importance of economic affairs for modern living, and its central influence in European and world affairs at the present time.

How we approach this understanding of context, and the particular importance we give to aspects of it, has also always been a matter of changing minds. Of course, we should not be surprised about such changes, for they are related in turn to a changing context. So Galbraith went on to note that although economic ideas are influenced powerfully by their situations, as that context changes so must the economic ideas 'if they are to retain their relevance'.[50] Addressing our context always needs to include taking economic matters seriously, yet how we interpret them must be responsive to the changing context. It is in this spirit that it can be argued that the signs of our times should now include the recognition of the importance for human living of market economies as well as liberal democracies.

Alan Booth, former Director of Christian Aid, moved to a similar conclusion before his death in 1990. In a seminal article[51] he came to terms with the end of Marxism, and then set out three 'normative characteristics' of an enlarged Europe: democracy, the rule of law, and a market economy. In what was a particularly bold conclusion, he began to come to terms with the applications of such rejections and affirmations for the ecumenical circles in which he had played such a prominent part. For he admitted 'the sustained attempt in ecclesiastical circles to play down traditional Western political values in order to make room for other cultures and systems'. For Alan Booth that could no longer be the case for Christians and Churches accepting the formative influence of their context on their thought and practice. The 'liberation theology phase' had to be replaced by a concern for public life which took seriously democracy, law, and market economies. It is a lesson that most church leaders, official bodies and theologians in the West, and the ecumenical movement, have yet to learn.

What, then, does it mean to discern the signs of the times, to read our context as Christians? That was the question I was asked to address with one hundred nuns, arranged in serried ranks, and to do so with reference to the contemporary political economy. It certainly began as a daunting experience, reminding one of Wellington's comment on his troops: 'I don't know what they do to the enemy, but by God they frighten me'! However, it soon developed into a splendid exchange of views on matters of much importance. One such was our understanding of signs of the times, my contribution attaining more clarities than usual because a reasonably sleepless night allowed more time for thought. Coming away from the meeting, I began to interpret signs as great movements of our times, which appear to be of providential importance for human purposes as we discern them in the light of our understanding of life and of God's purposes for the world.

The identification of such great movements therefore depends on the interaction between what we can isolate for discussion purposes as secular and religious understandings. (In reality, they are so interdependent as to make such an isolation the more dangerous the more it is dwelt on.)

The secular identification of disclosure movements emerges first out of the empirical recognition, by a significant proportion of people, disciplines and experiences, of certain movements as major trends in our times. Secondly, it consists of recognitions that represent the well-tried judgement, beloved of Maurice and J.S. Mill, that we are generally right in what we affirm and wrong in what we deny.[52] By these two tests, market economies are more confirmed than rejected as the most effective ways of managing economies in modern societies. The support of most practising economists underwrites this judgement.

The religious identification of key contemporary disclosure movements or trends has, for well over one hundred years, often included the secular evidence and arguments as integral to its Christian judgement. This is what lay behind F.D. Maurice's exhortation in *Politics for the People*, in 1848, that concerned men and women must

> consider the questions which are most occupying our countrymen at the present moment, such as the Extension of the Suffrage; the relation of the Capitalist to the Labourer; what a Government can or cannot do, to find work or pay for the Poor.[53]

Confirming such recognitions and deepening them by a critical conversation is the development of a historical perspective, beginning with, in Maurice's words, 'such history as I could connect with the events which I heard of as passing in our time . . .'[54] It was the function of such perspectives to contribute to 'a satisfactory image of the situation'[55] as an indispensable part of the Christian reading of the signs of the times.

In supportive and critical dialogue with such an image are the Christian understandings of God's purposes for human living. These emerge out of the communities of memory, the Churches, in their relationship with the Scriptures and wider Christian traditions. They are therefore wider than both the restrictive hindrances of narrow doctrinal bases, and the dangers of identifying God's will directly with specific events. The absurdity of the latter (a recurring disease in Christendom) is splendidly illustrated in the Reverend William Jones's *Popular Commotions Considered as Signs of the Approaching End of the World. A Sermon preached in the Metropolitan Church of Canterbury on Sunday, September 20th, 1787*. It was essentially directed against those opposing the divinely constituted authority of the current government!

A more significant example of this direct but questionable application of particular theological views to the details of contemporary life is provided by the *kairos* movement and school of thought. Paul Tillich, the great Americanized German theologian, creatively distinguished between *chronos* or chronological time and religious or *kairos* time, in which the historical movement is seen as bearing the power of the transcendent. Much contemporary religious reading of the signs of the times relates to the latter, and out of it have grown movements seeking to appropriate the present moment as a turning-point from a rejected status quo to a liberated future society.[56]

The danger of reading signs as *kairos*, apparent from its contemporary overuse, is its inbuilt propensity to seek to contain the 'unrefracted yes' of the 'unconditional' in a historical movement or idea.[57] It is the danger of pursuing the religious obligation to be involved in a movement to such an extent that the limitations of any involvement are overridden (the *obligatum religiosum* dominating the *reservatum religiosum*).

A related but opposite danger to such utopianism is the identifying of a secular trend as a sign simply because it is a secular trend. In other words, since it is part of the universe, then, as Carlyle said, 'by God, we had better accept'.[58] This is but a splendidly cruder nineteenth-century way of expressing Bishop E.R. Wickham's contemporary view of providence as leading us to 'look at the scientific and social revolutions of our time in a providential and prophetic way'.[59]

In contrast to all these views, it is suggested that our understanding of God's purposes is instead always a critical dialogue with secular understandings and experiences. It is never identified simply with those signs as providence or as *kairos* theology. The signs are therefore never God's will in any *direct* or *immediate* sense. They can be described more appropriately as 'fitting acts'; that is, they try to fit roughly with what we understand as both God's purposes and secular discernment.[60] So they are purposeful though provisional, related to a particular place and time, and never valid for all times and all places. They are our reading of our signs for our times. So the presence of such a strong element of self-interest, including ideological presuppositions, does not reduce their legitimacy. It rather reinforces their necessary provisional character, their *reservatum religiosum*. It is on this procedural basis that we can begin to argue the case for regarding liberal democracy and the market economy as signs of our times. It is principally with developing the latter case that the rest of this project is concerned.

Making the case: an introduction to the argument

It is normal practice to locate the introduction to a book at the beginning. However, the more I reflected on the emerging argument over market economies and what this could mean for Western Christian social thought, the more I came to see the multi-faceted nature of the case that had to be made. As a result, it seemed to be more consistent with the character of the case to put the introduction in the midst of actual contexts. This could then offer a better understanding of their use in Christian social thought. It would also allow me to express, through contemporary and associated historical events, some of the main themes, contributions and histories that relate to any serious consideration of market economies today. For example, themes like political democracy, capitalist economies, and the international character of modern life all contribute to the formation of the agendas of Christian social thought and the Churches. These relationships have been fostered by key organizations and individuals, some of whom have already been introduced but most of whom will be examined in more detail in later chapters. Running through themes and contributors has been the impact of contextual histories, of importance in their own right, and because of the central significance of 'communities of memory' in the formation of Christian traditions and contemporary church life.

The development of a Christian response to market economies is an indispensable part of the following argument. Although themes, contributors and histories will occupy an important place in building the content of the response, I have become more and more aware over these last few years how the way a judgement is formed connects to the content. I now see that both, in turn, are related to the shape of the Church's response to contemporary affairs.

I have also begun to recognize the function of additional factors in such an argument: namely, a necessary variety of styles and objectives. This conclusion is suggested partly by changes in our context, stimulating debates about post-liberalism and post-modernism. The former argues for the use of narratives and communities of memory in the formation of the Christian case and character. The American theologian Stanley Hauerwas is the best example of this trend. The latter, post-modernism, expresses a deep unease with the rationality associated with the great schemas like capitalism and communism, so influential in the modernization process.

However, the need for a variety of styles and objectives is also suggested by demands intrinsic to the argument about market economies. For example, it does appear to require a polemical engagement with well-established traditions and histories associated with the development of Christian socialism. It requires, too, an evaluative survey approach to the principal Christian responses to market economies.

The form of the argument is also influenced by the expressed purpose of the project. Thus the overall aim is to attempt to construct a more adequate Christian response to market economies because of their long history in Western societies, and their dominating position in today's world. Related to this wider aim are a number of dependent arguments and objectives. These include the contribution of a critical re-evaluation of the Christian social tradition of the mainstream liberal type. The significance of such a venture includes, but moves beyond, a personal agenda. It clearly *is* a personal agenda, though, because I have been a member of that tradition and type for over a generation, and owe so much to it. More important, that tradition and type have been the major influence on official church opinion in most Western societies, and have played an instrumental part in the early development of the ecumenical movement's social witness. It is still the major school of Christian social ethics in the USA and Britain. To challenge such a tradition and type has implications well beyond any personal agenda.

Other objectives include an appraisal of a powerful neo-conservative Christian tradition and of a radical Christian socialism. Both have essential contributions to make to the task of developing Christian social thought in response to the power of the market in the contemporary context. Whether or not that aim and these objectives are achieved, only time and contemporary judgements will tell.

Central to the project is the obvious need to come to terms with economics. (I say 'obvious' perhaps unwisely, because most theologians who have written in this field have not appeared to take economics seriously.) In this respect, over the last few years, I have become aware of how closely linked is the study and practice of modern economics with the reality of market economies. This gradual realization has affected profoundly my appraisal of the dominant Christian responses to market economies, and particularly the more radical Christian socialist type. The latter is notorious for its inability to understand basic economics in relation to market systems.

However, I have also become aware of how vulnerable economics and market economies are to wider issues. The result, I hope, is therefore in no way a justification of the absolute autonomy of economics, but it certainly seeks to respect and learn from the proper and relative autonomy of economics.

The economist Denys Munby was well aware of the dangers (and yet the necessity) of such a transcending of disciplinary divisions:

> Unfortunately, learning, wisdom and prophetic insight afford no guarantee that error will be eliminated, where technical knowledge is lacking. It is a tragedy of the growth of knowledge that people who try to enter on fields outside their own specialism cannot hope to master them all adequately. It is certainly no argument for not trying to make the attempt, because it is only by such attempts that we shall be saved from the follies of our specialisations.[61]

Since the project clearly requires an understanding of economics, it is at this point that the arguments may be at their weakest because I am not an economist, but instead a theologian. Others have tackled a similar task, but as economists who are also Christians. I have a high regard for them and have leant heavily on their wisdom, particularly in the following two foundational chapters on market economies. I hope my obvious limitations in this field will be forgiven, and repaired by others much better equipped to do so.

The difference between the expert Christian economists and myself is even more fundamental. Unlike them, I am clear that the contemporary theological task has to begin with the contemporary context. Invariably, they almost all begin with a theological exposition of a conservative and traditional kind.[62] They certainly all include the statutory theological chapter. Maybe they are attempting to correct Donald Hay's judgement that Christian economists tend to introduce theology as an afterthought to the economic argument.

However, distancing myself from them does not mean that I fall into Hay's trap for theologians writing on economic affairs: of being over-respectful of economics and reluctant to apply substantial theological insights to economics.[63] For beginning with the contemporary context, and pursuing a variety of objectives, themes, histories and contributions, is about a style of theological thought that is essentially a continual interaction between understandings of God's purposes mediated through our experiences of secular reality and through the Christian story and tradition. Explicitly Christian insights are therefore only a part of the whole theological task. I hope that this has become obvious even in this first chapter. It will certainly be explicitly and obviously part of the following chapters.

It will be evident that this venture does not fall into existing well-established camps – whether of types of Christian response to market economies, or of theological disciplines. The responses will be explored in Part Two. The question of theological disciplines is worthy of some attention at this early stage, although it will recur throughout the book, including in the final chapter.

Exploring market economies in the contemporary context is such an extensive and complex matter – crossing disciplines and experiences, and requiring the use of a variety of objectives and styles – that it cannot be contained within any one theological discipline. I have long accepted the inadequacy of dogmatic theology in addressing contemporary social affairs. Essentially speculative and deductive reflections have their place in the Christian programme, but it is strictly confined in relation to the tasks of practical theology. Biblical theology is at least as deficient in this field, as later chapters will confirm. It is not surprising that many have therefore regarded Christian social ethics as the most appropriate theological discipline for addressing modern social issues. However, the present project now suggests its serious limitations. It is not simply the complexity and multi-faceted nature of such a project that challenges modern tendencies to over-compartmentalize academic and professional disciplines (this will be seen to be a major problem of both current economics and theology). The problem is as much to do with modern Christian social ethics itself. For this arose as a moral response to industrialization, and so invariably reflects the propensity of Christians to assert the primacy of values over everything else.[64] In consequence, it makes the development of a properly interactive relationship between explicit Christian and secular understandings unlikely if not impossible. By over-promoting the moral, it ensures an inherent inability to promote ideas that are practically attainable. It makes practical theology impractical. In other words, pervasive realities like market economies demand a much broader and multi-disciplined approach from Christian social thought. Taking the contemporary context seriously makes the divisions of academic theology more and more out of touch with the realities of life. Once again, there is a growing need for new languages to describe new realities – whether for radical social programmes to replace socialism or for a form of Christian social thought to replace Christian social ethics.

The organization of what follows tries to engage these varied and important aims. At first sight, the title *Christianity and the Market* may seem to be singularly inappropriate for such a task. It will seem to some to be too reminiscent of other titles such as C.L. Marson's *God's Co-operative Society* (1930) and M.D. Meeks's *God the Economist* (1989). Following in that genre, why not 'God the Marketeer'? Yet to reduce God to a discipline or form of production is to open oneself to all the deficiencies of interpreting Christ through a dominant contemporary style or culture.[65] Such is to be taken over by the culture; it is not an engagement with it.

Christianity and the Market is not intended to be such a book. It is not an expression of religious belief in the market economy. That would be a nonsense, and would invite a repeat of Henry Scott Holland's attack in 1878 on my publisher, SPCK, for its 'one-sided Political Economy publications – condemning so strongly all trade unions and giving nothing but the master's view'![66] The title is therefore a declaration of intent to examine the relationship between Christian faith and the market economy. The subtitle, 'Christian Social Thought for Our Times', makes that explicit.

The book is divided into three parts. In Part One, an exploration of the nature and significance of the market is located first in a wider context (Chapter 2) and then explored in some detail in its own right (Chapter 3). Three classic types of Christian response to the market are then explored in some detail in Part Two (Chapters 4 to 6). In Part Three, the strengths and limitations of these responses to the market economy in that context form the basis of a reconstruction of a Christian response to the market. That response includes suggestions for the content of Christian comment, the method used, and its implications for the form of the Church (Chapters 7 to 9). The Postscript is a personal reflection on a continuing Christian journey out of socialism and through, and yet beyond, market economies.

Notes

1 T.G. Ash, *We the People: The Revolution of '89* (Granta Books 1990), pp. 50–1. Ash is a Fellow of St Anthony's College, Oxford. I am heavily dependent on his eye-witness account of the great upheavals of 1989. It is one of the most memorable examples of historical–political reporting.

2 Ash, p. 134.

3 Ash, p. 134, quoting A.J.P. Taylor.

4 Ash, p. 134.

5 Ash, p. 134, quoting Namier.

6 Ash, p. 135.

7 ibid.

8 J.C.D. Clark, *Revolution and Rebellion: State and Society in England in the Seventeenth and Eighteenth Centuries* (Cambridge University Press 1986), p. 169. Clark rightly warns against such a Whig interpretation of history.

9 R.N. Bellah, ed., *Habits of the Heart* (New York, Harper & Row, 1986), pp. 152–5.

10 Quoted in C.W. Stubbs, *Charles Kingsley and the Christian Social Movement* (Charles Kelly 1902), p. 69.

11 The full text of the placard can be found in S. Evans, *The Social Hope of the Christian Church* (Hodder & Stoughton 1965), pp. 152–3.

12 C.E. Raven, *Christian Socialism, 1848–1854* (Macmillan 1920), pp. 107–8.

13 E.R. Norman, *The Victorian Christian Socialists* (Cambridge University Press 1987), p. 10.

14 R.H. Tawney, LSE deposit, referred to in J. Atherton, 'R.H. Tawney as a Christian Social Moralist', Ph.D. Thesis (University of Manchester 1979), p. 90.

15 Maurice wrote to Kingsley on 2 January 1850, 'Competition is put forth as a law of the universe. This is a lie. The time has come for us to declare that it is a lie by word and deed. I see no way but associating for work instead of strikes' (F. Maurice, *The Life of Frederick Denison Maurice*, vol. 2, (Macmillan 1883), p. 32).

16 T. Christensen, *Origin and History of Christian Socialism 1848–54* (Aarhus 1962), pp. 108–9.

17 F.D. Maurice, 'Sermons on the Prayer Book and the Lord's Prayer, 3 December 1848', in *The Life of Frederick Denison Maurice*, vol. 1, p. 484.

18 Maurice, pp. 540–2.

19 F. Engels, *The Condition of the Working Class in England* (Panther Books 1969, introduction by Eric Hobsbawn), p. 75.

20 Quoted in D. Hay, *Economics Today: A Christian Critique* (Apollos 1989), p. 179.

21 Quoted in S. Mayor, *The Churches and the Labour Movement* (Independent Press 1967), p. 165.

22 *Three Letters to Chartists*, quoted in Christensen, p. 77.

23 Ash, p. 131.

24 Ash, p. 63.

25 Ash, p. 14. Ralf Dahrendorf, in his *Reflections on the Revolution in Europe* (Chatt. & Windus 1990), adopts Ash's distinction between refolution and revolution.

26 Ash, pp. 62–3.

27 Dahrendorf, pp. 76f.

28 Ash, p. 13.

29 Ash, p. 32.

30 ibid.

31 1 February 1990.

32 In *Beyond the Death of Socialism: Visions from Germany on Alternatives to Capitalism* (William Temple Foundation, Occasional Papers, no. 19, 1991).

33 Dahrendorf, p. 121, quoting Ash.

34 Ash, p. 96.

35 D. Marquand, *The Guardian* (9 November 1990).

36 Ash, p. 137.

37 *The Methodist Recorder*, 1 February 1990, prophetically commented concerning Gorbachev: 'His most critical problem, we still believe, is with the economy, for it is this that could bring him down.'

38 Ash, p. 151.

39 Dahrendorf, p. 23.

40 Ash, p. 156.

41 ibid.

42 Dahrendorf, pp. 22–3.

43 Ash, p. 73.

44 Ash, p. 56.

45 D.L. Edwards, *Christians in a New Europe* (Collins 1990), p. 51.

46 It is organized from the William Temple Foundation, Manchester Business School, Manchester.
47 Victor Hugo, quoted in Edwards, p. 23.
48 F.D. Maurice, Sermons on the Lord's Prayer, pp. 100–1. Quoted in M.B. Reckitt, *Maurice to Temple: A Century of the Social Movement in the Church of England* (Faber 1947), pp. 211–12.
49 J.K. Galbraith, *A History of Economics: The Past as the Present* (Penguin 1989), p. 1.
50 ibid.
51 *The Guardian* (16 April 1990) (or *Theology* (November–December 1990, vol. XCIII, no. 756)).
52 D.L. Munby, *God and the Rich Society* (Oxford University Press 1961), p. 12: 'In so far as these positive aims and ideals inspire trends, we can find the hand of God in them.'
53 F.D. Maurice, *Politics for the People*, no. 1, 6 May 1848. Quoted in Christensen, pp. 74–5.
54 F. Maurice, *Life*, vol. 1, p. 19. Quoted in Christensen, p. 12.
55 Munby, p. 16.
56 See *The Road to Damascus, Kairos and Conversion: A document signed by Third World Christians* (Catholic Institute for International Relations 1989). See also *Kairos Europa 1992*, an ecumenical movement linking Christian pressure groups in Europe with Third World liberation groups – as a challenge to the Single European Act of 1992.
57 In G.J. Dorrien, *Restructuring the Common Good: Theology and the Social Order* (New York, Orbis Books, 1990), pp. 74–6.
58 Quoted in D.L. Munby, ed., *Economic Growth in World Perspective* (SCM Press 1966), p. 23.
59 E.R. Wickham, *Ecumenical Review*, (April 1959), p. 265. Quoted in Munby, *God and the Rich Society*, pp. 15–16.
60 A concept used by R. Niebuhr, quoted in D.L. Munby, ed., *World Development: Challenge to the Churches* (Washington, Corpus Books, 1969), p. 97.
61 D.L. Munby, *Christianity and Economic Problems* (Macmillan 1956), p. 275.
62 I think of Sleeman, Munby, Hay and Griffiths.
63 Hay, p. 8.
64 Buchanan, *Ethics, Efficiency and the Market* (Clarendon Press 1985) preface, notes how philosophers (read theologians) are weak on efficiency and practicalities with regard to evaluating economic systems.
65 What Richard Niebuhr classified as 'the Christ of Culture' (the accommodation to culture) in his *Christ and Culture* (New York, Harper & Row 1951).
66 Paget's *Henry Scott Holland*, p. 97, quoted in Mayor, p. 200.

Two

Market Economies in a Changing World

So much of the breath-taking change in Czechoslovakia in the heady days of November 1989 was centred on the amazing Magic Lantern Theatre. It was there that the Civic Forum, the main opposition coalition, met, orchestrated by Vaclav Havel. One of the groups involved were economists from the Institute for Forecasting, nicknamed the Prognostics.[1] Like economists the world over, wherever two or three were gathered together, there were at least five or six opinions! Despite this, it was astonishing to hear in this official Institute of the Academy of Sciences in such a hard-line communist country that Dr Vaclav Klaus favoured the solutions of Milton Friedman, and Dr Thomas Jezek was a disciple and translator of Friedrich von Hayek. The two apostles of libertarian free-market economies were enthroned at the heart of a state socialist command economy!

And that was almost literally to happen within a month. For on Sunday, 10 December, Havel read out the names of the new cabinet to a celebrating crowd in Wenceslas Square. And there was Vaclav Klaus, 'the glinting Friedmanite', as the new Minister of Finance.[2] It was perhaps not surprising that a succession of free market economists were soon beating a path to Eastern Europe and the Soviet Union. Among them were our own Lords Harris and Griffiths. They represented the importance of economics for the difficult reconstruction of Eastern Europe, and the central role in that of market economies.

Such stories only reinforce the need to gain a greater understanding of market economies if we are to address effectively our contemporary context. This and the following chapter will seek to begin to make that case and increase that understanding.

Interpreting the market economy as a sign of our times is bound to be controversial, and this whole book is an extended argument about that. What can be noted about the concept itself is the advantage it possesses over two alternative concepts favoured in current Christian debates. On the one hand, it avoids the recent Christian obsession with the 'New Right'. The dramatic changes in Britain in the 1980s under Mrs Thatcher's premiership produced a surfeit of church conferences and secular books on the New Right. In many ways, this represented the Christian and radical tendency to jump on bandwagons, to reduce highly complex changes to the morally obvious, and therefore, generally speaking, to be quite inaccurate. There is now an understandable sense of *déja vu* about such moral reductionism. On the other hand, the concept of the market economy also avoids the obsession of many Christians with 'capitalism' as the key to open all doors: whether as the salvation or damnation of the world ('the riding the tiger' syndrome). It is more helpful to understand that both the New Right and capitalism point to broader and deeper changes and realities that must be taken into account in the development of Christian social thought. The term 'market economy' offers a better opportunity for doing this because it avoids the pejorative histories of capitalism and the New Right; it reduces the tendency to erect systems into panaceas for worship or demolition.[3]

It is important, too, not to reduce the market economy to the market as mechanism. This suggests a neutral machine which can somehow be divorced from a much wider context. It is not surprising that sociologists like Peter Berger have argued recently against any such reductionism by locating the study of contemporary capitalism in a social, political, economic and cultural context.[4]

The argument of this chapter comes to a similar conclusion. Because it begins with the contemporary context in all its plurality, as politics, economics, international, current and historical, it is driven to understand the market economy as an aggregate of perspectives. To describe it consequently involves the task of disaggregation: of isolating the various elements as part of a larger whole.

The argument is thus divided into two chapters. This first chapter concentrates on locating the market in its wider context – first by noting its international character, secondly by contrasting it with a state socialist or command economy, and thirdly by exploring its historical background. The following chapter addresses the market's economic character as the foundation of the market economy and, indeed, of modern economics. It then recognizes the socializing of the market through institutions and politics. Running throughout will be the development of themes and histories already identified, and the introduction of new ones, particularly in economics.

What emerges does not presume to be *the* definition of a market economy. It is rather a broad-based interpretation that crosses disciplines and histories, as befits a response to the contemporary context, and yet one that is centred on an economic understanding. Of course, many will argue that an 'objective' definition of such a controversial subject is impossible. It is too bound up with ideological debates about capitalism, throbbing as they are 'with prophetic pathos' on both Left and Right.[5] Yet interpretations of realities like the market economy cannot be reduced to ideology. Even if it could, the 'statements of fact' that enter into ideologies 'are not necessarily erroneous'.[6] In this, there is sufficient rapport among economists to build up a widely held understanding of an economic reality. For although they clearly differ in their interpretation of economics, there are certain general agreements. It is not 'as if one were speaking of music and the other of chemistry'.[7]

The greater danger in building up an interpretation of a market economy that is based on, yet broader than, an economic understanding, is that of generating a 'catch-all' concept. It is the problem of stretching 'explanatory categories so far that they lose their specific reference and become mere hold alls'.[8] Yet developing an interpretation of a phenomenon like the market economy through the contemporary context generates an understanding that no one discipline can grasp.[9] In the end, the development of the concept with all its limitations is part and parcel of the search for new common languages. In a period of great change, old languages become incapable of reflecting changing realities. They provide excuses for the continuation of outdated arguments and the avoidance of new understandings, practices and alignments. The use of 'the market economy' is an attempt to bridge such arguments of the past and whatever may emerge in the future.

In order to assist in the more economic part of this and the following chapter, use is made of economists who write from a Christian background. They include Donald Hay, John Sleeman, Denys Munby, Alan Waterman, Alan Storkey and Herman Daly. Particular church reports have also been helpful – including *Christian Values and Economic Life* (the major study conducted by the Federal Council of Churches in America in 1949), *The Ethics of Wealth Creation* (a report in 1991 to the British Methodists), and *Perspectives on Economics* (the 1984 report of the Industrial Committee of the Church of England).[10] Having worked through such a resource (one that is by no means exhaustive, as the Christian responses in Part Two will illustrate), I have been impressed by the content and quality of the Christian involvement in economics. It suggests the need to correct the myth that Christian social thought has neglected the field of economics.[11]

The Market in Context

A. *The international nature of market economies*

The emergence of market economies was part of the history of industrial capitalism and urbanization. They cannot be considered simply in their West European and North American forms. As the International Missionary Council acknowledged (held in Jerusalem in 1928 with Tawney in attendance), industrialization, particularly in its capitalist form, was a world-wide phenomenon. Its countermovement, the communist command economy, shared the same character. Locating the market in its international context is therefore a recognition of its universal nature, and its relationship to some of the most important debates in contemporary church life centred around liberationist movements and theologies. Its comprehensivity is also a corrective to those who associate it with homogeneity rather than great variety. To treat the market economy in South Korea and France as similar is to do violence to empirical realities and to perpetuate myths of international capitalist conspiracies.

The international nature of the market economy emerged partly as a result of the recognition by particular market economies that economic policies pursued in one country directly affected, and were in turn influenced by, policies pursued in others. A whole series of international bodies were developed to handle such interconnections, from the meeting of the seven most advanced economies (the G7) to the European Economic Community.[12] The 'extension of the market capitalist system from a single economy to a group of interacting economies'[13] has become a central feature of both market economies and their context.

In analysing that reality, most commentators have recognized it as 'a force of cataclysmic transformation in one country after another',[14] beginning in Western Europe and North America and spreading as far as East Asia. It has been a positive and negative force with the emphasis depending particularly on the stage of economic growth achieved.

With regard to markets as a positive factor on an international scale, observers from Marx to Tawney acknowledged the immense accomplishments of industrial capitalism in removing starvation as a recurring feature of life from the European and North American continents.[15] It was an achievement that was to lead to higher and higher individual living standards, with the accompanying enlargement of choice, and to constant improvement in education, health care and other social services. By 1938 four nations (France, the UK, Germany and the USA) were responsible for nearly half of the world's economic output, yet contained only 13 per cent of the population.[16] It was a domination by advanced market economies that has continued to this day, and one that has been endorsed and accentuated by the deep dissatisfaction with command economies. That rejection is all the more disturbing to the socialist alternative because of its occurrence in the European home of industrialization. Even more socialist-oriented societies have accepted that their economic agenda is now set by market economies as market socialism.

The growing dominance of market economies in wealth creation, with all its benefits, has become a more decisive trend even in Western economies in the last decade. It has not been restricted to the outburst of Thatcherism and Reaganomics in Britain and the USA, but it has affected Canada, France, Spain and Australasia, even under socialist governments. All have experienced major increases in economic growth.

Although originating in the West, the development of market economies cannot be so geographically restricted in the 1990s. They are now essentially a global phenomenon, particularly through their dramatic advance in East Asia. Indeed, that growth has been so powerful and distinctive that it can no longer be regarded as an extension of a Western reality. Berger understandably now argues that it should be treated as a 'second case' for market economies.[17] It is an argument built on the achievements of Japan, but increasingly followed by the

'Four Little Dragons' of South Korea, Taiwan, Hong Kong and Singapore.

Japan was the first non-Western society to become an advanced industrial society. Based on a carefully developed economic strategy, it was able to achieve a remarkable increase in national income of 8 per cent per annum between 1960 and 1970. The Four Little Dragons amplified and modified the Japanese story, but, unlike the latter, they have not yet become full democracies. However, they have each raised the standard of living of the majority of their populations through economic growth and a more effective income distribution. All five have been characterized by the interlocking of business and government in the promotion of national economic policy. Japan's Ministry of International Trade and Industry symbolizes this relationship and distinguishes the East Asian market economies from the outdated free market ideology pursued by Thatcher and Reagan.

With regard to market economies as a negative factor on the international stage, this has been manifested in the growing gulf with the Third World in terms of income per head, social provision and mortality rates. It is the precise nature of the relationship between the achievements of these 'two worlds' that has become the major source of division between them. That conflict has been epitomized in the case for and against the dependency theory. In its essence, this represents secular and church arguments against capitalism or market economies. It is personified in the theologies of liberation developed by theologians like Gutiérrez, Segundo and Duchrow (whom we will meet in Chapter 4), and by church bodies such as the Medellín Conference of the Latin American Episcopate (1968); the USA Roman Catholic Bishops' Pastoral letter entitled *Economic Justice For All* (1986); *The Road to Damascus: Kairos and Conversion*, a document signed by Third World Christians (1989); and many statements by the World Council of Churches.

Emerging in the late 1950s, radical dependency theory sought to replace ineffective and reformist development theory. Essentially anti-capitalist and neo-Marxist, it developed out of Lenin's theory of imperialism. This accounted for the increasing immiseration of the Third World by international capitalism's restless search for new markets.[18]

During the 1970s, dependency theory came to dominate much Third World thinking – particularly through the interpretations of

Fernando Cardoso. He linked it to the role of multinational corporations which rapidly became the 'major villains' of the game. They will be a recurring issue for Christian responses to international inequalities and their relationship to market economies. Third World poverty was thus now explained quite unequivocally as the result of First World success, whether through the United Nations' demand for a 'New International Economic Order' or the arguments of liberation theology. 'A central element in all of this is that the root causes of underdevelopment are sought *outside* the national societies, in the workings of the international capitalist system.'[19] Yet major arguments began to emerge over whether the relationship between First and Third Worlds could be expressed so simply. Most non-Marxist economists, including Donald Hay, were extremely doubtful whether capitalism had an intrinsic need to expand into the Third World. While accepting the exploitation of peripheral Third World nations by the centre of the capitalist First World, they attributed the underdevelopment of the Third World to a variety of causes – including the over-intervention of their inefficient governments in economic life and cultural factors. However, whatever the arguments about the relationship between advanced market economies and the underdeveloped Third World, all are agreed that the relationship is of the greatest importance for national and world economies. The increasingly international character of the market economy has ensured that this will be one of the great foundational questions in this generation.

B. *Command economies: the fatal deceit of politicization*

It is important to consider, however briefly, the significance of command economies. Any recognition of the contemporary context can do no other. State socialist centrally planned economies still dominate much of the world, from China and various Third World societies to the reluctant and increasingly ambiguous Soviet model. Historically, too, they emerged as the countermovement to capitalism or market economies. Sociologically, they can be regarded as a classic type: essentially, the only alternative to free market economies. Despite the command economy's possibly irremediable defects and its consequent rejection by more and more societies, it does reward further study – not least because of the way it highlights contrasting features of the market economy.

On 6 March 1990 the Supreme Soviet of the USSR approved a law authorizing 'private ownership of the means of production, so abolishing the state's virtual monopoly'.[20] Although the support for 'citizens' property' (the law studiously avoided the expression 'private property') was qualified and restricted to smaller enterprises, it did include the hiring of labour. For one radical deputy Alexei Yablokov, it represented understandably 'an enormous step forward'. Various proposals followed later in the year, including Stanislav Shalatin's plan to create a market economy in the Soviet Union in 500 days. These were astonishing events. As part of the movement of *perestroika* they complemented the events of 1989 in Eastern Europe.

And yet, one year later, we now realize how difficult is the task of transforming the Soviet Union into a modern society. At the heart of those obstacles may well have been President Gorbachev's reluctance to envisage a democracy with political pluralism and, connected to it, a market economy with economic freedom. The economic vision of *perestroika* appears static, with almost exclusively state enterprises competing for 'demand-determined' contacts. The Soviets appear to have missed the point of a market economy: the dependence on freedom to innovate, invest, and produce in a market environment; 'the market is a dynamic discovery process, not an improved method of computation'.[21]

It is at this point that we encounter the fundamental difference between market and command economies. For the latter is a predominantly *political* system, with the state, through the Party, overseeing all aspects of life, and especially the key sector of the economy. It is a system that tries to ensure that the central planning authority makes the basic economic decisions with regard to what to produce, in what quantities and qualities, and how it is distributed as commodities and incomes – including deciding between present consumption and investment for future production. The decision-making of consumers registering their wants through the price system, and producers deploying equipment and labour in response to consumer wants registered again through the price system, is replaced by a centralized bureaucracy. As an economy becomes more complex and consumer needs more sophisticated, it is a system doomed to failure. Such an economy cannot be planned and run 'like the post office'. Twelve million identifiably different products, 50,000 industrial establishments, and over 200 million consumers with all their varied wants, simply cannot effectively be co-ordinated by a central bureaucracy in order to deliver the required goods and services. 'It is not just a matter of technique plus accounting – arithmetic, as Lenin (before 1918) seemed naively to imagine.'[22]

The merging of all power into the state, and the consequent operating of a centralized planned economy, ensures rule by party-bureaucratic elites by a form of 'political patrimonialism'.[23] No wonder Tawney described Marx as the last of the medieval schoolmen. The problem of the domination of economics and economies by political or religious faiths is fundamental to this enquiry. The following discussion of the evolution of economics will confirm and elaborate this problem.

c. *The historical context of the market economy*

As the narrative account of the market evolves, various features in the contemporary and historical contexts have been identified for their contribution to our understanding of the market economy. Although the international, political and moral dimensions have been particularly significant in this regard, when considering the market economy in its intrinsically economic sense, its historical context assumes a key interpretative role. In order to emphasize this relationship, the history of the market should be seen as complementary and preliminary to the following chapter on the economic character of the market. Although this partly seeks to introduce people to economic thought, it must again be emphasized that it will bear all the marks of a layman straying into the area of economics.

The contemporary market economy, indeed economics as we know them, began in 1776 with the publication of Adam Smith's *An Inquiry into the Nature and Causes of the Wealth of Nations*. Most commentators on economics, including Marx, have regarded his contribution as a benchmark because of its decisive influence on the emergence of modern economics. 'Before Adam Smith there had been much economic discussion; with him we reach the stage of discussing economics.'[24]

However, the development of the market economy, like the

Industrial Revolution with which it was so associated, took generations to emerge. It was a procession characterized by slowness, irregularity and complexity.[25] It is a story that needs to explore the development of economics before Adam Smith, not least in order to explain the pivotal nature of the changes that he was so instrumental in promoting. Only then can many of the later amendments to economics be understood. Connecting three main stages in the history of economics (before Adam Smith, his contribution, and subsequent developments) is the great economist Alfred Marshall's definition of economics as 'a study of mankind in the ordinary business of life'.[26] For that is what economics is about, the bread and butter of life, whether in all its simplicity in the households of the ancient Greeks, or in the modern multinational corporation that supplies soap to space ships. Obviously, the use of the concept of the market economy refers to its contemporary character. Adam Smith and his successors referred to it as *laissez-faire* or the free market. His predecessors talked simply of the market.

Economics before Smith:
the ambiguity of historical antecedents

It is not difficult to read the origins of the modern market economy back into history. Brian Griffiths, and other evangelical Conservatives, have a tendency to do this with regard to the Old Testament.[27] Barry Gordon, in carefully describing Hesiod's views on economics in Greece in the eighth century BC, notes his acceptance of scarcity as a basis for choice and therefore competition as 'good conflict' for allocating resources.[28] The ambiguity of such interpretations is that they become sources of misunderstanding as well as illumination. The trap is to go back into history in ways that discern in it signs of hope for a modern case, and reject or neglect signs that contradict that case. The British tradition of Social Christianity, led by R.H. Tawney, has been particularly guilty of this. By drawing a clear decisive break between the regretted end of the medieval moral–theological regulation of economic life in the sixteenth and seventeenth centuries, and the welcomed (re)emergence of Christian socialism in the nineteenth century, it failed to recognize the development of quite major amendments to the former and the equally significant earlier alternatives to the latter. Both deviations grasped the changes in economic life with far more accuracy than mainstream Social Christianity.

Reading a theme back into history can, however, also be a source of contemporary illumination, especially with regard to recurring questions. The role of ethics in relation to economics in general, and to the issue of value as use or exchange in particular, has direct consequences for the continuing debate about interest (usury), prices and money. When interpreted in a pre-modern sense, they occupy prominent places in the work of theologians like Duchrow and Meeks, and such contemporary organizations as the World Council of Churches. This suggests that the tendency of many modern economists to regard Adam Smith as the father of economics is unhelpful if it rules out the recognition that the history of pre-modern economics continues to influence contemporary debates.

A layperson surveying the development of economics will be struck by the importance of context. For example, the changes in the late eighteenth and early nineteenth centuries, which witnessed the emergence of the Industrial Revolution, were related intimately to the development of modern economics. The great inter-war depression provoked J.M. Keynes to reform neo-classical economics. In the case of the pre-Adam Smith context, the most dominant characteristic context is the essential continuity in economic understandings throughout some 2,000 years. It generated a predominantly static understanding of the economy and society. From Aristotle to Aquinas, economic thought reflected the centrality of the household and its involvements in local, restricted markets.

For Aristotle's household economy (remember that the very word economy is derived from the Greek for household (*oikos*) and law or management (*nomos*)), production was predominantly for and within the household context. There was no wage theory, because most work was done by slaves. The prices of goods were not determined by their exchange value in response to the forces of supply and demand in competitive markets. The value of the limited goods related to their use in the household, and in relations between households in terms of their equivalent value for the procurement of other goods. Exchange value therefore depended on the use value, on the satisfying of a need in the household: there was a clear recognition of the primacy of use values in economic reasoning.[29] What is particularly interesting is Aristotle's recognition of the fundamental problem of value as reflected in prices. This is illustrated by the fact that water, which is so useful, is worth so little in exchange value, whereas diamonds, which are of so little intrinsic use, are so valuable in exchange. The solution of that problem, so central to modern microeconomics, was not solved until the end of the nineteenth century.

The limited use made of money therefore related only to its use as a medium of exchange. It was regarded as barren and incapable of 'breeding'. Consequently, accumulation of money could only be for personal consumption; there was no recognition of the use of money as capital investment for future productive purposes. Interest was rejected because, in such a context, it could only be an imposition by the rich on the poor seeking the essentials of life; it contradicted the belief in the household supplying all its members' needs. Aristotle's deep rejection of money as of value in its own right (and so regarded as a commodity) spilled over into his unease with the trading function involving, as it would, financial exchange systems (in which money would gain, in part, a value in itself).

The task for Aristotle, and for well into the Middle Ages, was to maintain life, including the economy, at its existing basic level so that people could be released for the more important affairs of political life. It was to manage what is given by nature; it was not to transform it by enterprise.

How would such a mind-set engage the economic problem of scarcity? Essentially by philosophical arguments about moral purposes. The means to such goals, including economics, existed to serve that greater good. There was no understanding of economics as the allocation of scarce means, irrespective of the ends. Economics was therefore subordinated to ethics which in turn related to a primarily static view of the good life. It was in no way regarded as a distinct field of study in which 'the How and Why of economic mechanisms' are worked on.[30]

It was such a view of a relatively unchanging world, with its uneasy attitude to wealth creation, which (when linked to Old Testament views) shaped the New Testament context. 'Creative and elaborately planned enterprises, for example those of modern industry or wholesale business with its keen desire to open up new countries, could not thrive on this soil where the impulse of gain is tied down.'[31] We face two quite different mind-sets; it was not necessarily or essentially a matter of ethics.

It was these views that Aquinas inherited and developed, and so influenced the medieval mind (and, until the 1960s, Roman Catholic theology). His study of economics, which occupied a subordinate part of his theological work, certainly addressed issues of money, interest, value and price. However, it did so through a study of the economic relationship of individuals and households, and not through an analysis of the actual economic context. Again, all was subordinated to ethics and the good life: economic techniques had no significance in their own right. His work on usury and the just price reflected these perspectives.

And yet, beginning in the twelfth and thirteenth centuries, through the contributions of individuals like Nicolas Oresme (d. 1382) and philosophical reorientations like nominalism which rejected abstract universal concepts, there emerged a new willingness to reflect on what was actually happening in economic life. Thus the debasement of the coinage provoked a recognition of the need to protect money by accepting that it had a value in itself. Only then could people use it to trade with one another in confidence. Yet to do so placed it within the influence of market forces. It is this issue of money and capital as a commodity that still shapes the thinking of some liberation theologians, including Duchrow.

The needs of expanding commerce, particularly in the northern Italian towns, also began to change attitudes to the lending of money for commercial ventures. Despite the illegality of usury, exemptions began to emerge, including a recognition that the lender could claim loss because he could have put the money to a more profitable alternative use (the argument *lucrum cessans*, or what we now call the opportunity cost). All these developments were related to the regularization and institutionalization of commerce and consequently of finance. The arguments about economics were beginning to acknowledge the need for exchange systems, and therefore for value in exchange and not simply in use.

It was such changes that influenced theologians like Leonard Lessius (1554–1623). His contribution often seemed closer to nineteenth-century economics than to the mercantilists and physiocrats of the eighteenth century. For him, economic relations were not conducted between two isolated individuals, but rather in organized markets. And these varied from markets for commodities to finance, all sharing a unity of theory.[32]

It was such developments challenging the Tawney tradition of Christian social thought that mourned the ending of the domination of economic life by theology and canon law. Their attempted regulation of economics failed because of the increasing gulf between precept and practice. Dogma was rejected because it no longer reflected an adequate analysis of society. That was not the fault of economics, but of theology and an ecclesiastical mind-set. The attempts of thinkers from Oresme to Lessius should be a reminder that the increasing irrelevance of Christian social thought was rooted in the dominant tradition of the schoolmen of the Middle Ages, including Luther and seventeenth-century examples such as Baxter. The official Church had ceased to count in economics because it had ceased to think many centuries before the eighteenth.

Adam Smith: the founder of modern economics and the market economy

The excursion into economic thought before 1776 indicates the profound nature of the transition to economics as we know them. That development was linked inextricably to the emergence of the modern market economy. The ground rules for both were set out in the work of Adam Smith.

In its essentials this represented a comprehensive rejection of previous economics and economies in general and, in particular, as exemplified in the static philosophy of mercantilism. *The Wealth of Nations* represented 'history's most climactic assault of ideas on policy'.[33] Yet, as is so often the case, such a seminal work was as much a response to, as an interpretation of, an emerging context. It represented the transformation of the household economy, operating in local restricted markets, to an economy characterized by specialization, the division of labour, and the consequential dependence on the interdependence of markets as we know them. It was a world in which people made products for sale in the market and not for personal use, and so the price obtained, and the price paid for what people wanted, both became essential parts of economic life. It was a change symbolized by the industrialist replacing the merchant.

Out of the early stages of these developments, Smith emerged as the supreme 'prophet of its achievements and the source of its guiding rules'.[34] So it was that *The Wealth of Nations* came to map out the field of future economic enquiry in terms of private property, enterprises, the market, labour, value, price, demand and supply, rent and interest. His contribution can be divided into three parts.[35]

1. His view of the broad forces that motivated economic life influenced profoundly the nature of the economic system. Complementing his exploration of benevolence in his earlier *The Theory of Moral Sentiments* (1759), he recognized the importance of self-interest as the basic motivator in the economy. 'It is not from the benevolence of the butcher, the brewer, or the baker, that we expect our dinner, but from their regard to their own interest. We address ourselves, not to their humanity but to their self-love.'[36] In pursuing that interest privately and competitively, the consequences served the common good, whether intended or not. In other words, the individual

> is in this, as in many other cases, led by an invisible hand to promote an end which has no part of his intention. . . . I have never known much good done by those who affected to trade for the public good. It is an affectation, indeed, not very common among merchants, and very few words need be employed in dissuading them from it.[37]

It was this approving acknowledgement of the relationship between self-enrichment and public good that represented a fundamental break with medieval and biblical authority.

2. He pioneered new explanations of price formation, and their relationship to the distribution of the income created as wages, profits and rent. What is now called microeconomics became central to the economic task, even though Smith's inadequate answers were to be superseded by the theory of marginal utility at the end of the nineteenth century.

3. He addressed the issue of public policy in relation to economic growth. He was clear that the creation of wealth involved the rejection of the protectionism, statism and monopolies of mercantilism, and the promotion of free trade, large markets

(required by the division of labour), competition, and state intervention restricted to defence, the administration of justice, and very limited public works. The market economy was to be freed from heavy-handed government. Adopting a slogan of the French physiocrats, he advocated that things be left alone, and they would then work themselves out (*laissez faire, laissez passer*).

After Adam Smith: the emergence of 'the system'

With these and other developments 'the history of economics took its longest step'.[38] In the next hundred years, economists produced modifications to the emerging 'system' of 'the classical tradition' of economics (a concept used by both Marx and Keynes). By these means, it was able to keep abreast of the changing industrial and economic order, in ways Christian social thought and Marxism had failed to do.

The early modifications to the classical system were ambiguous in their consequences and influenced economic and social policy up to the present. For example, Jean Baptise Say (1767–1832) reinforced the system's tendency to regard itself as a self-correcting equilibrium. He was clear that the production of goods would always generate sufficient demand to purchase all the goods. There could be no overproduction or shortage of purchasing power (Say's law). It was this belief in the self-regulating nature of the market that was to be exploded by the Great Depression and the work of J.M. Keynes. Parson Malthus (1766–1834), as Marx called him, concentrated on establishing the link between the growth of population and food supplies. Without checking the former, famines and wars would result. Just as important, and in contrast to Say, he recognized that in the economic system the demand for goods might be inadequate, with overproduction and stagnation being the result. 'For the first time, in English economic theory at any rate, the possibility of crises arising from causes inherent in the capitalist system was admitted.'[39] No wonder economics became known as the dismal science! Malthus will figure prominently in the emergence of Christian Political Economy, explored in Chapter 4.

It was with David Ricardo (1772–1823) that the economics of Adam Smith began to be transformed into the modern discipline of economics. In contrast to Smith's inductive method based on empirical observation, Ricardo was a theoretician. He worked from assumptions about the behaviour of economic man (the classical *homo economicus*), including the belief that he would always strive to achieve maximum advantage in competition. Many have attacked this fundamental assumption as a fictitious view of human nature – what the philosopher A.N. Whitehead called 'the fallacy of misplaced concreteness'.[40] What can be argued more convincingly is the recognition that the associated influence of utilitarianism on economics impeded the attempt to construct economics as a value-free science.

Important as these modifications to the classical system were, they failed to explain the nature of prices; they had not resolved the age-old Aristotelian dilemma of value in relation to water and diamonds. It was not until 1871, with the work of William Stanley Jevons (1835–1882), professor of economics at Manchester, that the answer emerged as the theory of marginal utility. For it is not the satisfaction from the *use* of a product that gives it value; rather, it is the satisfaction from the last and least wanted item. In Western societies, water (unlike diamonds) is generously available; the last glass has little or no utility, and its lack of exchange value sets the value for the rest. In other words, 'the utility of any good or service diminishes, all else equal, with increasing availability; it is the utility of the last and least wanted – the utility of the marginal unit – that sets the value of all'.[41] Its power as an explanation of value in the market economy was revealed in its ability to settle problems of prices, wages and interest. No wonder Galbraith talked of 'the magic of marginality'![42]

By 1900, the neo-classical system was fully in place, and expressed in the works of Alfred Marshall, the great Cambridge economist. At the centre was a theory of prices determined by the ever-moving equilibrium between supply and demand, and it remains part of the teaching of economics to this day. It illustrates too the increasing domination of economics as and by a profession, and the central role of the British in this formative period.

As a system evolving in response to changing contexts, it displayed a remarkable resilience, despite its major defects with regard to inequalities of reward and power, 'the great black hole of mainstream economics'.[43] It was these that Marx highlighted. In particular, he observed the inherent tendency of unrestrained capitalism to generate monopolies and cyclical unemployment. However, through the macroeconomic management of economies complemented by welfare policies, market economies have adapted the system to moderate many of these deficiencies; 'the development of economic society has not been kind to Marx'.[44]

It has been this ability to amend with circumstances in a framework of continuities that has proved such a strength of the market system. The work of economists like Joan Robinson in identifying the tendency to monopolistic competition, and Joseph Schumpeter in acknowledging the key role of the entrepreneur and 'the creative destruction' of technological change, bear witness to this ability to respond to emerging trends. However, it was perhaps J.M. Keynes (1883–1946) and his *The General Theory of Employment Interest and Money* that best illustrated this resource for change. Responding to the Great Depression, he recognized that the classical system did not ensure an equilibrium at full employment; that required the injection of demand through the macroeconomic management of the economy. The decisive problem of economics had moved from determining how prices were formed and incomes distributed (microeconomics) to 'how the level of output and employment is determined'.[45] This later developed into the concern for economic growth. Other developments, more internal to the profession of economics, included the mathematical formulation of economic relationships and the building of econometric or computer models of the economy, leading to the use of economic forecasting.

Facing up to the contemporary context is profoundly about engaging the modernization of the economy and economics in the last two hundred years. A startling illustration of this presumption is that the economist J.K. Galbraith has known personally most economists for *a quarter of that time*. The same could be said about Ronald Preston and John Bennett in the related field of Christian social ethics. These are modern disciplines responding to changing modern realities.

The nature of that change as a comparatively recent phenomenon is brought home to us by the dramatic and related emergence of economic growth. It has been the story of the movement in the last two hundred years from essentially zero growth to a self-sustaining growth. So dynamic has been that development, that within our lifetime there will be more economic change than in previous tens of thousands of years.

It ought not to surprise us that economics and such economic change are bound inextricably together. 'Economic ideas are not very important, when and where there is no economy.'[46] The influence of a changing context was reflected increasingly in the dominance of market economies and the related yet separate discipline of economics.

Such changes and relationships raise profound questions of contemporary Christian thought, for most Christian leaders, theologians and Churches have never accepted or understood the revolutionary impact and character of these changes. They have been so decisive as to render redundant any attempt at a 'return philosophy' to previous contexts. Occasionally a Christian thinker will glimpse this. F.D. Maurice did, writing about the emergence of national societies and the role of the Church. He observed that:

> The establishment of outward law, the formation of national societies . . . [were] parts of God's great scheme for developing more fully the nature and character of Christ's Kingdom. . . . This change [from the ancient world], I affirm to be not merely one in outward and material happiness, but one connected with the very ends for which the Church exists.[47]

It is such a positive and discerning reading of the signs of the times that has been so absent from informed Christian opinion. This is partly because the rise of modern markets and economics has presented an unequivocal challenge to the domination by theology of economics and economic life up to the decisive changes 'inaugurated' by Adam Smith. That domination no longer exists. Yet the question of the nature of the relationship between ethics and economics remains, but needs to be completely reformulated in Christian social thought. What does not help is the perennial temptation for theologians to return to pre-modern understandings, and the confusion it generates over the relationship between economics and market economies. So when Meeks promotes the superiority of a 'household' economy over contemporary market systems, or Duchrow rejects the findings of modern economics on interest for a qualified biblical and medieval rejection of usury, and David Jenkins rejects the market system as a 'fatal mistake'[48] irrespective of its intimate connections with economic discoveries, then we are faced with failures to understand contexts and changes. They represent an inability to come to terms with the reality that 'Economics in all modern manifestations centres on the market . . .'[49]

Notes

1 T.G. Ash, *We the People: The Revolution of '89* (Granta Books 1990), p. 87.
2 Ash, p. 124.
3 G. Williams, *The Economics of Everyday Life* (Penguin 1951), p. 8.
4 P. Berger, *The Capitalist Revolution: Fifty Propositions about Prosperity, Equality and Liberty* (Wildwood House 1987). He talks of an 'economic culture' theory of capitalism which can explore 'the social, political and cultural matrix or context within which these particular economic processes operate' (p. 8). M. Novak, in *The Spirit of Democratic Capitalism* (American Enterprise Institute/Simon & Schuster 1982), refers to the political, economic and moral–cultural dimensions of capitalism.
5 Berger, p. 31.
6 Schumpeter, quoted in J.P. Wogaman, *Christians and the Great Economic Debate* (SCM Press 1977), p. 31.
7 J.P. Wogaman, *Christian Perspectives on Politics* (SCM Press 1988), p. 10, discussing a definition of politics.
8 J.C.D. Clark, *Revolution and Rebellion* (Cambridge University Press 1986), p. 103.
9 Clark, p. 94.
10 J. Bennett, ed., *Christian Values and Economic Life* (New York, Harper & Row 1954); *The Ethics of Wealth Creation* (The Methodist Division of Social Responsibility 1990); *Perspectives on Economics* (CIO Publishing 1984).
11 Theologians in the mainstream liberal tradition, like Preston and Wogaman, have all contributed to this myth – as, indeed, have I.
12 J. Bennett, ed., pp. 101f.
13 D. Hay, *Economics Today* (Apollos 1989), p. 248.
14 Berger, p. 3.
15 R.H. Tawney, review of V.A. Demant's *Religion and the Decline of Capitalism*, in *The Observer* (July 1950). (Quoted in D.L. Munby, *Christianity and Economic Problems* (Macmillan 1956), p. 244.)
16 Williams, p. 44.
17 Berger, pp. 140f.
18 Interestingly, Hobson's work on capitalism's need for markets, and investment opportunities for surplus capital, predated and influenced Lenin.
19 Berger, pp. 124–5.
20 *The Guardian* (7 March 1990).
21 M. Wolf, review of *Perestroika in Perspective* (Padma Desau Tauris 1989) in *The Financial Times* (2 September 1989).

22 A. Nove, *The Economics of Feasible Socialism* (Allen & Unwin 1983), p. 33.
23 Berger, pp. 184f. (referring to Max Weber's use of the concept).
24 Sir Alexander Gray, quoted in B. Gordon, *Economic Analysis before Adam Smith: Hesiod to Lessius* (Macmillan 1975), pp. xii.
25 J.C.D. Clark, *English Society 1680–1832* (Cambridge University Press 1985), p. 65 – describing the Industrial Revolution. The work of Archdeacon Cunningham, and Ashley at the end of the nineteenth century, emphasized the value of understanding economics through its historical evolution.
26 Quoted in J.K. Galbraith, *A History of Economics: The Past as the Present* (Penguin 1989), p. 5.
27 This will be discussed in Chapter 4.
28 Gordon, p. 5.
29 Gordon, pp. 36f.
30 Gordon, p. 123, quoting Schumpeter.
31 Gordon, pp. 88–9, quoting J. Weiss, *Earliest Christianity*, vol. 2, 1897 (New York, Harper & Row, 1965), p. 593.
32 Gordon, pp. 260–2.
33 Galbraith, p. 44.
34 Galbraith, p. 58.
35 I am here following Galbraith's discussion of Smith, pp. 64f.
36 A. Smith, *The Wealth of Nations*, Book 1, ch. 2, quoted in Galbraith, p. 64.
37 Smith, Book 4, chapter 2.
38 Galbraith, p. 73.
39 Galbraith, p. 80, quoting E. Roll, *A History of Economic Thought* (New York 1942).
40 Quoted in H. Daly and J. Cobb, *For the Common Good* (Merlin Press 1990), p. 36.
41 Galbraith, p. 108.
42 Galbraith, p. 110.
43 Galbraith, p. 115.
44 Galbraith, p. 138.
45 Galbraith, p. 233.
46 Galbraith, p. 2.
47 F.D. Maurice, *The Kingdom of Christ* Everyman edn, vol. 2. pp. 234, 239–40, quoted in D.L. Munby, *God and the Rich Society* (Oxford University Press 1961), p. 39.
48 *The Guardian* (24 May 1991).
49 Galbraith, p. 25.

Three

The Economic and Social Character
of the Market

There is considerable agreement 'on what is [the market economy] undoubtedly one of the most important moral, social and political issues of our time and of the foreseeable future'.[1] Written in 1985, this is a judgement confirmed by the late 1980s and early 1990s. Events in Eastern Europe, Western societies and East Asia have seen the market economy rise to new prominence. The growing problems of the only major alternative, the command economies, and their resort to market mechanisms to stem their decline, have only served to heighten the market's prominence.

Yet important though these contextual factors are for building a fuller picture of the market economy, they do not describe adequately what lies at its heart. For that is profoundly a matter of economics, as the survey of its history began to reveal. That distinctive emphasis now needs elaborating, through a survey of the economic character of the market economy. This can then lead on to a recognition of its social character, including its basis in institutions and politics.

Facing up to reality: the market as economics

For the steadfastness of Balaam in refusing to turn aside when the creature on which he rode refused to go forward, is precisely the steadfastness of our country gentlemen, be they High or Low Churchmen, and false prophets. They do not believe that facts are the angels of the Lord, saying 'Thus far shalt thou go and no farther'.[2]

Facing up to the realities of life, particularly in their more empirical form, has never been easy for many Christians. Even in 1992, almost 150 years after Darwin's pioneering work on evolution, there are still many who reject his discoveries because of a

48

fundamentalist reading of the Scriptures. Much more disturbing, because it is more representative of mainstream church opinion, has been the questioning of the discoveries of economists. A stark example of this faith perspective will be noted in the following discussion on the key economic assumption of scarcity. The rejection of the hypotheses and methods of economics has been exacerbated by the failure of official church opinion to distinguish between economic realities as the basic economic problems such as scarcity, which all economies have to engage, and as the ways in which the problems are dealt with by particular economic systems.[3] The inter-relationship between problems and systems encourages that confusion, for the economic task includes both.

Before trying to develop our understandings of distinctions and confusions, we need to recognize the Christian misuse of economics is not simply the result of theological confusions over the realities of life. It also lies deep in the character of economics itself, with regard to the validity of its scientific and factual basis. To what extent must its discoveries be accepted as beyond theological argument? If it includes a scientific dimension, what weight can be placed on it? All these matters have been part of a continuing debate in economics from the ancient Greeks to the present and particularly with regard to two kinds of experience that are distinguishable yet not fully separable. On the one hand, there are human purposes and commitments and, on the other, a body of more empirical information about the world and the skills for analysing it.[4] It is a distinction that economists now describe as the difference between the normative and the positive, between what ought to be and what is, between social theory and scientific method. Are basic economic problems in the field of positivist economics, and therefore to what extent are they beyond moral questioning?[5]

All these questions are the subject of continuing debates. For example, there is much dispute over scientific method, about whether it can be objective and value free. In the eighteenth century the philosopher Hume began a tradition that rejected reliance on the senses as a basis for factual information, and in the twentieth century Karl Popper argued that there is no logical basis for our selection of facts given their infinite number. Scientific method, including its use in economics, is always 'theory laden'. Yet for the purposes of this argument it is assumed, despite these qualifications, that science has necessarily 'a metaphysical faith in the existence of regularities in our world', a faith without which 'practical action is hardly conceivable'.[6] What is crucial is that such understandings, whether applied to basic economic problems or systems, should be open to falsification by empirical evidence (so all swans can be presumed to be white until a black one arrives). Out of these debates it is therefore possible to argue for a view of economic theory as a kind of 'theoretical realism'; when tested by empirical data it can be regarded as a provisional handle into complex realities. For no economic theory, whether concerned with basic economic problems or systems, will ever correspond fully to 'reality'. Yet they can be described as 'operationally meaningful theorems'.[7]

Out of these arguments there begins to emerge a view of economics as problems and systems that appear to be appropriate for dealing with the project of market economies. Like J.M. Keynes, it suggests the use of a combination of models appropriate to the task in hand, in the light of one's intuitions and immersion in the facts of the situation. It leads to understandings of economic problems and systems that are provisional because of questions about scientific method and theories, and yet purposeful because of the weight of evidence suggesting that such understandings are less inaccurate than any others. With these working agreements, the question of basic economic problems and systems can be engaged.

Scarcity as the economic problem

Whatever the economic system, whether command or market economy, it has to address questions relating to scarcity and how to meet people's wants. In modern economics these are connected to a context influenced by specialization and the subdivision of labour.

There is almost universal agreement among economists that scarcity is the fundamental economic problem. Essentially, this is the recognition that in the world as we know it there are always more wants than the resources to meet them. As a result, the economic task becomes how to allocate scarce resources to satisfy these wants.

It is important to understand what scarcity means because its definition in economics is more complex than its normal usage. First, it is a recognition that we have only a finite amount of resources to meet our wants. By 'resources' are meant the natural elements of soil and minerals (called land), the man-made element of factories, machines and the infrastructure (called capital) and the human effort (called labour). These three constitute what economists call the factors of production, the means by which our wants are satisfied. Secondly, it is an acknowledgement that finite resources can be brought together in different combinations to produce different goods and services. The question is which to produce, and in consequence what not to produce. For the full cost of using land for a tennis court also includes the cost of not using it for growing vegetables (the opportunity cost). Finally, scarcity also arises out of the problem of timescale: of having to choose between meeting present wants or investing to meet future wants.[8]

Set against these limited resources are people's wants as goods and services, which become more varied as a society becomes more prosperous.[9] Indeed they are now so diversified as to be regarded as limitless, fed by what Dr Johnson called 'the hunger of imagination'.[10]

It is the putting together of infinite competing wants and finite resources that produces scarcity as the fundamental economic problem and assumption. There are always more wants than the resources to satisfy them.

Economics is consequently about facing up to the realities of life as they really are. 'Economising only arises in a world where things are scarce, and choice has to be made. In heaven no problem of scarcity arises, and in hell no possibility of choice exists; economics is a science dealing with the conditions of human life in this world.'[11] Yet the economic problem is not simply about facing up to the contemporary situation, for scarcity will almost certainly be the case for as far into the future as we can envisage: 'no foreseeable increase in the quantity of economic means appears to be sufficient to overcome the harshness of the struggle for wealth'.[12] Indeed, scarcity was recognized as a deciding factor of economic life in pre-modern society. It was Hesiod, in eighth-century Greece, who declared 'The gods keep hidden from men the means of life.'[13]

It is precisely this fundamental assumption and problem of

economics that has been questioned by some theologians. For them, the biblical testimony suggests that belief in God's blessings will lead to the overcoming of scarcity. The latter is regarded as the product of human injustice rather than finitude.[14] With the Marxist faith in communist abundance, it is a dogma shared by all who cannot accept the 'limitations of choice in space and time'.[15] It is the assumption of this project, shared with most economists, that facing the realities of our economic context is about facing up to scarcity: 'The Science which studies human behaviour as a relationship between ends and scarce means which have alternative uses.'[16]

Following such a definition, the basic economic task of all systems concerns the allocation of scarce resources to meet people's wants. Tasks centre on what and how to produce, and for whom,[17] and fall into four basic functions:

1. The demand problem of how to decide which wants should be met (and therefore which will not be).

2. The production problem of how to combine the resources of land, labour and capital to produce the goods and services.

3. The exchange and distribution problem of how to share out the product to those who produce and those who cannot.

4. The savings and investment problem of how to divide the product for present and future use (investment).[18]

The price mechanism

The influence of scarcity on the economic task developed into modern economics through the Industrial Revolution. Production then began to be determined by specialization and the subdivision of labour. Both depended on the growth of larger, more complex and impersonal markets, replacing exchange through barter. In a remarkable passage in her autobiography, Beatrice Webb describes these changes as they transformed the personal relationships of the household economy. Recording a visit in her youth to her poor relations in Bacup, a textile town in north-east Lancashire, she observes the transition from the bartering of the moorland farms to the market relationships in the newly industrialized valleys:

Once again, therefore, by a conjunction of co-operative and trade union organisation, we must bring the producer and consumer face to face. I do not mean that the boot-maker can sell his boots to the weaver, while the weaver disposes of his cloth to the farmer's wife; this personal relationship is no longer possible in a commercial system transformed by the industrial revolution. Barter between individuals must be superseded by negotiations, through authorised representatives, between groups of workers and groups of consumers. Individualist exchange must follow individualist production, and give way to collective bargaining.[19]

Industrialization provided both structure and motivation for the transformation of basic economic problems and tasks into modern economics and market economies.

Most economists argue that the fulcrum of that transformation was the emergence of the price system or mechanism. In a remarkable way it provided answers to basic economic problems in the context of an increasingly populated urban-industrial society. The task itself was awe-inspiring in its complexity. In its essence it was how to co-ordinate the demand and supply of many thousands of different goods and services produced by many thousands of firms for millions of households. Such developments were required by the rise of specialization and the subdivision of labour. Thus individuals no longer made goods for their own use, but for sale in a market. As a result, the price obtained for the goods produced and the price to be paid for what the individual wanted became of vital importance. As Beatrice Webb observed, barter between individuals ceased to be the manner of exchange; the market system did away with 'the need for reciprocal coincidence of wants and supplies' which was so restrictive of economic growth.[20]

The problem of course was how to co-ordinate the demand of consumers and the supply of producers so that both were satisfied; by that is meant the provision of the required goods and services in terms of quantity, quality and price, at prices that enabled the producers to make sufficient profit to stay in business.

It was these realities and problems that modern economics and the market economy rose to meet. And the latter has provided consistently the dominant model in terms of economic effectiveness, when compared to the only other dominant model: the command economy. It has been noted already how the latter tried unsuccessfully to face basic realities and problems with the central planners of state-owned enterprises deciding what and how to produce, and the manner in which the proceeds should be distributed.

At the heart of the market economy's response to realities and problems lay the price mechanism or system. Indeed it was so dominant that some economists have referred to the market as 'the price economy'.[21] Relying on private ownership particularly of the factors of production like land and capital, and on money as the medium of exchange and not barter, the price mechanism had two main functions: as incentive and as signals of information. Regarding the former, the owners of resources like capital could switch them from falling to higher returns. Regarding the latter, prices signalled two kinds of information to be harmonized or co-ordinated. First, prices indicated the intensity of the consumer's demand for a product. Secondly, prices indicated the costs incurred and the resources or factors needed to produce that product. A rising price signalled to the producer the value of obtaining more resources to produce more of the product, the information and incentive functions of prices thereby overlapping. As a result, the consumer was seen to buy more as prices were lower, and the producer to produce more (and therefore achieve greater profit) as prices moved higher.

The two, the prices indicating consumer demand and producer costs, were seen to meet at the point where the demand of the consumer matched what the producer would supply. It is this equilibrium price that reflects the satisfaction of consumer demand and the producer's sale of the goods and, in particular, as described through the theory of marginal utility.[22] If the price goes above that level, the goods are not all sold because consumers buy fewer. As a consequence, the reduced demand results in the reduction of the price until it returns back to the equilibrium point. If the price falls below the point, demand increases, the goods are all sold, and so the price rises because the demand is no longer satisfied. Again, the price moves until it reaches the equilibrium point. The interests of consumers and producers are therefore reconciled by the way both respond to the price signals. This in turn then determines the output of products.

It is where consumers and producers encounter one another

that the market comes into being: 'A market is simply a meeting of buyers and sellers.'[23] Despite the value of such an observation, the market mechanism begins to acquire a complexity and substance that means simple descriptions mislead. Irrespective of the intricacy of consumer-producer price relationships, the concept of market has to be regarded as an aggregate term for a variety of markets. For example, the commodities market refers to the final goods and services purchased by consumers from companies. The decisions regarding the output of such goods are determined principally by the interaction of demand and supply. The factor market for the resources of land, capital and labour provides producers with the essential means for the production of commodities. Again, as a market for buyers and sellers the interaction of demand and supply determines the price of the resources of land and capital. However, the price of labour is not determined by higher prices generating more supply. Other influences also play a major part, including training, geography and social class. What cannot be regarded as the primary determinant of labour costs are the needs of the workers:

> A man's family does not require any less food for healthy existence even if he does not produce so large an output or if its value in the market decreases; yet an employer who based his workers' wages on their needs, rather than on the value of their work, would soon find himself in Queer Street.[24]

This economic understanding of the labour market contradicts the claims of Christian organizations and leaders – such as the Christian Social Union and William Temple – that the reasonable pay of the worker must be the first claim on the industry.

Finally, in capital markets financial intermediaries such as banks allocate the savings deposited with them, including passing them on to borrowers for investment purposes. The advantage of such a market is that there is no need to match savers and borrowers, and the risk of lending for investment is spread. Again, as with the other markets, 'prices', like interest rates, provide essential information and incentives. In other words, despite the variety of markets each with their special features, they are linked in a fundamental unity of economic theory and practice. They operate, as we have seen, 'according to the same basic set of principles'.[25] They emerge as the coherent centre of the market economy.

Operating in this market of markets are a number of key actors. Apart from the state, they consist principally of consumers and producers. The latter include firms who purchase factors in the factor market, organize production to meet the particular demands registered through the price mechanism, and then sell to other firms or consumers. The prices suggest how best to allocate or deploy the resources in order to anticipate the demands of the market.

The former, the consumers, consist of individuals and households with sufficient income to purchase final goods and services in the commodity market. They also act as suppliers in the factor market of labour and capital (there is a circular flow of the income received for labour being used to purchase goods or invest). For consumers, the prices of goods and services enable them to assess their relative value and so prioritize their wants. Certain wants, including some foodstuffs, are relatively inelastic in the sense that their demand does not reduce if the price rises.[26] Prices therefore enable the consumers to achieve the most satisfaction out of their income. The market, by increasing the standard of living, enables those choices and wants to be enlarged.

It is at such points that Christian belief has been challenged, with the Church frequently giving the impression that it is 'ill-disposed towards the pretensions of men to exercise choice'.[27] Yet the actual working of basic economics (including as the market economy) questions such indiscriminate moral judgements, for the expansion and meeting of choice is an indispensable part of economic reality. However, Christian ignorance of the complexity of economics cannot be corrected adequately by the equally indiscriminate justification of increased choice by theologians like V.A. Demant: 'The enlargement of human choice, whether through an expanding economy or through the discoveries of science or art or literature, is all part of God's design for men.'[28] Accepting the economics of choice can never be associated with a blanket approval of decisions. Both judgements betray the absence of a discerning engagement with economic realities.

In relation to the two principal economic actors, the businessman is regarded by many economists as playing a central role.[29] As mediator between consumer and producer, he performs two important functions in the market economy. On the one hand, he initiates production by forecasting demand and so takes the risk of assembling the resources necessary to meet it. In this:

> Chance and luck play a part more important than plan and foresight; a cool nerve is a more valuable asset than a wide-ranging capacity to see all sides of a problem; the power to take rapid and firm action is more likely to be successful than the ability to judge wisely.[30]

It is these entrepreneurial skills that exemplify the dynamism of a market economy in contrast to its absence in a command economy.

On the other hand, the businessman also seeks to co-ordinate production in order to meet the price messages from consumers by bringing together the requisite resources to produce what is demanded at the lowest cost. The probability of profit acts as incentive to the businessman to make such decisions; he consistently acts through 'the sieve of profitability'.[31]

It is this function of co-ordination that is also one of the principal characteristics of the price mechanism and consequently of the market economy. It is this feature that stands in such contrast to the planned economy because the character of market co-ordination is profoundly about *decentralization*; it is achieved without a central bureaucracy, by the individual actions of consumers and producers each acting in response to price signals; there is no direct link between consumers and resources; planners are replaced by prices. The market economy therefore 'relies upon the impersonal working of the price mechanism to do the job of bringing consumers into contact with resources'.[32] No wonder the economist Peter Donaldson, writing out of the labour movement's base at Ruskin College, Oxford, could declare, 'That is the magic appeal of the market system: that without any planning intervention whatsoever, consumer demands are met as fully as possible.'[33]

Competition, profit, self-interest, conflict and usury

There are important issues associated with the economic base of market economics and price mechanisms. Indeed, they are so integral to both, and to modern economics, that a brief consideration of them is more than justified. It is warranted additionally because they play an over-significant part in Christian social thought. The charge of overdramatization is sustainable partly because they have been considered rarely in the context of economics and the market economy. They have been treated instead as isolated phenomena, without the necessary discernment. What follows corrects some of these deficiencies by locating them in the economic context. Although called issues, some call them 'virtues'.[34] Most are associated with the root economic problem of scarcity and complexity.

'We have been turned out of Paradise. We have neither eternal life nor unlimited means of gratification.'[35] A modern economist confirmed Hesiod's acceptance of scarcity as a fundamental determinant of economic life. Accepting the scarcity of resources has many implications. For example, it means there is an impetus to use them more efficiently to meet the expressed wants of consumers. The alternative is to accept the waste of scarce resources, the knowingly less efficient use of resources. *Competition* between producers ensures that resources are deployed in the least costly production. It also becomes a test of efficiency. For such competition to exist requires many buyers and sellers so that none are so large as to over-influence prices, and there is free entry and exit for them from the markets. Consequently, if the price moves up, more would enter the market, and vice versa. Excess profit would therefore eventually be eliminated. By the 1930s, however, economists began to recognize the growing presence of the imperfect competition of monopolistic capitalism, with the impact on markets of larger and larger companies. However, a modified but none the less legitimate and valuable role for competition continued to influence economic thought. There was a general understanding of competition not as rivalry, but as what Hesiod called 'good conflict', the existence of alternatives for buyers and sellers so that none could determine the price. 'Competition is what keeps profit at the normal level and resources properly allocated.'[36] The role of the state was to resist its over-deterioration into quasi-monopolies. For competition was the opposite of monopoly, not co-operation. Thus a major misunderstanding of the Christian socialists, with their promotion of co-operation as the remedy for competition, was traceable to their defective grasp of economics.

Profit is similarly related to basic economic problems and the response of market economies. Essentially, it represents 'the surplus of revenue over costs'[37] of those able to use capital in production. Of course, most people are motivated by the desire for gain, if only by working harder for more pay, or buying the same goods cheaper in one supermarket than another. In the allocation of scarce factors for the production of goods and services, making profits serves two functions vital for the efficient operating of the market economy: it acts as an incentive and it provides information. These ensure that resources can be used more efficiently to satisfy declared wants, and generate a criterion to test the extent of that achievement. Both combine to keep 'the particular units of our economy in tune with the needs of the whole'.[38] Profits also provide the primary source of saving for industrial investment for future production. The real problems of excessive profits can only be located in this context.

The importance of *self-interest* has been acknowledged in the history of economics. At the heart of Adam Smith's discoveries was his recognition that the pursuit of self-interest by individual consumers and producers also delivered the unintended consequences of the public good. Conversely, the pursuit of altruism in economics would result in economic harm. What is also apparent is the intimate relationship between self-interest and the 'virtues' of competition and the profit motive. Their combined effects contributed greatly to the emergence of a dynamic economy.

Integrally part of that free market economy are inevitable *conflicts* of interest between the owners of the factors of production (capital and labour), managers and managed, producers and consumers, and rich and poor. For increasingly large markets and companies only accentuated fundamental differences generated by specialization and the subdivision of labour. Schumpeter's description of capitalism's technological change as 'creative destruction' is equally applicable to these disturbances. Yet it also suggested that the cause of conflict contained the possibilities of its regulation, through the price mechanism. Conflicts between different groups in the market can be settled through price changes. When they change, people have to adapt; so the conflict ceases to be between people because the price mechanism provides 'the objective factor' to which they have to adapt.[39] The voting procedures of liberal democracies provide a similar impersonal way of facing up to inevitable conflicts of interest.

Examined in the same context, the essentially economic character of interest assumes a significance that Christians throughout history have rarely understood. There are still important voices that use biblical and medieval condemnations of *usury* as the basis of moral judgements on economics. Some of these historical arguments have been noted, including the process of increasing amendments to that traditional opposition under pressure of changing economic realities. These consisted of the growing need for capital, no longer for personal use, but for the production purposes of commerce and then industry. Money ceased to be regarded as 'barren' and not for 'breeding', but as credit, as command over necessary resources: so 'the lender forgoes a certain amount of command over resources and makes it available to the borrower'.[40] It was this purchasing power, as capital, that was used to purchase factories and 'mixed' with labour and raw materials. As 'stored-up wealth in the form of capital', it made possible the creation of more products from a given amount of labour and natural resources. It made possible industrialization and the modern economy.

In this process, all three factors of production – labour, capital and natural resources – were essential. To isolate one, capital, as Marx and his successors have done, including liberation theologians, is to misunderstand totally the plural nature of economic growth and modern economics. Similarly, it is also important to distinguish in the economic process between payment as interest for the use of capital, and the distribution of the ownership of capital. Regarding the former, economic theory understands interest to include reward for abstinence from present consumption or waiting for greater returns, and reward for sacrificing liquidity, the ability to use money now. A risk element is also identified as warranting reward by rate of interest.

All these functions are as essential as labour for the economic process. It is vital for human living now to divert resources from present consumption, or liquidity, to investment for future production; it is essential to allocate capital between varying risks. All need to be encouraged by incentives, all require regulation and allocation by mechanisms. It is to these tasks that a varying rate of interest contributes, by acting as a price mechanism and allocating the supply of capital between competing uses or demands. And again, as with self-interest, conflict, competition and profits, interest is open to grave abuse, although its economic value cannot be overridden by its misuse: despite misapplications, 'while steps can be taken to anticipate their consequences, they cannot be eliminated altogether by any alteration of the economic system, however radical'. Given the need for modern economies and economics, the choice is not between interest or a usury-free society. It is about coming to terms with the economic realities of life and seeking to modify them in the light of human purposes; it is not about pursuing utopian alternatives: 'Monetary panaceas, like all forms of panacea, are therefore based on an over-simplification of the issues involved.'[41]

The consideration of issues like profit and interest has been undertaken in relation to the context of basic economic problems and the market system. It has been a survey with omissions and inaccuracies. Yet its concern has been to recognize the importance of economics for such issues. It thereby stands as a correction to theological judgements which consider such matters as predominantly ethical. This interpretation is a reaction against such divorcing from context.

What emerges from these considerations, including the central role of the price mechanism, is the fundamental importance of basic economic problems and the response of the market economy. Indeed, so dominant is the latter in the modern economy and context that it is not surprising how many superlatives it has attracted, even from moderate economists; Donaldson refers to the 'magic appeal'[42] of the market system and the 'mesmeric appeal of the price mechanism'.[43] The legacy of Smith's 'hidden hand' continues to be very obtrusive!

Faced with the temptation to overemphasize, it is important to correct misunderstandings of the price-market economy by confirming the interpretation beginning to emerge in this study. What this rejects is any attempt to inflate its achievements by removing it from the constraints of the realities of life on earth. Denys Munby recognized this danger when he argued that 'economists have been tempted to bow down and worship this marvellous automatic regulator of man's affairs, partly at least because they alone understand it, and what we understand, we begin to love, and then to adore'.[44] It is that 'fatal deceit'[45] of the tendency to idolatry that can be detected in the contemporary works of F.A. Hayek and, to a much lesser degree, in Britain's Lord Harris. It is a deceit that can be traced to Adam Smith's view of the market as a 'natural' phenomenon of the same order of reality as Newton's laws of gravity, and to Herbert Spencer's Social Darwinism in the late nineteenth century. Daly and Cobb rightly correct these gross misunderstandings by recognizing the market as an essentially human construct which brings order out of potential chaos, and originates in a way comparable to language.[46]

The emerging picture of the market economy must also be distinguished from its ideal type as developed in more theoretical economics. This assumes that consumers bid rationally and freely for goods in the market, that prices reflect costs, that competition is unrestrained and therefore removes excess profit, and resources go to the most efficient firms. Although such theorizing is essential for the development of any academic discipline, and is reflected in some of the arguments in this chapter, the understanding of the market economy that has to emerge relates more to the general characteristics of actual market economies as they have developed particularly in the West. This means that the undoubted, and I would argue essential, contributions to human living of the market economy in more advanced societies have to be qualified by its equally undoubted but highly significant defects, even when measured against its ideal type. Thus actual firms are often not in full competition, so prices do not fully reflect costs and firms do not simply respond to consumer demand. Yet despite universally agreed defects, there is a general recognition that no effective substitute exists, whether of a socialist command economy or a substantial 'third way'. As the secular economist Donaldson observes, supported by the lay theologian Hay, 'until we devise some clear alternative techniques for coping with the enormously complex problems of allocating resources in a modern industrial economy such a view remains utopian'.[47]

It appears, therefore, that the market economy remains the least harmful way known to us of operating a modern economy. Indeed, so significant is it, in its complexity and achievements, and despite its defects, that one becomes unable to use some traditional concepts to account for it. For example, Polanyi[48] was right to warn against elevating it into the actual determinant of society itself. Yet to reduce the market to a small 'm', to a mechanism alone, to a 'serviceable drudge',[49] equally misses the mark. The concept of a market economy avoids such disadvantages. So the complexities of economics and contemporary society in a changing context again heighten inadequacies of traditional language, not least in Christian social thought.

Facing up to reality: the socializing of the market

To exalt the market system into a hard determinist ideology of a libertarian type,[50] not only distorts the evidence of most econom-ists with regard to its immense contribution as an essentially human construct, warts and all, but it also fails to accept its location within the wider framework of society. For the first century of modern economics this broader understanding was reflected in the use of the concept 'political economy'. Pointing to the connection between economic and political theory and practice in any understanding of wealth creation in society, it was replaced by 'economics' as the specialist-operating concept before the end of the nineteenth century. In recent years there has been a renewed interest in the older concept, among theologians as well as others. So Meeks includes four components in political economy: power, property, work as production, and needs as consumption.[51]

Despite its greater accuracy as a more 'suggestive concept', it is doubtful whether its rediscovery reflects sufficiently the complexity of the contemporary context. Revivals rarely allow for the new challenges of a contemporary context, partly because they are so associated with the past. The value of the 'market economy' is that it can be interpreted to include both modern economics as basic economics and system, and its intimate connections with contemporary institutions and political life. It is that essentially economic base and its wider linkages that comprise the modern market economy.

Having noted that, of course, there is an immediate need to acknowledge that the processes of socialization have influenced increasingly the formation of the contemporary market economy, beginning in the mid-nineteenth century. The unequivocal oper-ating of a pure *laissez-faire* was inflicted on British society, if at all, for only a limited period. Legislation, for example as Factory Acts, began to curtail its worst excesses almost from its inception. By 1950 the state, through macroeconomics, played a decisive role in the maintenance of economic activity and employment. All advanced market economies are thus now organized on the basis of such an 'impurity principle'.[52] The effective functioning of a market economy now includes, quite centrally, a social dimension.

All these developments combine to question previous classifications of market economics. Reflection on them again suggests clarifications for the task of reformulation and redefinition. For example, the connotations between *laissez-faire* capitalism and the 'free' market indicate their inappropriateness for describing the complex socioeconomic reality of today's market economy. The use by Thatcherism and Reaganomics of the 'free market' served the useful function of criticizing the corporate state of the 1970s, but it hardly does justice to the social and economic needs of people in advanced societies, as their successors John Major and George Bush soon acknowledged. With regard to 'capitalism' itself, that concept is so identified with the earlier 'free market' variety and the understandable reaction of socialism against it, that again it appears increasingly inappropriate as a description of contemporary Western market economics. It was Bishop Oxnam in 1954, writing out of the old Social Gospel tradition in the USA, who (with others) acknowledged the inaccuracy of the old concept of capitalism to describe its socially reconstructed contemporary successor.[53] The rise of the powerful modern state, political democracy, social welfare policies and institutions, and a greater business responsibility, have transformed the market into its current reality.

Within the Western tradition, the market economy now manifests itself in a number of forms. These vary from the social market of Germany and the social democracy of Sweden, to the more primitive socialization of the USA, in some ways closer to the market economies of East Asia. A major symbol of this trend has been the commitment of the European Community to the Social Charter as an integral part of the market economy, despite the foot-dragging of the British administration.

The necessary socializing of the market economy should also be distinguished from the processes of modernization, for these stretch beyond the system of market economies and include command economies. Most important of all, they centre on the technological transformation of modern life – producing what Peter Berger has described as 'the revolution of rising expectations',[54] and affecting social mobility and class structures. Clearly, market economies are part of such processes as their principal historical initiator through the combining of capitalism and industrialization, and as their most effective sustainer. Yet modernization and market economies are not fully coterminous given the growth of modern command economies.

The intimate relationship between the two forces certainly includes the emergence of post-industrial societies. By this is meant the steep decline of traditional manufacturing employment in advanced economies, and the complementary rise of the service sector spearheaded by the growth of the new knowledge class associated with the new technologies.[55] Yet even these developments cannot be restricted to market economies, but are present also in command economies, 'the twin manifestations of modernity'.[56] That is why so many of the critical judgements of capitalism by Marxists are so inaccurate. For they ascribe to capitalism alone what is part of the wider processes of modernization, even though they are focused in it. Using the concept of market economy allows a discerning representation of all these trends in ways that take greater account of the nuances of actual economic and social processes.

To examine major characteristics of the socializing of the market economy, two areas of influence, institutions and politics, have been selected. Both have enabled the market economy to reject raw *laissez-faire* capitalism and yet retain a central commitment to the market-price system.

1. Institutions

There was early recognition of the need for a social framework within which the market could operate, to provide what was regarded as an essential support and constraint. It was in 1759 that Adam Smith observed that, '[Men] could safely be trusted to pursue their own self-interest without undue harm to the community, not only because of the restrictions imposed by the law but also because they were subject to built-in restraint derived from morals, custom and education.'[57] The major institutions of society, in particular property and values, made significant contributions to the sustaining and restraining of the market.

Property

The nature and significance of property in society has been a matter for debate throughout history. That has been the case certainly with regard to the functioning of economics, and particularly in terms of the ownership and deployment of the factors of production, land, labour and capital. With the dismantling of feudalism and mercantilism and the rise of *laissez-faire* capitalism, new understandings of property began to play a central role in the development of market economies. It is not surprising therefore that many commentators continue to define the market system with reference to 'the market with private property in the means of production'.[58] Others regard the institution of private property as one of the two essential features of a 'capitalist market economy'.[59] It is on this private ownership of the means of production that the opposition to market economies, led by the Marxists, has concentrated. By replacing it with the collective, social, state ownership of the main factors of production, it formed the basis for the command economy of state socialism. Given the intractable problems of operating such economies, other socialists have sought to use the market price mechanism, but in association with the state ownership of the major means of production.[60] It is with such a major modification to the communist economic project that the Chinese have experimented in recent years.

What is clear from this brief survey of the relationship between property and market economics is the centrality of the issue, and it is this that Christian commentators have acknowledged. Many liberation theologians follow the communist position, but most theological opinion in the West has accepted the importance of private property (including the means of production) for the effective functioning of modern societies. Within that acceptance, however, there has been a wide spectrum of opinion. This extends on the one hand from an unqualified support for private ownership, supported by the contemporary libertarian American philosopher Nozick, but also present in much neo-conservative Christian thought today and in early modern Roman Catholic teaching.[61] On the other hand, there has been strong support for a balanced approach to private property. Reinhold Niebuhr represents this perspective best, acknowledging the indispensability of private property for individual liberty and self-expression, yet also understanding that its concentration would lead to its use as a means of oppressing others.[62] Brian Griffiths exemplifies those who argue strongly from Scriptures for private property, but refuse to absolutize it because the sovereignty of God relativizes all ownership.

The broad acceptance of private property, particularly in the means of production, is now an indispensable part of the effective functioning of the modern market economy. Recent events in Eastern Europe and the Soviet Union have confirmed the relationship between market economies, liberal democracies, and civil liberties, and the unobtrusive but central role of private property in all of them. Arguing for private property as a basic determinant of a market system reflects these realities. It is a position confirmed by the observation of economists that, 'The trading of property rights is the essential feature of a market economy.'[63] Envisaging the operating of the price mechanism, particularly in its co-ordinating and incentive roles, without the existence of widespread private ownership, is extremely difficult. There have been no substantial examples in history of advanced economies maintaining their growth rates over generations without such an institutional basis.

Within this broad acceptance of the role of private property and its variety of modern forms, there are a number of qualifications. For example, there is no general support in theory, and certainly not in practice, for the extreme libertarian defence of absolute, unqualified, private ownership. At most, philosophers like Nozick have influenced temporarily wider opinion, but they will not be determinative in the long run. The trend has been to develop a series of modifications to the regulating model of private property. Thus market economies now accept that all property does not need to be in private ownership. Public services like education, roads and parks illustrate the legitimacy and feasibility of this development. The growth of the modern state has confirmed and extended this trend. While performing the key function of defending property rights and contracts, both indispensable to the market economy, the state has also been the principal agency for restraining the undue use of these rights in contravention of the public good or as a means of oppressing others. Beyond these qualifications is the historical character of the relationship between private property and market economies. This suggests that neither should be elevated into a central role for all economies in all places at all times: 'What is desirable at one time will not be desirable at another, as the technical and economic possibilities alter.'[64] It is therefore appropriate and necessary to argue only that the relationship appears to be essential for market economies at this stage of history.

Values

Adam Smith argued from experience and not abstract theory (unlike many later economists) that the effective operating of the market depended on the support of values as resource for market behaviour and restraint of its tendency to imbalance. The former included truth, honesty, obligation and trust, which the market system did not provide, and yet without which it could not survive: 'Market relations are so pervasive in a capitalist economy, that it would be impossible to regulate every transaction by a legal contract. An element of general social assent to standards of honesty and truth is also needed.'[65] Many of these values are historically part of Christianity initiating and sustaining virtues in the private and public realms. It is not surprising that the languages of faith and economics are so interconnected, with their talk of trust, debt and redemption. The role of the Protestant work ethic in the development of capitalism is another indication of this connection between Christianity and economics.

The restraining function of values in the market relates particularly to the use of self-interest as the principal motivating force in economic life. Its sheer power, if unrestrained, develops into selfishness, and the damaging of the intrinsic operating of the market through the creation of monopolies and the erosion of trust relationships. Among the greatest enemies of the market are the casino economy operators who promote greed as the primary economic virtue. Yet the untrammelled use of self-interest has equally harmful implications external to the market mechanism through its disturbing social consequences. The damage to individuals and communities through unemployment and deprivation is closely related to the functioning of an unregulated free market with uncontrolled self-interest at its heart.

The role of values as resource and restraint and their ambivalent relationship to the market economy are well illustrated through the necessary but ambiguous virtue of individualism. Its reality infects all classical economics, including the works of Marshall and Keynes. It is certainly present in contemporary Christian defenders of the free market – those such as Brian Griffiths. Again, this should not surprise us. Modern economics has given a primary role to the individual as consumer and producer acting in a rational, calculating and self-interested mode. Its tendency to develop sometimes into 'hyper-individualism', and rights only as entitlement,[66] into what Preston and MacPherson[67] have described as 'possessive individualism', should not be regarded as too over-dominant. It should certainly not be allowed to obscure its essential contribution to market economies, liberal democracy and civil liberties. As personal responsibility, initiative, rational and calculating choice, it provides an essential complement to the need for community. Indeed, the liberation of the individual from the corporatism of feudalism and mercantilism was achieved partly at the continuing cost of traditional human solidarities. Once again, there emerges the need to balance the excesses of individualism in the market with the communitarian habits promulgated by families and a wide variety of mediating structures or intermediate associations. It is here that the Church as institution has an essential role to play in nourishing those values that both resource and restrain the performances of market economies. It confirms the identifying of the cultural – moral realm as an order of creation, and as an indispensable institution, an intimate correlate of the market economy.[68]

2. Political life

The importance of politics for human living and its connections to economics has been acknowledged throughout recorded history. Thus the ancient Greeks maintained orderly household economies to free them for the more valued life of the *polis*. The relationship continued even into the modern era, with the rise of classical economics and their early naming as political economy. Recent attempts to revitalize the concept witness to the persistence of the concern to locate economics in a wider framework, and indeed to subordinate it in the end to the political task. The work of two leading Christian social ethicists, Wogaman and Preston, is committed to such priorities.

The importance of the relationship itself has been revived by the events of 1989. The principal participants regarded market economies and liberal democracies as two sides of the same coin. Before examining that connection, the nature of the link between the modern state and the market economy needs to be registered as both essential contribution to the socializing of the market and necessary preamble to a discussion of democracy and capitalism.

The market and the state

The modern state in Western market economies has emerged only in the last 100 years and is characterized by its complexity and size. Now, over 40 per cent of national income is allocated regularly to funding state activities and services over a whole range of social and economic fields. As the modern democratic state, it awaits theological interpretation, almost as an essential complement to this project. For, like the market economy, it is part of the modernization process, emerging in the West in relation to the development of capitalism and industrialization.

The modern state performs two essential functions with regard to the market economy.

First, it is an acknowledgement of the need for a framework wider than the market economy for it to operate more effectively. That in turn raises the question of participation and accountability in the wider framework. If, as Lord Harris argues, 'man should have the reins of his destiny so far as possible in his own hands', [69] then the consequence is an argument for involvement in political as well as economic power, a development to which Harris fails to pay sufficient attention. Given the sheer size of the modern state and economy, the issue of involvement in the one invariably and necessarily spills over into the other.

Secondly, the state is required to support and restrain the market economy. On the one hand it supports it by legitimizing and protecting private property and contracts. Since the Second

World War, through the development of macroeconomics, it also seeks to oversee economic activity by using, for example, fiscal and monetary policies. The maintenance of high employment, economic growth and low inflation are valued objectives shared with economic actors, but no longer left to them. Indeed, recently emerged East Asian market economies, along with France and Germany, now foster the closest collaboration between government and industry in carrying out industrial policies and activities. Japan's Ministry of International Trade and Industry (MITI) is the prime example of this development. Similarly, supporting the population through the collective provision of key services like education and health are regarded as essential contributions, as well as a counter-balance to economic activities. On the other hand, the state also acts as an essential corrective to known defects in the market economy. So it promotes anti-monopoly policies, corrects the externalities deficiency of the market, and pursues a whole host of regulatory interventions in the market, including the labour market as proposed in the European Community's Social Charter.

Despite the essential contribution of state activities to a modern market economy, there is an equal agreement that too much intervention can be counterproductive. The presumption has to be in favour of the free operating of the price system. So the last decade has seen the restoration of economic imperatives to a central place in economic management. Even with a strong modern state, 'it will still be necessary to make the price mechanism as a guide to efficiency'.[70]

The market and democracy

Once again, the market economy appears to be connected in the most substantial way with another sphere of reality, in this case liberal or political democracy.[71] The intimate nature of that relationship has been confirmed by recent events in Eastern Europe. After years of living under a totalitarian regime, the attraction of market and democracy was partly as 'an institutionalized limitation of the power of government'.[72] That certainly accounts for some of their success in North America, Western Europe and now Japan. E.R. Norman wisely sets these achievements in a longer-term perspective, when perhaps 'Europe and North America in the nineteenth and twentieth centuries, will prove to have been the one time in human development when a serious attempt was made to allow effectively free institutions'.[73]

From the perspective of the market economy, it can be argued that the relationship with democracy is essential because intrinsic to both projects is the decisive separation of the political and economic arenas. Without this degree of autonomy it is highly unlikely that the market-price economy would be able to operate effectively. So:

> There are elements of truth . . . in classical economies which remain a permanent treasure of a free society, since some forms of a 'free market' are essential to democracy. The alternative is the regulation of the economic process through bureaucratic – political decisions. Such regulation, too consistently applied, involves the final peril of combining political and economic power.[74]

It is just such a mistake that command economies made because they subordinated economics to a political ideology in ways reminiscent of the pre-modern societies of mercantilism and medieval Christendom. They stand as a warning against the dangers of political power without diminishing its necessity. They point to the value of the market economy for liberal democracy, since the effective functioning of each depends upon their relative autonomy within a wider framework of interdependence.

Despite their close relationship, important clarifications need to be registered. To begin with, their differences must be emphasized. Thus there will always be conflicts of interest between them, partly because democracy functions as a countervailing power to the market as well as contributing to a framework in relation to which it needs to operate. The growth of the government's role in economic affairs in the modern state only confirms the argument for liberal democratic politics. Democracy and the market are also not fully coterminous because although democracies are more likely to be market economies, not all market economies are democratic. It is a timely reminder to the Novaks of this world that a majority of the black citizens of the USA and a minority of citizens in Northern Ireland were not able to exercise their democratic rights effectively until the late 1960s. The political position is worse in the 'Four Little Dragons', although there are some signs of progress in them.

Despite these distinctions and caveats, there are strong tendencies at work that urge us to take account of the growing links between democracy, the market economy and civil liberties. Choice in politics appears to be an increasingly essential complement to choice in the economy, particularly as societies develop into more advanced economies. Such convergences obviously support Milton Friedman's claim that 'freedom is one whole'.[75] Yet equally, the exercise of choice is at least as much, if not more so, about finding *proximate* solutions to sometimes *intractable* problems, which the necessary interdependence of democracy and market also confirms. It is as much about what Ash noted so poignantly and realistically in Poland, after the first flush of revolution: the return of 'normal politics'. For the ability to exercise freedom in a Western democracy and market economy is about the precious gift of 'normal politics' and 'normal economics'. It is far more true to actual life, to the context itself, than the ideologically pure freedom of the Friedmans.

Facing up to our contemporary context with any degree of adequacy must surely include facing up to the market economy. What at first sight appears to be a straightforward task becomes, on closer inspection, a web of interlocking perspectives. At its heart is the market itself, focused on the price mechanism, a reality 'so familiar that it is difficult to convey its full significance'.[76] Its seminal importance, including its relationship to modern economics, is both confirmed and clarified by reflection on its historical context. Yet even such necessary focusing is misleading because it does not convey the dynamic and changing nature of the market with all its inherited defects and deficiencies. Emerging challenges in the wider context are making these shortcomings more apparent.

Again, the market cannot be considered in isolation from this broader context, not least because of its international character but more especially because as the First World it is enmeshed in the whole complex business of Third World development. The recent collapse of Second World command economies can only heighten dramatically that relationship.

Yet even without a wider perspective, the market cannot be viewed as economy alone. From its very inception, and gathering pace throughout its history, its survival and growth has been dependent upon powerful forces of socialization. These have varied from forces arguably almost intrinsic to it, like private property and economic virtues, to external forces closely and increasingly connected to it. The relationship of the market to liberal democracy best summarizes that part of the complex web. Because of the growing significance of the relationship it is unhelpful as well as inaccurate to assert the primacy of either market or democracy, particularly given the failure of politicized economies in Eastern Europe. The relationship should be viewed rather as symbiotic, as two necessary realities in interactive relationship with one another.

To aggregate and then conceptualize this web of forces and relationships is no easy task. What becomes more and more apparent is the inadequacy of traditional language. As we have noted, certainly 'capitalism', like 'the word *laissez-faire*, is dead'.[77] Yet other language, more preferred by Western Christian social thought, is also redundant. For example, the concept of a mixed economy no longer does justice to the changing context, with its emphasis on the market as socialized and its recognition that over-interference with the market mechanism produces damaging consequences outweighing preferred benefits. The events of 1989 only confirm the obsolescence of a mixed economy 'in which the state in various ways controls and plans the activities of private businessmen, and itself engages directly in economic activity as an entrepreneur',[78] even though private businessmen play an important role in it.

The market economy has been confirmed overwhelmingly as a working concept for the next part of this project because it encapsulates more adequately than any other the complex web of forces and relationships that has so far emerged.

Notes

1 A. Buchanan, *Ethics, Efficiency and the Market* (Clarendon Press 1985), p. 1.

2 F. Maurice, *Life*, 1885, vol. 1, p. 441.

3 M. Novak, in *The Spirit of Democratic Capitalism* (American Enterprise Institute/Simon & Schuster 1982), p. 240, distinguishes between the economic realities present in every economic system in every age, and the evaluation of economic systems. He also notes an equivalent distinction made on

Marxism in the papal encyclical *Pacem in Terris*, 1963, between historical movements (comparable to basic economic problems) and philosophical teaching (comparable to economic systems), pp. 251f.

4 Roger Shinn, 'From Theology to Social Decisions – and Return', in Block, Brennan & Elzinga, eds., *Morality of the Market, Economic Perspectives* (Fraser Institute 1985), pp. 188-9.

5 D. Hay, *Economics Today* (Apollos 1989), pp. 92–3. I am much indebted to his discussion of positive and normative economics.

6 Hay, p. 95, quoting K. Popper, *The Logic of Scientific Discovery* (Hutchinson 1968), p. 252.

7 Hay, p. 110, quoting P. Samuelson, *The Foundations of Economic Analysis* (New York, Atheneum, 1965).

8 J.F. Sleeman, *Basic Economic Problems: A Christian Approach* (SCM Press 1953), p. 22.

9 G. Williams, *The Economics of Everyday Life* (Penguin 1951), pp. 112–13.

10 M.D. Meeks, *God the Economist: The Doctrine of God and Political Economy* (Philadelphia, Fortress Press, 1989), quoted on p. 159.

11 D.L. Munby, *Christianity and Economic Problems* (Macmillan 1956), pp. 44–5.

12 J. Bennett, ed., *Christian Values and Economic Life* (Harper 1954), p. 186.

13 B. Gordon, *Economic Analysis before Adam Smith: Hesiod to Lessius* (Macmillan 1975), p. 4.

14 Meeks, pp. 171f.

15 Munby, *Christianity and Economic Problems*, p. 262.

16 L. Robbins, *The Nature and Significance of Economic Science*, 1934, quoted in P. Donaldson, *Economics of the Real World* (BBC and Penguin 1973), p. 22.

17 R. Benne, *The Ethic of Democratic Capitalism: A Moral Reassessment* (Fortress Press 1981), chapter 6, quoting Samuelson.

18 J.F. Sleeman, *Economic Crisis: A Christian Perspective* (SCM Press 1976), chapter 7.

19 B. Webb, *My Apprenticeship* (Penguin 1971), pp. 386–7.

20 Hay, p. 148.

21 G. Williams, chapter 2. Munby, in chapter 9 of *Christianity and Economic Problems*, refers to it as 'the price system'.

22 As noted above in the history of economics section, marginal utility for the consumer relates price to the value of the last item consumed; for the producer, the value of the resource or factor relates to the marginal contribution of the last unit of the resource used when it is equal to the cost of any alternative use. See H. Daly and J. Cobb, *For the Common Good* (Merlin Press 1990), pp. 47–8.

23 Donaldson, p. 23–4.

24 Williams, p. 177.

25 Gordon, p. 262.

26 Williams, pp. 23f.

27 D.L. Munby, *God and the Rich Society* (Oxford University Press 1961), p. 42.

28 Munby, *God and the Rich Society*, p. 43, quoting V.A. Demant, *God, Man and Society* (SCM Press 1933), p. 49.

29 For example, see Munby and Hay.
30 Munby, *Christianity and Economic Problems*, p. 164–5.
31 Munby, *God and the Rich Society*, pp. 202f.
32 Donaldson, p. 23.
33 Donaldson, p. 25.
34 Sleeman, pp. 55f.
35 Gordon, p. 4.
36 Daly and Cobb, p. 49.
37 Munby, *God and the Rich Society*, p. 82.
38 Munby, *God and the Rich Society*, p. 83.
39 Munby, *God and the Rich Society*, p. 122.
40 I am heavily dependent on Sleeman's *Basic Economic Problems*, pp. 152f, for this section on interest.
41 Sleeman, p. 166.
42 Donaldson, p. 25.
43 Donaldson, p. 143.
44 Munby, *Christianity and Economic Problems*, p. 205.
45 The title of Hayek's latest work – an attack on socialist and political interference with the market!
46 Daly and Cobb, pp. 44f.
47 Donaldson, pp. 147.
48 Daly and Cobb, p. 61.
49 A favourite concept of R.H. Preston's, adapting one of Tawney's. It resonates with Meeks's view of it, quoting M. Polanyi, as an 'institutional gadget' (Meeks, p. 50).
50 For example, David Friedman, son of Milton, does this.
51 Meeks, p. 8.
52 G. Hodgson, *The Democratic Economy* (Penguin 1984).
53 Bennett, ed., pp. 24f.
54 P. Berger, *The Capitalist Revolution: Fifty Propositions about Prosperity, Equality and Liberty* (Wildwood House 1987), chapters 1–3.
55 These developments have been charted in my *Faith in the Nation*, and in other more substantial works.
56 Berger, p. 11.
57 A. Smith, *Theory of Moral Sentiments*, in A.W. Coates, ed., *The Classical Economists and Economic Policy* (Methuen 1971).
58 A. Buchanan, *Ethics, Efficiency and the Market* (Clarendon Press 1985), p. 2.
59 Hay, pp. 146–7.
60 Developed by Oskar Lange and Fred Taylor in the 1930s.
61 See the papal encyclical of Leo XIII, *Rerum Novarum*, 1891, para. 35.3: 'We have seen this great labour question cannot be solved except by assuming as a principle that private ownership must be held sacred and inviolable' (Catholic Truth Society 1983). This position has since been modified.
62 R. Niebuhr, *The Children of Light and the Children of Darkness* (New York, Charles Scribner's, 1944), pp. 117–18.
63 J. Le Grand and R. Robinson, *The Economics of Social Problems* (Macmillan 1976), p. 153.

64 Munby, *God and the Rich Society*, p. 192.
65 Hay, p. 149. V.A. Demant in *Religion and the Decline of Capitalism* (Faber 1952) argued, along with others, that capitalism was parasitic on such external values and would gradually consume them.
66 See R. Bellah, ed., *Habits of the Heart*, (New York, Harper & Row, 1986).
67 See R.H. Preston, *Religion and the Persistence of Capitalism* (SCM Press 1979), and his use of C.B. MacPherson's *Theory of Possessive Individualism* (Oxford University Press 1962).
68 On the Reformed tradition regarding the Orders of Creation, see Preston, pp. 75–6, and Novak.
69 Peter Vandame, interpreting and responding to Ralph Harris in *The New Right and Christian Values*, Occasional Paper no. 5, 1985, Edinburgh, New College.
70 J.E. Meade, *Efficiency, Equality and the Ownership of Property* (Allen & Unwin 1964), p. 13.
71 By 'democracy' is meant 'a political system in which governments are constituted by majority votes in regular and uncoerced elections' (Berger, p. 74).
72 Berger, p. 75.
73 E.R. Norman, *The Denigration of Capitalism* (The Standing Conference of Employers of Graduates, Annual Lecture, May 1977).
74 R. Niebuhr, *The Irony of American History* (New York, Charles Scribner's, 1952), p. 93.
75 Berger, quoted on p. 78.
76 Hay, p. 147.
77 Munby, *Christianity and Economic Problems*, p. 233.
78 Munby's definition, in Munby, *Christianity and Economic Problems*, p. 234–5.

Part Two

Christian Responses to the Market Economy: Three Great Communities of Memory

Because the church exists for the sake of God's love of the world, there can be no sound teaching about the church that does not include the relationship of the church to our society's economy and the world's economy (M. Douglas Meeks, *God the Economist: The Doctrine of God and Political Economy*).[1]

It is commonplace to argue that 'there exists no serious disciplined body of theological reflection on the history and foundation of economics'.[2] The next three chapters will try to demonstrate that the myth of the commonplace, as usual, collapses when faced with a survey of actual Christian responses to market economies. It compelled me to change *my* mind.

The general objective of Part Two of the project is to clarify the principal Christian approaches to economics in the contemporary context. To do so is a valuable exercise in its own right. There is a constant need for 'the enlightenment of Christians on complicated matters with which they should be concerned as citizens or members of particular groups in society'.[3] The market economy is certainly such a matter, as previous chapters have revealed. Yet so also are its Christian responses, and these too warrant equally careful and detailed analysis. By bringing context and responses together in a critical appraisal it should then be possible to undertake a second objective: to reformulate Christian social thought.

A study of current Christian engagements with the economy reveals a rich and varied fare. It provides a wealth of resources for those concerned about contemporary society whether from the perspective of international issues, economic affairs, the struggle for political democracy or the moral–cultural arena.[4] All these concerns become apparent as we identify three main

Christian responses to market economies, their characteristics, key representatives, the history of their traditions or communities of memory, their influence on the responses of the Church to economics, and the theological method used. Reflection on the relationship between these aspects of Christian life is particularly rewarding. Its importance was brought home to me when I realized that deficiencies in what the liberal tradition said about economics not only lay behind the Churches' pronouncements on the economy, but was also reflected in a defective theological method. There is an intimate and formative connection between them all, and their histories. It is another example of the dangers of restricting an enquiry into such a complex reality as the market economy to the narrow confines of a particular theological discipline like Christian social ethics. This study drives one unremorsefully into a web of themes, histories, personal stories, church life and witness, and methodologies. Because they play such an important part in the following chapters, further introductory comment is justified.

To bring order into such complex material, three main Christian responses to market economies have been identified: the conservative, the radical, and the liberal. Each illustrates a 'generating centre' or tradition of Christian thought on economic affairs[5] (what the US theologian Stackhouse referred to as the 'major accents' in an area of study).[6] The value of such typologies or viewpoints for sharpening understanding of important issues is well known. Yet their dangers are equally obtrusive. Thus it is important that they should not be confused with pure types that rarely exist in reality, particularly in a complex, radically changing context. They can then indicate actual trends and emphases, and point to certain historical continuities and developments as bases of identifiable traditions. They also obviously overlap with 'generating centres' in secular responses to economic matters. This should not surprise or disturb even those Christians who are tenaciously concerned to promote and defend a distinctively Christian way of life. For overlap is inevitable if we are dealing 'with an objective world shared in common'.[7]

The three chosen responses should elicit no surprise. They are so obvious as to require little justification. Yet they are none the less important because they do indicate the dominant trends in Christian thought – which either work closely with market economies, which reject them, or which try to subordinate them to other purposes by reducing them to the status of a mechanism.[8]

What is surprising is what is omitted. For example, there is no recognition of 'green' Christianity as a fourth response, what Wogaman calls 'economic conservationism'.[9] This is partly because such economics are not developed sufficiently to constitute a new dominant type; it is equally because they reject so much basic economics common to existing systems as to suggest the repudiation of economic systems in themselves. In contrast, the radical critique is included precisely because it seeks to replace the market system with a socialist one. However, because conservationism represents such a vital perspective in the contemporary and emerging context, it does occupy a prominent place in the *final* part of the argument: in the reconstruction of Christian social thought. For similar reasons, the powerful anarchist–pacifist Christian tradition is not included. Running through all these alternatives, although to a lesser extent, is the panacea disease that Denys Munby so ruthlessly criticized in the 1930s Christendom group and its pursuit of the elixir of a distinctively Christian sociology. All are characterized by 'brilliance of intellect and imaginative grasp of problems unhampered by any solid knowledge of the realities of the issues with which they tried to grapple, and any willingness to learn from experts'.[10]

The development of the three responses is essentially a series of conversations. Beginning with their main characteristics, each is then expressed through the particular contribution of a Christian who best exemplifies that tradition. Again, there are obvious dangers in such a decision. Choices reflect preferences if not prejudices, yet provided that reasoned arguments support the decisions, then that deficiency is neutralized. More challenging is Wogaman's concern that the purpose should be 'not so much to classify thinkers as it is to explore issues'.[11] I am much less reticent because I recognize the value of stories and individuals in the development of Christian social thought. This is another indication of the break with the liberal tradition, which Wogaman exemplifies, and the acceptance of some post-liberal arguments.

After careful thought, I decided to select three *contemporary* examples of the responses. The acceptance of the key role of the contemporary context ruled out any other choice, despite the contributions of figures like R.H. Tawney to these traditions.

In the formation of Christian social thought, the centrality of the contemporary context cannot be avoided. Consequently, the Christian responses and their representative figures must be equally contemporary. This judgement is only confirmed by the growth in the 1980s in the quality of the Christian debate on economic affairs.[12]

The three representatives were also selected for a number of other reasons. For example, each had to have a proven track record in terms of the quality and substance of their engagement with the contemporary market economy from the perspective of a particular tradition. Because of the international character of the market economy, the ecumenical dimension had to be represented in both senses of the word: as multinational, and reflecting different denominations and the ecumenical movement. The conservative response is therefore illustrated by the work of Brian Griffiths writing as a member of the Church of England; the radical response by Ulrich Duchrow, a (West) German Lutheran who has also been involved recently in an official capacity with the World Council of Churches; and the liberal response by J.P. Wogaman, a Methodist in the USA.

Obviously, they do not represent all denominations or countries! To counter this deficiency, considerable attention is paid to other nations, denominations and contributors. Thus Roman Catholicism is reflected in the comments on *Economic Justice For All* (the Pastoral Letter of the US Bishops) and in the frequent references to the work of Michael Novak. The absence of Third World liberation theology is a more substantial and disturbing omission. After much thought, I decided that being faithful to our context and the central role of market economies could only be attempted from their basis in the Western tradition of advanced economies. It reflects my growing conviction that the days of the hegemony of unequivocal liberationist socialist theologies are coming to an end. Yet the international character of market economies and the dominating presence of poverty in the Third World require such perspectives to feature prominently in the arguments of this book. The contribution of Duchrow consciously provides a substantial link with the liberationist traditions of the Third World. The absence of other Christian economists (Griffiths is the only one of the three trained in the discipline) is compensated for by the dependence on economists like Hay, Sleeman, and Munby in Chapters 2 and 3.

The 'conversation' then moves on from contemporary responses to their history, to those communities of memory or traditions that matter to the responses and their representatives. Because the project is written from and addressed to an essentially British context, where the representatives are not British then the brief stories of British 'deputies' are used as entry points to the British traditions of the responses. R.H. Tawney fulfils this role for the radical response, and Ronald Preston for the liberal. In doing so, we need to be aware of the danger of 'linear history', of reading back into history from a present stance, and so being open to the charge of serious misinterpretation. Clearly, the intention is not to do that. It is rather to work with the history of a tradition with the aim of refining, developing and contextualizing an important strand even further.[13] This will involve important reinterpretations of tradition, given the challenge of the contemporary market context.

The final layers of the responses relate to their implications for church life and theological method. Regarding the former, the formation of a response to an issue as complex and dominant as the market economy is almost inevitably reflected in an equivalent form of the Church. The liberal response provides the prime contemporary example of this connection, with its domination of the social statements of leaders of the Western Church and official church bodies. Yet the relationship also affects the others. For example, the radical response seeks to convert the Church into an opponent of the status quo and exemplar of an alternative economy. The conservative seeks to use the Church to legitimize the market economy.

The implications for theological method are more complex, yet linkages do exist between deficiencies in the economic judgements of the liberal response and the method used. In contrast, the conservative and radical responses are prone to use a more direct method, moving directly from the Scriptures or Christian doctrine to detailed judgements on contemporary economic questions. Given the inadequacies of all three responses in this field in a period of great change, it is important to discover whether a major development in theological method is being signalled. The historian Jonathan Clark's judgement points beyond historical

83

method to the possibilities that the development of Christian responses to market economies begins to present to Christian social thought and the Churches: 'The generality of scholars are only driven to a discussion of method in times of crisis within their subject, when an orthodoxy is threatened or breaking up.'[14] This suggestion is examined in Part Three.

Notes

1 Philadelphia, Fortress Press, 1989, p. 23.
2 M. Novak, *The Spirit of Democratic Capitalism* (American Enterprise Institute/ Simon & Schuster 1982), p. 237.
3 D.L. Munby, *God and the Rich Society* (Oxford University Press 1961), p. 165.
4 Novak, p. 14.
5 J.P. Wogaman, *Christian Perspectives on Politics* (SCM Press 1988), part two.
6 M.L. Stackhouse, *Public Theology and Political Economy* (Grand Rapids, MI, Eerdmans, 1987).
7 Wogaman, p. 9.
8 Wogaman's types include the anarchist–pacifist, the liberationist, the neo-conservative, and the mainstream liberal (part two of *Christian Perspectives on Politics*). This resonates with my approach more than his earlier *Christians and the Great Economic Debate* (SCM Press 1977).
9 In his *Christians and the Great Economic Debate*.
10 Munby, p. 158.
11 Wogaman, *Christian Perspectives on Politics*, p. 31.
12 Raymond Plant's judgement in J.C.D. Clark, ed., *Ideas and Politics in Modern Britain* (Macmillan 1990), p. 117: 'The quality of the debate has improved enormously over the period in question and reveals very important features of the attitudes of the protagonists.'
13 R. Hole, *Pulpits, Politics and Public Order in England, 1760–1832* (Cambridge University Press 1989), p. 265.
14 J.C.D. Clark, *Revolution and Rebellion: State and Society in England in the Seventeenth and Eighteenth Centuries* (Cambridge University Press 1986), p. 16.

Four

The Conservative Response.
Affirming the Market Economy:
The Tradition of Christian Political Economy

Wherever markets are allowed to work, the result is an increase in prosperity and jobs. The remarkable contrast in economic performance between Asia-on-the-Pacific and Latin America over recent decades can be traced to the superior wisdom of faith in the market over faith in the state (Brian Griffiths).[1]

The devoted affirmation of market economies has been a growing phenomenon in the last fifteen years. It played a central part in the revolutions in Eastern Europe in 1989, and is a recurring symbol of the tortuous struggle for reform in what was the Soviet Union. Less surprising but as significant, and connected to these great upheavals, has been the remarkable resurgence of interest in strong market economies in 'capitalist' societies. Overshadowed by the charismatic leadership of President Reagan and Mrs Thatcher, similar commitment to the market was also occurring in countries as diverse as Canada, France, Spain and Australasia. This was certainly not a resurrection, because all these economies had been market-oriented for many generations. Yet it was a dramatic revival from the stagflation of the 1970s, and the post-war rule of the corporate state of Keynesianism and Welfarism. These developments were best characterized by the rise to power of the New Right or neo-conservatism[2] in the USA and Britain at the end of the 1970s. Although the replacement of Thatcher and Reagan by Major and Bush heralds a greater awareness of the social context of the market, the commitment to its dominant role remains. This is likely to continue for the foreseeable future, particularly with the spectacular decline of command economies as the only feasible alternative. They suggest good arguments for

85

interpreting the response through the contemporary importance of neo-conservatism.

The neo-conservative response to market economies has always been part of a broader movement just as the emerging understanding of market economies has included more than economics. Its principal features have therefore focused on the central role of the free market, a commitment to private ownership, a reduced role for the state, a strong belief in authority and democracy, and a recognition of voluntary bodies and personal responsibility. It has always been implacably opposed to socialism.

The Christian involvement, particularly in neo-conservativism, has been notable if not remarkable for its practice and theory, especially in the USA and Britain. In America, neo-conservative Christian political influence affected the highest levels, from Presidents Reagan and Bush to some of their most senior advisers and officials. Theoretically, this response's authority equalled its practice. Led by leading theologians like Richard Neuhaus, Ernest Lefever and Michael Novak, their contribution greatly benefited from such think-tanks as the Institute for Religion and Democracy (itself partly funded by the American Enterprise Institute).[3]

In Britain, the story followed a similar pattern but lacked the resources and intellectual power of the Americans. The political influence was expressed through Mrs Thatcher, as Prime Minister, and Brian Griffiths as head of her Policy Unit. Strong support was provided by Douglas Hurd, Chris Patten, Lord Hailsham and John Selwyn Gummer. Think-tanks played an even bigger part in the development of neo-conservatism in Britain, particularly in the formative years out of office in the 1960s and 1970s. The Institute of Economic Affairs under Lord Harris's direction, and the Social Affairs Unit under Digby Anderson, were important in this regard.

Besides these individuals and groups there are others, from theologians like Robert Benne in the USA[4] and E.R. Norman in the UK,[5] to organizations like CABE (the Christian Association of Business Executives). They come from all the major denominations and traditions, from the evangelicalism of Brian Griffiths to the Anglo-Catholicism of John Selwyn Gummer.

Despite variety, the tradition has a coherence that distinguishes it from extremists like the libertarians Friedman and Hayek, the evangelical fundamentalist Gerry Falwell, and the moral majority movement. What emerges is predominantly a responsible and impressive Christian response to market economies which needs to be treated with a discerning judgement lacking in the official Churches and their leaders.[6] Wogaman rightly observes that its representatives have tried to be creative, not just reactionary, in their theology and practice. It is a tradition to respect and learn from.

Characteristics of the response

It can be as confusing as illuminating to set out the principal features of this response, particularly as Christian neo-conservatism.[7] For example, the American strand is more committed to democratic capitalism than to the market economy. However, this can be regarded as complementary to the understanding of the market economy already beginning to emerge. Although this included market economics at its centre, institutions and politics were also integral to its development in advanced societies.

There are six characteristics relevant to the enquiry into market economies:

1. *A fundamental commitment to the market economy as an economic system* In comparison with the command economy, the free market is regarded as superior because of its efficiency and support for basic human freedoms. Consequently, it encourages only as much state intervention compatible with a democracy and a social concern for the basic welfare of all citizens. However, the recognition of the proven value of the market-price mechanism is never taken to the excess of libertarians like Hayek, Friedman and Harris. They tend to regard these forces and structures as unalterable laws in human nature, speaking of them 'as religious people speak of the numinous'.[8] There is no such strong tendency to idolatry in this Christian response, but there is a powerful understanding of the importance of wealth creation in the Scriptures and wider Christian tradition. It is regarded as a means of life and undertaken for the greater glory of God. The practice of modern economics is seen as central to this task. It is therefore committed to promote competition by restricting the tendency to monopoly by companies, trade unions and professional associations. Private ownership as the dominant

form of stake in society is acknowledged to be indispensable to the market enterprise.

2. *The dedication to political democracy as government by majority rule, regular free elections and fundamental civil liberties.*[9]   This is connected to a high valuation of what William Temple called intermediate associations. Standing between the individual and the state they act as bulwarks against state encroachment, and provide more accessible 'schools' for learning democratic skills. Underwriting such organizations and activities, certainly for Novak, is the principle of subsidiarity. Deeply embedded in the teaching of papal social encyclicals to the present day, subsidiarity declares that, 'It is a fundamental principle of social philosophy, fixed and unchangeable, that one should not withdraw from individuals and commit to the community what they can accomplish by their own enterprise and industry.'[10]

The relationship between democracy and the market (called 'capitalism' by the American strand) is of particular importance. For example, it reflects the necessary separation of the major arenas of life, especially politics and economics. In is argued that both reflect biblical insights into human dignity and sin. Thus democracy 'sustains the possibility of humane government in a necessarily unsatisfying world'.[11]

Although democracy and market are treated as the 'definitive political and economic values',[12] neither are regarded as the centre of value; God is above all systems whether political or economic. The suggestion is that both should be promoted as the clearly preferred, least harmful systems known to us.

It also claims democracy exists only in market economies, although the latter are not always democratic. In advanced societies, the two exist as a complementary whole, human freedom requiring both. This avowed relationship between political and economic functions in the market economy is also acknowledged by liberation theologians – but instead to justify their rejection, including Western political democracy!

3. *Curtailing the power of the state and politics in modern society.*   The extension of the power of the state and politics in the twentieth century is regarded as detrimental to liberty and the efficient functioning of the market. The state's contribution to economic life is therefore limited parallel to its restriction in wider society by the role of intermediate associations. However,

the state is expected to promote justice in defence of the vulnerable and to ensure that all citizens have the basic minimum necessary for life in a modern society, including income.

4. *The importance of religious values in resourcing democracy and the market.*   The response rejects the idea or feasibility of a totally free market society or ideology, operating without the constraints and support of institutions, values and politics. What are seen as the forces of secularism and their development from the Enlightenment are also rejected, and in particular their attempted exclusion of religion from the public and economic arena. This is one of the few points of agreement between the conservative response and the US Bishops' *Economic Justice For All*. Both are concerned with the dangers caused by the contemporary erosion of 'accumulated moral capital'.[13] Both link the reform of capitalism with spiritual renewal. Indeed, Novak goes further by advocating a plural society, and the support of values wider than Christian ones.[14] Capitalism, or the market economy, is regarded as profoundly about economics, and yet therefore inevitably and necessarily about more than economics.

5. *The rejection of communism and socialism as forms of idolatry.*   They are certainly seen as 'deeply flawed' and as 'the enemy'. As a sign of the times, the Christian project has to be unapologetically anti-communist, because communism is 'incompatible with a Christian understanding of humanity and historical destiny'.[15] Yet despite this intractable opposition, Christian neo-conservatives do not commit the excesses of McCarthyism in the early 1950s.

Associated with this rejection, in the USA rather than Britain, is the Christian legitimation of the USA as the key countervailing power in the world. The response is deeply disturbed over the mainline Churches' refusal to continue to underwrite this role. As Neuhaus comments, 'much of the leadership of mainline Protestantism cannot contribute to the moral legitimation and definition of the American experiment because, when all is said and done, it no longer believes in that experiment'.[16] The English Christian conservatives accept that judgement with regard to their own Churches.

6. *The recognition of many of the market's limitations, but within an overall framework of acceptance.*   The response's major concern over Third World poverty reflects this priority. While treating it

as a dominant international problem, along with the contribution of multinational corporations, it refuses to attribute this disaster principally to the market economy. Instead it regards Third World economies, their governments' policies, and cultural context, as the major cause of poverty.

Essentially, the response therefore takes the market economy very seriously. It tries to understand its economic base, its strengths and its connections with other spheres of life, and it does so for theological, economic, political and cultural reasons. It is an impressively consistent and coherent response, promoted with great conviction.

Brian Griffiths: the moralist of the market-place

In so many ways, Brian Griffiths is a classic convert. Brought up in a Welsh working-class family he travelled the well-trod route for self-made men: via the grammar school, the London School of Economics, and academic life (as Professor of Banking and International Finance at the City University, London), to become a non-executive director of the Bank of England.

Griffiths's political transformation was as dramatic and paralleled his social progress. Standing in the socialist tradition, he learned the importance of justice and a concern for the poor, and he continues to express his admiration for the labour movement's achievements in the nineteenth century.[17] The 1960s, however, changed all that. Through the economic mismanagement of the Wilson government, he jettisoned Keynesianism in favour of the free market system and monetarism. It was these understandings that were expressed so strongly in his tract for the times in 1985, *Monetarism and Morality: A Response to the Bishops*.[18] He became an admirer of Mrs Thatcher,[19] and in 1985 was chosen by her to head her Policy Unit. He remained a key influence on economic and social policy until their departure from office in the autumn of 1990. It was the classic journey from socialism to neo-conservatism undertaken by leaders from Novak to Paul Johnson, and stereotyped in Kristol's immortal assertion that, 'A neo-conservative is a liberal who's been mugged by reality.'[20]

The final conversion was from the closed ranks of the Plymouth Brethren to the established Church of England in the late 1970s where he became a devoted and committed member: as church warden, lay preacher, member of the national Church's Industrial and Economic Affairs Committee, and resourceful supporter of the dialogue between the Church of England and the Conservative Party. He remains a committed evangelical.

In so many ways Griffiths therefore represents the Christian neo-conservative response. As a self-made man on the Right of the Conservative Party, he clearly places a free market economy at the heart of its programmes. Yet he is aware of the market's connection to social policy and institutional life, and especially its dependence on moral values.[21] Indeed, it was partly because of his clarity over the latter that he was chosen by Mrs Thatcher as a major resource for her concern to capture 'the moral high ground' of national life. It was a remarkable combination that generated a 'Sermon on the Mound' free market economy.[22] Its impact spread well beyond Conservative Party and nation, even though most commentators stressed how little impact Mrs Thatcher's stewardship had had on voters' beliefs even after ten years in office. Yet that deficiency was more than compensated for by what Frank Field called her 'conversion of the Labour Party to a free market'![23]

At the heart of Griffiths's response to the market are strongly held Christian convictions, carefully elaborated in two important books, *Morality and the Market Place: Christian Alternatives to Capitalism and Socialism* (1982), originally given as the evangelical London Lectures in Contemporary Christianity, and *The Creation of Wealth* (1984), produced at the invitation of the Christian Association of Business Executives. Both are written in a deceptively simple style, yet careful reading reveals a well-read, disciplined theological mind. It comes as no surprise to hear him express his preference for a different way of life, one teaching Christian ethics! In contrast to Novak's intellectual breadth and fluency, Griffiths's unaffected arguments might appear pedestrian (a charge often made when comparing American and British social theology). Yet as a combination of theological reflection and practical experience, Griffiths's approach might well have the edge. He should certainly be regarded as a leading lay theologian.

What Griffiths does, essentially, is to make a clear Christian moral case for the market economy which is all the more per- suasive because, unlike Novak's, it recognizes its major defects.

These he seeks to remedy by arguing for its reform according to basic Christian principles. As an evangelical, influenced by neo-Calvinism,[24] he derives these norms very clearly and unequivocally from the Bible.

Since they are so central to his thinking and practice, the seven biblical guidelines for economic life are worth noting. They are: the positive mandate to create wealth; the need for private property rather than state or collective ownership; that each family should have a permanent stake in the economy; that the community should seek to relieve poverty rather than promote equality; that the government should remedy economic injustice; that materialism should be guarded against; and that accountability and judgement are integral parts of economic life.[25]

These guidelines emerge out of his interpretation of great biblical themes as they speak to the fundamentals of economic life. They vary from: the nature of creation, with its commitment to the goodness of the created order and our relationship to it through work and stewardship; the nature of the Fall with its implications for scarcity and the impossibility of economic utopias; the Mosaic laws as they provide a framework for political economy within which economic issues like property, the regulation of capital markets, prices, wages, taxes and redistribution are dealt with.[26]

Interestingly, such biblical political economy is heavily dependent on the Old Testament, leading one theologian to describe it as a 'Torah economy'.[27] In this, Griffiths is close to the radical response to the market of Ulrich Duchrow and the liberation theologians. Constituting fundamentally opposing views, they use the same basic literature and are committed to a biblically informed political economy as the basis for reforming society. In contrast to the radicals, however, Griffiths does not communicate a life-and-death hands-on wrestling with the Scriptures and contemporary capitalism. His work rather suggests an attempt to hedge the market round with governing principles; it is essentially an exercise in Christian social ethics. In the style and ethos of his theology, Griffiths stands in the tradition of rational evangelicalism. He is a 'keeper of the faith' and 'companion of the soul' with regard to political and economic life.[28]

Brian Griffiths confidently locates economic questions at the centre of his treatment of the market economy. He considers them in terms of 'the analytical tools of economics' and as an economic system.[29] What he therefore presents is a carefully reasoned case for the free market in a Christian framework. He does this through the foundational theme of the biblical and human importance of wealth creation.

For Griffiths, the market economy is undoubtedly the best way to achieve the creation of wealth. Historically he notes its remarkable record in increasing goods and services between 1790 and 1939. Compared with other existing systems, he records its greater effectiveness in generating economic growth and improving the living standards of citizens.[30] At the heart of these achievements he detects an increasing efficiency in the use of resources principally through the application of technological and human skills. Yet he is also aware that a central place in this take-off to sustained growth has to be accorded to the price mechanism. He regards it as provider of crucial information and incentives[31] for the efficient allocation of scarce resources to the process of wealth creation. Associated with this mechanism are major features of the market system, including private property, a stable state and legal system, and supportive values. He regards such analysis, and its distinctions between basic economics and economic systems, as essential in order to avoid the pitfalls of simplistic moral judgements. It is such economic and moral confusion that he detects in official church criticism of market economics in general and monetarism in particular.[32]

The commitment to the market-price mechanism must be distinguished from Griffiths's theological rejection of the free market as hard determinist ideology. Friedman and Hayek's view of the market as a spontaneous order, with no overall purpose, guaranteed harmony or equilibrium, and based on a view of economic man as rational isolated individual, is unacceptable to Christian opinion, contradicting, as it does, Christian beliefs in creation, providence, stewardship and human relationships.

From such libertarian distortions, the theological task is to rescue the market by locating it in 'the bounds of Christian justice'.[33] Its theological and economic advantages allow no other response. That is Griffiths's reply to Friedman's question to him: 'How can you be a Christian and advocate the market economy?'[34]

The rejection of the market as 'pure system' complements his opposition to the command economy because of its fundamental economic flaws, including its discarding of the price mechanism.

Its 'scientific' pretensions are similarly unacceptable, along with its disastrous record on civil and political liberties. The fundamental contradictions of communism are so unmanageable that even its existence as modified socialism cannot be condoned. Griffiths gives the last word to Solzhenitsyn, speaking about those who reject communism but fail to grasp 'its implacable nature . . . the failure to realise that communism is irredeemable, that there exist no "better" variants of communism . . .'[35]

In contrast to both hard determinist ideologies, he argues for a market economy which, although designated in a fallen world as the least harmful,[36] none the less can and must be 'persuasively argued' for.[37] Such a case, however, can never be the baptism of the market,[38] yet 'there is nothing to suggest in the whole of Scripture that the basic institutions of capitalism are incompatible with a Judaeo-Christian world-view'.[39]

What is also central to the case for the market, and distinctive of Griffiths's understanding, is the recognition that the market can only be rescued in Christian eyes and in terms of its own survival by the promotion of Christian values. The only feasible way forward for the market economy is as one of the 'Christian alternatives to Capitalism and Socialism'.[40] For this to happen requires the market being bound by 'Christian principles of justice'. It is a position close to V.A. Demant's belief, shared by T.S. Eliot, that society's 'cultural values and economic and political achievements will not survive without a Christian basis'.[41]

Such a Christianizing of the market is not just essential for Christian support; it concerns the very survival of the market. For Griffiths claims that the market economy was in deep crisis in the 1970s, challenged by unemployment, pollution, social dislocation and Third World poverty. Their root cause was the 'false values of secular humanism',[42] which distorted the values undergirding the market and derived from the Enlightenment. From that same source sprang the two fundamental economic distortions of the libertarian and communist ideologies, the one corroding the market from within, the other from without. The crisis of the market was at root a matter of values. Its redemption was equally a values issue to be solved by Christianizing the market. Only then would it be possible 'to implement what at least to economists appear to be technically feasible solutions to our problems'.[43]

The reform of the market according to biblical principles

therefore becomes his great concern. The 'logical outcome'[44] of the transformation of secular humanist capitalism will be a market economy compatible with Christian beliefs. For Griffiths that objective is not utopian. Setting out the kind of reforms needed to achieve it in 1980, in the lectures for 'Morality in the Market-Place', his 'The Conservative Quadrilateral' in 1990 gave numerous examples of how they were being accomplished. For example, the reform of the institutions of the corporate state had proceeded apace. So the assumption that the government should solve all problems, whether in economic life or social policy affairs, was discarded as an operating principle in national life. Privatization programmes, the tight control of public expenditure and borrowing, the reduction of direct taxation rates, the introduction of market criteria into the welfare state, and the drastic curtailment of local government powers – all these symbolized this transfer of authority. Complementing the change of emphasis was the commitment to localized managerial and financial decision-making in the health and education services, and the increase of consumer and producer participation. The latter was promoted through wider share ownership; the former by encouraging people to buy their own homes and to participate in the local management of schools.

Equally dramatic were the major reductions in trade-union monopoly powers and their greater democratization. Restrictive practices in other professional associations were also addressed, but with less success. More progress was made in the promotion of competition policy and the deregulation of financial markets.

All these changes were highlighted by Griffiths in reaction to what he regarded as David Jenkins's selective attack on the Conservative Quadrilateral of the individual, choice, the market, and wealth creation. In reply, he constructed what is essentially a Christian framework for the Conservative Quadrilateral based on biblical principles. The result was his balancing of individual and community, choice and responsibility, markets and welfare, and wealth creation and trusteeship. In this way, he was able to inform the reforms of the 1980s with theological principles.[45]

Within this biblically organized economy, Griffiths deals with four issues essential to the operating of a market economy: the state, political life, intermediate associations, and private property. With regard to the state, the reforms to dismantle the corporate state should not condone a minimalist negative view of the state. He is clear, on biblical grounds, that the state must be more than the guarantor of law and order, property rights and contracts. Unlike the libertarian market, the state must also be an active promoter of justice for the poor.[46]

Political life is also treated in a positive way, because economic freedom is regarded as a condition of political freedom, and yet insufficient to ensure democracy. The dignity of the individual drives Christianity to be deeply implicated in both.[47] Unlike Novak, he does not give the highest place to democracy, yet the whole tenor of his arguments in the Conservative Quadrilateral suggests it, with its references to individual and community, choice and responsibility, market and welfare, wealth creation and trusteeship. It is not surprising that in the end he turns to the 'modern concept of a social market economy'[48] as a close approximation to Christian beliefs. And that cannot be envisaged without political democracy. Interestingly, what he is not prepared to develop is the case for economic or industrial democracy, which he regards as an unjustified obstacle to economic efficiency, good decision-making and flexibility.[49] Yet he does accept the need for the radical reform of company law, including the concept of limited liability with its erosion of personal responsibility, and he encourages profit-sharing and employee-share ownership.[50]

Such understandings of state and politics are heavily dependent on a strong commitment to intermediate associations. As the first step to the love of nature and humankind, they are regarded as essential for the flourishing of private and public life, as means to greater participation, and a defence against the encroachments of the modern state: 'To be attached to the subdivision, to love the little platoon we belong to in society, is the first principle (the germ as it were) of public affections. It is the first link in the series by which we proceed towards a love of our country and to mankind.'[51]

Finally, much of his understanding of the market economy is dependent on his high estimate of private property, the justification for which is 'rooted in creation'.[52] Yet he rejects the libertarian view of unconditional private ownership, and would never argue that, 'The individual in market society is . . . proprietor of his own person.'[53] Despite these qualifications, the need for exclusive rights to property as a basis for the exchange rights of ownership in the market[54] means that his Christian attempts to control ownership may be as utopian as Baxter's attempts to regulate usury in the seventeenth century.

The economic efficiency of the market economy is not sufficient to justify Christian support. Central to its economic functioning are certain 'virtues' that require careful Christian appraisal. They include the profit motive, self-interest, competition, inequality and individualism. Two other issues associated with the market, unemployment and Third World poverty, also require examination.

In exploring each of the five 'virtues', Griffiths displays an ethical sensitivity to the major criticisms that they have attracted. Yet for economic and moral reasons, he accepts their legitimacy in a Christianized market economy. Thus he argues that self-interest and the profit motive function in all areas of life, in the family and community, as well as in business.[55] The pensioner seeks to obtain the best interest rates on her savings, the trade union fights for its members' interests. Similarly, no company can survive for any length of time unless it makes a profit. What the market economy does is to develop an economic system based on man as he is, including self-interest, as a means to greater general prosperity. Competition, too, reflects a recognition of reality as scarcity, and therefore of competitive markets as 'superior to other practical forms of economic organization in terms of allocating resources'.[56] None of these are Christian ideals for living in the Body of Christ, yet all are part of the Christian facing reality.

Again, for the Christian, some inequalities of resources, but not of intrinsic worth, are necessary for dignity, freedom and justice. Yet these can never be pursued in isolation from the Christian responsibility to share resources with others. The Christian stands as much against the libertarian promotion of the rights of property without responsibility, as against the egalitarian promotion of the responsibilities of property without its rights. The Christian holds a distinctive balance between rights and responsibilities. Not surprisingly with such views, Griffiths rejects the individualism of the Enlightenment, of Adam Smith and David Hume, yet he does recognize the importance of human individuality in creation, with its correlates of liberty, respect for the individual, and personal responsibility for community.[57]

What distinguishes Griffiths from other Christian supporters of the market, such as Novak, is his economic realism. He therefore regards unemployment as 'one of the most disagreeable features of capitalism'.[58] Yet that same realism also means that he recognizes the difficulties in the post-1970s of maintaining low unemployment, low inflation and economic growth. Tackling these complexities involves basic economics as well as economic policy. Yet with a right sense of proportion he acknowledges that the more formidable challenge to the market economy is in the international field, in what he calls 'Third World poverty and First World responsibility',[59] and is part and parcel of the global conflict. Like Novak, he is very aware of the devastating proportions of the problem and, like him, sees the issue of poverty itself, not inequality, at its heart. The task is therefore not about catching up with the West, but how to encourage countries to develop their own resources, skills and cultures. The problem is not caused primarily by exploitation of the Third World by the West, and in particular by multinational corporations (although he does accept some criticisms of their activities, and therefore of the need for some regulation).[60] For wealth creation is not a zero-sum business, whereby the increasing wealth of some is always at the expense of others. It is rather a positive-sum game in which wealth creation increases the total for the benefit of all. The common argument that poverty is about inequality and the plight of classes not individuals, about external causes and not home-grown ones, and concerns the responsibility of governments not individuals, is an understanding that 'totally distorts and undermines a Christian perspective on global poverty'.[61] For him, international poverty is caused significantly by non-economic factors, including cultural restraints on economic modernization, unstable and corrupt governments, and the adoption of economic systems inimical to wealth creation. He therefore rejects the Brandt Report's claim that 'all cultures deserve equal respect, protection and promotion',[62] and the Third World's proposals for a 'New International Economic Order'. The latter's rejection of market economies, its politicization of economic life as a global corporatist welfare state, and its redistribution of wealth from First to Third Worlds (including by the former accepting a nil growth policy), go against all economic and political wisdom. In contrast, he advocates encouraging the creation of wealth, including through multinationals, fairer trading structures, development aid, and world evangelism. There is no alternative to the market economy, in either First or Third Worlds, for the creation of that wealth without which international poverty will never be relieved.

In the end what emerges from Griffiths's work is no crude Christian justification of neo-conservative policies. His reflections on wealth creation and the Conservative Quadrilateral go far beyond this. However, because of this reasoned moderation, it is equally wrong to reduce his contribution into the parameters of the mainstream liberal tradition by suggesting he is proposing a kind of welfare state with a market economy.[63] What Griffiths is arguing for is first and foremost a market economy, with market economics at its heart, in a Christian framework. Hay's judgement captures this distinctive character better, although in doing so he raises a further problem when he observes that, 'What Griffiths succeeds in showing is that a market capitalism founded on the values of faith would look very different from one founded on the values of Mammon.'[64] The problem for Hay, therefore, is that his understanding is 'too dependent on a revival of Christian social values'.[65] Actually, what we are presented with in reality, in the light of what happened in the 1980s, is instead a clear Christian conservative response to the market economy, which is essentially and substantially an affirmation on the basis of careful theological and empirical arguments.

From Malthus to Chalmers: the remarkable narrative of Christian political economy

The story of the use of one of the great books of history can be almost as informative as its content. So it is with Adam Smith's *The Wealth of Nations*. In the late 1780s Thomas Malthus obtained his degree at Jesus College, Cambridge, and began to prepare for ordination into the Anglican ministry. Preferring to study political economy rather than theology, he borrowed *The Wealth of Nations* from the College library. It was a sentiment not shared by fellow-ordinands – or even by most of the Church of England since then! In the next fourteen years it was taken out on only five more occasions. Some three years later, in 1792, and hundreds of miles away on the Fife coast of

Scotland, twelve-year-old Thomas Chalmers also read *The Wealth of Nations*. Thus were linked, through the influence of Adam Smith, and unbeknown to themselves, the two great masters of Christian political economy, described by Marx as 'Parson Malthus and his pupil, the arch-Parson Thomas Chalmers'.[66] It was to be the publication by the former of *An Essay on the Principle of Population* in 1798 which marked the emergence of Christian political economy, and the publication of the latter's *Bridgewater Treatise* in 1833, which indicated its end.

Even though it was such a time-limited movement, it was far more extensive than the much briefer first phase of Christian socialism (1848–54) and, it can be argued, had at least as formative an influence on Church and society in Britain. Its neglect is a result partly of the misinterpretation of history by the dominant mainstream liberal tradition of Christian social thought. This tendency has justified that dominance by the classic ploy of regarding 1848 as the commencement of modern Christian social thought and rejecting anything before it in conflict with its premises.[67]

It has been an unfortunate development, to say the least, because it has allowed fundamental misunderstandings of the economic task and market economy to continue to dominate Christian social thought and church pronouncements. The tradition of Christian political economy is remarkable partly because it provides a major corrective to this defective analysis and interpretation. But its most important contribution was to the development of classical economics and, through it, to the Christian conservative response to the market economy.

Its end was no less informative than its beginning. By the early 1830s its principal architects had been promoted to bishoprics, and thus no longer gave the priority to economics needed to keep up with its increasingly technical nature. They lost touch, too, with the changing context and its modification of raw *laissez-faire*. Chalmers's rhetoric was more and more divorced from a strong base of scholarship. Using a classic aphorism of Tawney's in a way quite opposite to his intention, 'The social teaching of the Church had ceased to count [in economics], because the Church itself had ceased to think.'[68] By then, however, the tradition had made its great impact: 'the most influential of the church leaders were all soaked in the attitudes of Political Economy'.[69]

It took the Christian socialists over three generations to reverse the position.

What was Christian political economy? Alan Waterman, whose scholarship has done most to illuminate the subject, defines it as 'a label for the intellectual enterprise of combining classical political economy with Christian – specifically Anglican – theology in normative social theory'.[70]

Always behind such definitions lie a complex of ideas and histories. Before elaborating them, it is worth developing our understanding of the tradition. Essentially, Christian political economy sought to bring together economics and an economic system. So, on the one hand, it played a key role in the development of what the great American economist Samuelson called 'the canonical classical model of political economy', with its work on the nature of production, distribution and exchange. Malthus, Chalmers, Whateley, Sumners and Copleston all made contributions to classical economics, often in close contact with great secular economists like David Ricardo; the latter conducted an extensive correspondence with Malthus and had a high regard for the work of the others. On the other hand, the tradition's activities in economics strongly favoured the principal features of a normative free market system, including private property, free competitive markets, free trade, and economic inequalities. In doing so, however, it should not be over-associated with the old Tory defence of the *ancien régime*, which remained in full and harsh control of British constitutional changes until 1832. It was much closer to the emerging liberal tradition of Peel, which presented a major challenge to the *ancien régime*. The continuing linking of the tradition with an unthinking, reactionary stance does not do justice to these complexities.[71]

How were these two, economics as positive and normative, combined? Most people believed the task was impossible. The founder of the Drummond Chair of Political Economy at Oxford (the first in Britain), and a pre-millenialist,[72] assumed that 'like other branches of Politics, [political economy] is a ticklish one for a Christian to meddle with: they cannot be conducted upon Christian principles, nor ever will be, till The King reigns in righteousness'.[73] Carlyle and Coleridge agreed, but for different reasons; they regarded political economy as a contradiction in terms of basic Christian beliefs, representing as it did men 'grown mechanical in head and in heart, as well as in hand'.[74] Others believed they could be combined, but only by reasserting the traditional Christian hegemony over all disciplines. The original use of the concept 'Christian political economy' in France actually reflected this interpretation.[75]

The British tradition of Christian political economy believed neither, but rather sought to understand the different tasks of theology and economics and how they could be related. For over thirty years it therefore generated a continuity and development of ideas that warrant the designation of 'tradition'.[76] It did so, too, in response to the clear and strong challenges of a rapidly changing context. For example, Malthus wrote his *Essay* (1798) in answer to the egalitarianism of the French Revolution, so brilliantly promoted by William Godwin's *Political Justice* (1793). It generated, in other words, a powerful response to the emergence of a new economically determined society. It was an early attempt to come to terms with the realities of a modern context in which, as Whately observed, 'political economists, of some sort or other, must govern the world'.[77]

As a tradition, it was of course comprised of the contributions of a number of major leaders of the Church, whose 'stories' warrant recounting.

Thomas Robert Malthus

The founder of the tradition was Thomas Robert Malthus (1766–1834). He developed the secularization of Christian eco-nomic theory in ways that William Paley achieved for political thought.[78] Like the Archdeacon of Carlisle, he contributed to the seismic change in Christian understanding from a deontological view to an equating of God's purposes with what seemed just and right. Essentially, his *Essay* expounded what he discerned as the law governing the growth of population. This suggested that population is limited by the means of subsistence, and that it increases when those means allow and does so geometrically, while food supply can only increase arithmetically. The resulting imbalance can only be redressed by moral restraint or starvation. However, running through these arguments was the polemical intention of criticizing Godwin's promotion of an egalitarian society. Out of these discussions emerged major understandings for the development of modern economics and its relationship to Christianity.

First, he rejected Godwin's view that the plight of society in the harsh 1790s was the result of unjust institutions, the reform of which would produce the good society. For Malthus, although this was a beautiful vision, it ignored the life of 'man on earth' and 'the grinding law of necessity'[79] so closely connected to the scarcity of resources. An increase in population in such a perfect society would subject it to all the conflicts and stresses associated with scarcity; it would encounter the 'severe touch of truth' that is the nature of the economic problem itself.[80] Changing structures would not overcome that scarcity and problem. Related to these insights was Malthus's recognition of the economic law of diminishing returns and the inability of the market itself to avoid cyclical crises.

Secondly, in trying to face up to scarcity, Malthus accepted private property and self-love in the market as a major contribution to meeting the needs of a controlled population. There would never be a stage, as Godwin claimed, when such means could be jettisoned. Man would never be able to 'safely throw down the ladder by which he has risen to this eminence'.[81] None the less, Malthus's acceptance of the market as the least harmful way of operating an economy was not intended to support the reactionary politics of Burke and the ultra Tories. Yet it was equally a rejection of economic utopias. Sadly, his insights were more likely to be appropriated by the former.

John Bird Sumner

The problem of John Bird Sumner (1780–1862), according to Ricardo, was his determination to apply himself to theology and church life, and so turn his back on economics; thus in 1818 Ricardo wrote, 'I am sorry to hear that Mr Sumner does not intend writing any more on Political Economy – his whole attention in future is to be devoted to the study of Theology.' The great economist added the ironic rider, 'Whether in this future pursuit he will have an equal chance of benefitting mankind, as in the former, I have great doubts, or rather I have no doubt at all.'[82] So, in 1848, they made him Archbishop of Canterbury!

The high regard in which Sumner was held by economists was

based on his *Treatise on the Records of the Creation* (1816) in which he sought to reconcile Malthusian economics with the 'wisdom and goodness of God'. Comparing the poverty of many in more prosperous societies with the poverty of the majority in others, he observed that the former operated on free market principles. Despite the obvious problems of such societies, he sought to demonstrate that 'political economy also reveals that the genuine evil associated with the inevitable outcome is remediable'. He therefore advocated local charities, friendly societies, and parochial savings banks.[83] In these and other ways he helped dissipate the gloom that still surrounded Christian political economy.

Edward Copleston

Edward Copleston (1776–1849) wrote his famous *Two Letters to Peel* in 1819, the first addressing the problem of post-war inflation and its relationship to monetary policy, and the second dealing with the increase in poverty. Like Sumner, he was clear that political economy should be concerned with the increase of national wealth and, in consequence, the treatment of poverty. Again, Ricardo had a high regard for his work. Out of his contribution it began to be possible to make the distinction between positive and normative strands in economics, to recognize the importance of both, and to progress their relationship. He was certainly not concerned to underwrite extreme *laissez-faire* economics, and recognized the significance of the question of the poor and their right to self-preservation. After thirteen years as Provost of Oriel College, Oxford, he became Bishop of Llandaff.

Richard Whately

Richard Whately (1787–1863), with Malthus, made the most important contribution to Christian political economy. Both should exercise considerable influence on the development of Christian social thought in relation to modern market economies. More so than Malthus, Whately saw the vital significance of economics for Christianity because he understood its increasingly central role in modern life, and saw the need to clarify the relationship between economics and Christianity. The latter was required for the good of both parties, and certainly to prevent the domination of economics by irreligious philosophical radicalism. This clarity of thought came out in a letter, written to a friend, on why he accepted nomination for the Drummond chair of political economy:

> Religious truth . . . appears to me to be intimately connected, at this time especially with political economy. For it seems to me that before long, political economists, of some sort or other, must govern the world. . . . Now anti-Christians are striving very hard to have this science to themselves, and to interweave it with their own notions.[84]

Whately's task was to address that question from the chair, which he did far more successfully than F.D. Maurice, who tried to obtain the chair in 1837 and failed.

As Schumpeter observed, he was not 'profound or very learned', but he was a 'leader of the formative type, an ideal illustration of what it means to be a key man'.[85] With these skills and a commitment to economics, he influenced a generation of Oxford graduates and economists. He did this by distinguishing between religious and secular knowledge – the latter being concerned with theories tested by 'observable phenomena', the former with faith. As a result, he was able to assert that, 'Scripture is not the test by which the conclusions of Science are to be tried.'[86] The ancient hegemony of theology over all other disciplines was rejected. Political economy was to be concerned with the means, by a study of 'the nature of wealth, its production, the causes that promote or impede its increase, and the laws which regulate its distribution'. Theology should be concerned with the complementary study of ends informed by moral principles, and so freed to recognize the proper role of economics in their 'efficient pursuit'.[87] The Church therefore had a part to play in the debate about economic policy, and should oppose the attempt of philosophical radicalism, and especially utilitarianism, to control policy and economics. His great hope, despite his departure for the see of Dublin in 1831, was

> that Political Economy should have been complained of as hostile to Religion, will probably be regarded a century hence . . . with the same wonder, almost approaching to incredulity, with which we of

the present day hear of men's having sincerely opposed, on religious grounds, the Copernican system . . .[88]

Thomas Chalmers

In some ways, Thomas Chalmers (1780–1847) comes closer to contemporary radical and conservative responses by his advocacy of a Godly Commonwealth. Given the dislocation of traditional Scottish society through urbanization and industrialization, he proposed an ideal Christian society based on the parochial system and communities of pre-industrial Scotland. By evangelism, personal visiting and parish schools, and the use of the free market, society would be revitalized into the Godly Commonwealth. His book *An Enquiry into the Nature and Stability of National Resources* (1808) provided the economic basis for his programmes, and his *Christian and Civic Economy of Large Towns* (1826) elaborated his social policy. It was to be the latter that attracted most attention by its harsh attack on the 'meddling hand' of the state through its poor laws, and by its promotion of parish visiting, and direct charitable giving to support self-help. Despite his great influence on the public and politicians, he was essentially too moral after his conversion in 1812 when his religion began to dominate his economics. He became a moral generalizer on complex subjects, 'too apt to suffer one great idea to fill up the whole field of his intellectual vision, to the exclusion of other objects which, by being taken in, would have corrected his false perspective'.[89] He came closest, too, to baptizing classical political economy, seeing both God's hand in the economy and the economic benefits of morality. It is perhaps not surprising that he also viewed the Church as a religious movement. In this, as in his economics and social policy, he seemed 'crassly oblivious of the subtler difficulties of the subject and of the attempts of his predecessors . . . to deal with them'.[90]

Brief as these stories are, they should give sufficient indication of the quality and substance of the tradition of Christian political economy. They suggest insights for the development of the contemporary conservative response. Four such insights have been selected to illustrate this potential:

1. In association with the powerful evangelical movement of the early nineteenth century, the tradition contributed to those

values or 'habits of the heart' that were so important for the effective functioning of the market economy. It is easy to deride the impact on popular manners of books like Wilberforce's *A Practical View of the Prevailing Religious System of Professed Christians in the Higher and Middle Classes in the Country Contrasted with Real Christianity* (1797). So often moral exhortation did merge into Burke's 'preventive police of morality',[91] underpinning extreme *laissez-faire*. Yet the promotion of public probity, frugality, professionalism, and personal rectitude, along with the strong evangelical belief in economic life as a place of trial,[92] did help to generate a culture that influenced the emergence of the market economy. The formative impact of such values on the economy is perhaps what Sir Peregrine Worsthorne had in mind when he criticized *Faith in the City* for merely pressing for more houses and jobs in the inner cities. What it should have done was to shock ordinary people into 'the paths of righteousness for fear of eternal punishment'.[93] This was not too far from Mrs Thatcher's conviction that 'economics are the method' but 'the object is to change the heart and soul' (1981).[94] What the Christian political economists and the evangelicals did was to affect such value changes, but on the formation of economics and not vice versa.[95] They helped to achieve what Demant and Preston, and Adam Smith before them, had acknowledged as essential for an effective market economy: the formation of a supportive value culture.

What contemporary neo-conservatives have failed to do is to recognize that a changing context also amends the nature and significance of such values. So the Limited Liability Act of 1855 was attacked by evangelical opinion because it removed much of the risk, test and responsibility from business. Yet the economic need for such a Bill, particularly to encourage the capitalization of industry, carried the day. Thus 'the virulent phase of *laissez-faire* capitalism (since about 1780) came to an end in 1856 when it was enacted that in future the blood of bankrupts should be sprinkled only, and not spilt'![96] Values, like religious ideas, cannot be pursued regardless of the realities of life.

2. The tradition made a major contribution to the 'canonical classical model' of political economy. Until the 1820s, Christian and secular economists like Malthus, Ricardo, Chalmers, Sumner and Copleston were close in personal contact and views. Before the rise of philosophical radicalism and the decline of Christian

political economy changed all that, Christian economists had made important contributions to the understanding of scarcity as the fundamental economic problem, and as a central organizing principle of social science (thus Darwin's work on natural selection owed much to Malthus). From this basic shift in the habit of thought emerged the definition of modern economics as 'the study of rational choice in the face of scarcity'.[97]

3. In the light of this achievement, the tradition continued the process of theology's coming to terms with the relative autonomy of economic and political thought. By distinguishing between religious and scientific knowledge, and the positive and normative strands in economics, it enabled Christian social thought to develop an appropriate contribution to economic policy. That few church leaders have understood and capitalized on these clarifications is one of the great misfortunes of Christian history.

4. The Christian political economists demonstrated that modern Christian social thought cannot be based on Christianity alone. The nature and significance of economics was such that Christianity had to understand it in order to influence it. The developments of economic life had a ruthless way with those 'who fell back on a mindless affection to the past'.[98] No longer could Christian social thought return to the seventeenth century and before, when theological and economic knowledge were the same, and the Church could require obedience to its social doctrines. The emergence of distinctions between religious and secular understandings in the seventeenth and eighteenth centuries meant such a return could never be effective. The differences had to be faced theologically. R.H. Tawney observed this dramatic change, but drew quite the wrong conclusions: 'Objective economic science was beginning its disillusioning career, in the form of discussions on the rise in prices, the mechanism of the money-market, and the balance of trade, by publicists concerned, not to point a moral, but to analyse forces so productive of profit to those interested in their operation.'[99] Because the seventeenth and eighteenth centuries abandoned the Church's economic discipline, Tawney therefore assumed that the social teaching had ceased to count because the Church had ceased to think. Yet it was precisely when the Church began to think, with the work of Paley and the Christian political economists, that its traditional teaching ceased to count. Because Tawney

failed to accept that political economy and Christianity could relate creatively as well as critically to each other, he failed to recognize the implications of his argument and helped to ensure deep deficiencies in contemporary church responses to market economics. The work of the Christian political economists is a major corrective to these misinterpretations of history, and a major source for the reconstruction of a more adequate Christian social thought.

Addendum on Church and theology

What a response does and says about the market economy affects its understanding of the Church's function and the theological task. So neo-conservatives encourage the Church to play a vital role in the reform and maintenance of the market economy. In turn, that programme is informed by a way of doing theology. All are connected.

Generally speaking, neo-conservatives have a high estimate of the Church and the contribution it should make to economic life. Their commitment to the market economy as the preferred economic system is not unconditional. It is dependent upon location in a Christian framework informed by biblical principles like justice and stewardship. Within that framework there is a mutual recognition of the dependence of the market on certain values like truth and trust which are not generated by the mechanism, but which bodies like the Church can nurture. Without the support of framework and values, neo-conservatives do not believe either that the market warrants Christian support or that it will survive and prosper. Some exponents, like Michael Novak, regard the religious task as wider than Christianity. Others, like Brian Griffiths, restrict it to the Church. All agree its centrality,[100] including non-Christians like Roger Scruton. The justification and extent of this support in England is reflected in a long history, for most of which the Church has been bound inextricably with the established orderings, including the economy.

Despite general support for a reformed market economy, questions arise from within the response's experience about the feasibility of such a programme for the Church. To begin with, the tradition has not dominated the official Churches' response to the market economy for many generations, although it is likely to be more representative of ordinary church members. As a result, it is hostile to existing leaders of the Church and governing bodies, which it regards as unrepresentative of the nation's life. Indeed, some would argue that the statements of church leaders and bodies often indicate an absence of belief in the governing institutions of Western societies, like the market economy and liberal democracy. For Neuhaus, 'much of the leadership of mainline Protestantism cannot contribute to the moral legitimation and definition of the American experiment because, when all is said and done, it no longer believes in that experiment'.[101] There is a deep and bitter rejection of the intellectual captivity of the Churches by the mainstream liberal tradition.

The inability of the neo-conservatives to influence the decision-making in the Church so important for its programme is reinforced by another problem again intrinsic to the response. Despite its historic identification with established orderings, the contemporary response has a tendency to sectarianism partly because of its commitment to an ideal Christian society. Its conviction politics resonate more with pressure group politics than the plural nature of the actual Church. Like Thomas Chalmers in the early nineteenth century, it mistakes the institutional Church for a movement. Again, it has to be said that Novak, in a very different American context, supports a plural society and a civic religion more in tune with major trends in American life and culture. Even so, it is unlikely that this response could reflect the varied views of an advanced society with its religious, moral, political and economic interests.

When the actual proposals of the response are scrutinized they add to the uncertainties and ambiguities surrounding the feasibility of its influence over the Church. For example, the proposed church support for the values necessary for the survival and prosperity of the market turns out to be no simple accreditation or legitimation of the cruder kind. The recognition of the importance of transcendent beliefs to give meaning to society acts as resource and criticism of existing social and economic values.[102] Thus both Bellah in the USA, and Griffiths in Britain, do not regard the function of a civic religion simply as a resource for the required values, but also as a challenge to values like selfishness and dishonesty.[103] There is no underwriting of *laissez-faire* capitalism.

The response's understanding of the theological task confirms and elaborates some of these insights into the Church's function in society. Theological method inevitably plays a forceful and explicit part in the response because of its active concern to Christianize the market economy. This is revealed at its clearest in the evangelical, biblically based work of interpreters like Brian Griffiths, but it is also present in the cultural-Catholicism of Michael Novak. With the English neo-conservatives, the Christian framework and values are derived from the Scriptures, the ultimate objective being a Christian political economy. Before its achievement, the Christian task is to influence the existing social order according to Christian principles so that it conforms more closely to the ideal.

It is not surprising that this approach has been called direct theology[104] in Christian social ethics. By this is meant that it reasons from insights and guidelines perceived in Scripture or natural law to what should be promoted in a particular society with regard, for example, to economic life. We have seen how Griffiths uses this method to support a reformed market economy and its key features, like private property. Yet the term 'direct', though helpful, is also a confusion if it allows people to assume that the reasoning is directly from the Bible to today's particular economic problems, without any hindrance. For that is not the case. On the one hand, Griffiths is aware of the technical constraints and complexities of economics and of its relative autonomy. He therefore develops 'general guidelines' from 'key elements in a Biblical view of economic life',[105] which are essentially derived and mediating principles of a particular kind and cutting edge. Another evangelical lay theologian, Donald Hay, uses a similar method and describes his working biblical guidelines as 'derivative social principles'.[106] On the other hand, the term 'direct', when used in association with ideals like a Christian political economy, can suggest the use of biblical principles as a blueprint for an ideal society to be achieved in an existing context. Again, such is not the case, for both Novak and Griffiths are well aware of the limitations of finitude and sin and the dangers of rational utopias. Their economics and politics of imperfection reject any such blueprint achievable on earth. Maybe the time has come for the development of new concepts to describe actual theological method. For, in other ways too, the neo-conservative response has been seen to justify serious re-appraisal if our primary task really is to face up to the realities of our contemporary context. That must surely be an essential prerequisite for the reconstruction of Christian social thought. However, before that can be seriously attempted, the other responses require similar treatment.

Notes

1 B. Griffiths, 'The Conservative Quadrilateral', in M. Alison and D.L. Edwards, eds, *Christianity and Conservatism: Are Christianity and Conservatism Compatible?* (Hodder & Stoughton 1990), p. 232.

2 J.P. Wogaman's concept in *Christian Perspectives on Politics* (SCM Press 1988).

3 K. Leech, 'Moving Right for Jesus', *New Statesman and Society* (25 August 1989).

4 R. Benne, *The Ethic of Democratic Capitalism: A Moral Reassessment,* (Philadelphia, Fortress Press, 1981).

5 E.R. Norman, *The Denigration of Capitalism* (The Standing Conference of Employers of Graduates Annual Lecture, May 1977).

6 Leech (in 'Moving Right for Jesus') does not recognize sufficiently these distinctions and instead suggests the various strands in the Christian Right are united only by 'fear and intolerance'.

7 Wogaman's *Christian Perspectives on Politics* includes a fine survey of current Christian responses to political life. His 'neo-conservative' type has been a considerable influence on this section, and indeed on equivalent sections in the following responses.

8 M.D. Meeks, *God the Economist: The Doctrine of God and Political Economy* (Philadelphia, Fortress Press, 1989), p. 65.

9 Novak's Institute for Religion and Democracy has a Foundational Statement which sets out these and other criteria for an effective democracy (Wogaman, p. 74).

10 Pius XI, *Quadragesimo Anno* (1931).

11 Wogaman, ibid., quoting *Christianity and Democracy* (Washington D.C., Institute on Religion and Democracy, 1981), p. 5. Novak confirms Reinhold Niebuhr's support for democracy in M. Novak, *The Spirit of Democratic Capitalism* (American Enterprise Institute/Simon & Schuster 1982), ch. 19.

12 Adapted from Wogaman, p. 73.

13 'The Evangelical Protestant Perspectives on American Economic Life', R. Mouw, quoting I. Kristol, *Three Cheers for Capitalism* (New York, Basic Books, 1978), pp. 65–67, in C.R. Strain, ed., *Prophetic Visions and Economic Realities: Protestants, Jews, and Catholics Confront the Bishops' Letter on the Economy* (Eerdmans 1989), p. 33.

14 Novak.

15 Wogaman, pp. 79–80.

16 Wogaman, pp. 82–3.

17 B. Griffiths, *Morality and the Market Place: Christian Alternatives to Capitalism and Socialism* (Hodder & Stoughton, 1982 edn), p. 43.

18 B. Griffiths, *Monetarism and Morality: A Response to the Bishops* (Centre for Policy Studies 1985).

19 'I am a great admirer of the Prime Minister, it is a great privilege to be able to work with her' (*The Observer*, 6 October 1985). (I owe this reference, and other insights, to Bob Dickenson, one of our research students at Manchester University.)

20 Quoted in Strain's *Prophetic Visions and Economic Realities*, p. 117.

21 His description of 'Economic Conservatism' through Mrs Thatcher's vision summarizes the main features of his vision – including a property-owning democracy, privatization, the movement from the corporate state, and the reform of the welfare state (*Monetarism and Morality*, p. 12).

22 So named after the famous speech by the Prime Minister, on 21 May 1988, to the General Assembly of the Church of Scotland, meeting on the Mound in Edinburgh.

23 F. Field, review of *Morality and the Market Place* in *The Independent* (25 May 1989).

24 Griffiths's concern for a reform of the market and its institutions according to biblical principles does connect with the Dutch neo-Calvinist tradition of Abraham Kuyper and Herman Dooyewaard. This has influenced evangelical social thought, particularly on economics. Dr Tony Cramp, the Cambridge economist, and Dr Alan Storkey of the Oak Hill Theological College are examples of this tradition. For further information on the Dutch neo-Calvinist tradition, see R. Preston, *Church and Society in the Late Twentieth Century* (SCM Press 1983), pp. 77–81.

25 Griffiths, *Morality and the Market Place*, pp. 91–9.

26 Griffiths, *Morality and the Market Place*, pp. 77–85.

27 Meeks, *God the Economist*, pp. 85f.

28 R. Oakley, 'Profile of Brian Griffiths', *The Times* (17 March 1988).

29 B. Griffiths, 'The Conservative Quadrilateral', in Alison and Edwards, eds, p. 232.

30 Griffiths, *Morality and the Market Place*, pp. 15f.

31 Griffiths, *The Creation of Wealth* (Hodder & Stoughton 1984), p. 33.

32 Griffiths, *Monetarism and Morality*, Conclusion.

33 Griffiths, *Morality and the Market Place*, p. 39.

34 Griffiths, *Morality and the Market Place*, p. 7.

35 Griffiths, *Morality and the Market Place*, p. 70.

36 'If we are to have institutions in our society which can cope with the reality of a fallen world then we must look for something much more robust than the spontaneous sharing of the early Church' (Griffiths, *The Creation of Wealth*, p. 63).

37 Donald Hay's judgement on Griffiths's case for the market economy, *Economics Today: A Christian Critique* (Apollos 1989), p. 170.

38 John Stott is clear that Griffiths does not baptize the market (Foreword to *Morality and the Market Place*).

39 Griffiths, *The Creation of Wealth*, p. 63. It is such statements that presumably

led Hay to criticize Griffiths's tendency to elevate the market into a biblical ideal: 'It may be compatible with some or all aspects of biblical ideals, but it is not an ideal in itself' (Hay, p. 79).

40 Sub-title of *Morality and the Market Place*.

41 T.S. Eliot, *The Idea of a Christian Society*, (Faber & Faber and Harcourt, Brace 1939), quoted in R.H. Preston, *Religion and the Persistence of Capitalism* (SCM Press 1979), p. 14.

42 Griffiths, *Morality and the Market Place*, Foreword by John Stott, p. 10.

43 Griffiths, *Morality and the Market Place*, p. 26.

44 Griffiths, *Morality and the Market Place*, p. 100.

45 Griffiths, 'The Conservative Quadrilateral'.

46 Griffiths, *Morality and the Market Place*, pp. 33–9.

47 Griffiths, *The Creation of Wealth*, pp. 89–90.

48 Griffiths, 'Christianity and Capitalism', in D. Anderson, ed., *The Kindness that Kills: The Church's Simplistic Response to Complex Social Issues* (SPCK 1984), p. 110.

49 Griffiths, *Morality and the Market Place*, pp. 119f.

50 Griffiths, *Morality and the Market Place*, pp. 119–20.

51 A favourite quotation from Burke, in Griffiths's 'The Conservative Quadrilateral', p. 224.

52 Griffiths, *Morality and the Market Place*, p. 92.

53 Meeks, *God the Economist*, p. 110 quoting C.B. Macpherson, *The Political Theory of Possessive Individualism: Hobbes to Locke* (New York, Oxford University Press, 1962).

54 Griffiths, *The Creation of Wealth*, p. 58.

55 'In terms of motivation it is impossible to isolate profit and the business community from other parts of our economic system' (Griffiths, *The Creation of Wealth*, p. 67).

56 Griffiths, *The Creation of Wealth*, p. 73.

57 Griffiths, *The Creation of Wealth*, p. 80–3.

58 Griffiths, *The Creation of Wealth*, p. 84.

59 Griffiths, *Morality and the Market Place*, p. 125.

60 He therefore rejects the classic position as described by Nyerere – 'In one world . . . when I am rich because you are poor, and I am poor because you are rich, the transfer of wealth from the rich to the poor is a matter of right' (Griffiths, *Morality and the Market Place*, p. 129).

61 Griffiths, *Morality and the Market Place*, p. 136.

62 Griffiths, *Morality and the Market Place*, p. 143.

63 To some extent, Ronald Preston gets close to doing this in his 'Brian Griffiths on Capitalism and the Creation of Wealth', in his *The Future of Christian Ethics* (SCM Press 1987), pp. 148–9.

64 Hay, p. 171.

65 Hay, p. 173.

66 I owe this reference to Alan M.C. Waterman's *Revolution, Economics and Religion: Christian Political Economy, 1798-1833* (Cambridge University Press 1991), p. 223. I am greatly in debt to his scholarship, as this section will reveal.

67 For further examples of such misinterpretations, see J.C.D. Clark,

Revolution: State and Society in England in the Seventeenth and Eighteenth Centuries (Cambridge University Press 1986).

68 R.H. Tawney, *Religion and the Rise of Capitalism* (Penguin 1938), p. 188. Tawney's judgement included the period in which Christian political economy flourished!

69 Waterman, p. 258, quoting E.R. Norman, *Church and Society in England, 1770–1970* (Clarendon 1976), pp. 136–7.

70 Waterman, pp. 11–12.

71 It is a complexity misread not just by the mainstream liberal tradition, but also by conservative revisionists like Clark.

72 The belief that the second coming of Christ would precede the reign of felicity on earth.

73 B. Hilton, *The Age of Atonement: The Influence of Evangelicalism on Social and Economic Thought, 1785–1865* (Clarendon Press 1988), p. 45. I regard this as another major source for this tradition.

74 Carlyle, quoted in Hilton, p. 37.

75 Alban de Villeneuve-Bargimont's treatise *Economie politique chretienne* (1834) did not distinguish between science and theology in the way the British were beginning to do (Waterman, pp. 12–13).

76 E.R. Norman does not recognize that 'a pattern of development in Christian political and social ideals can be clearly discerned'. Quoted in R. Hole, *Pulpits, Politics and Public Order in England, 1760–1832* (Cambridge University Press, 1989), p. 265. This relates to his inability to detect such a pattern in Christian socialism: E.R. Norman, *The Victorian Christian Socialists* (Cambridge University Press 1987).

77 Quoted in Hilton, p. 46.

78 Again, there is a major myth which regards Paley as representative of the accommodation of Christian thought to a reactionary establishment. He was, in fact, strongly opposed to the ultra Tory reactionaries, arguing for the need to correct the 'real imperfections of our existing institutions' (Waterman, p. 134).

79 Waterman, p. 15.

80 Waterman, p. 41.

81 Waterman, p. 49.

82 Waterman, p. 157.

83 Waterman, p. 170.

84 Waterman, p. 206.

85 Waterman, p. 204.

86 Waterman, p. 208.

87 ibid.

88 ibid.

89 Waterman, p. 239.

90 Waterman, p. 250, quoting the *Eclectic Review*, 1832.

91 Quoted in Hole, *Pulpits, Politics and Public Order in England, 1760–1832*, p. 136.

92 So there was a regular use made of the parables of the talents and the wise steward (as now with Brian Griffiths). The modification of *laissez-faire* capitalism later in the century saw these replaced by an

appeal to the parables of the Prodigal Son and the Good Samaritan! (Hilton, p. 116).

93 Hilton, p. 373, quoting the *Sunday Telegraph*.

94 Hilton, p. 374.

95 To illustrate this influence of moral religion on economics (which E.R. Norman quite underestimates), one historian has coined the concept 'soteriological economists' for the Christian political economists (Hilton, pp. 6f).

96 Hilton, p. 297.

97 Waterman referring to Samuelson, p. 259.

98 Waterman, p. 204, reflecting on Whateley's contribution.

99 Waterman, p. 263.

100 The Christian business executive Alan Gregory, writing in the Church of England report *Growth, Justice and Work* (Board for Social Responsibility, Church House Publishing 1985), regards the Church's 'over-riding duty as to foster that moral awareness throughout society' (p. 20).

101 Quoted in Wogaman, pp. 82–3.

102 Wogaman, quoting Bellah, p. 131.

103 Wogaman, p. 135.

104 See Duncan Forrester's critique of middle axioms in 'What is Distinctive in Social Theology', in M.H. Taylor, ed., *Christians and the Future of Social Democracy* (Hesketh 1982), p. 38; and in R. Preston, *Religion and the Persistence of Capitalism* (SCM Press 1979), p. 8.

105 Griffiths, *Morality and the Market Place*, p. 91.

106 Hay, pp. 309f.

Five

The Radical Response.
Rejecting the Market Economy:
The Tradition of Christian Socialism

Compromise is as impossible between the Church of Christ and the idolatry of wealth, which is the practical religion of capitalist societies, as it was between the Church and the State idolatry of the Roman Empire (R.H. Tawney).[1]

The basic ethos of capitalism is definitely anti-Christian (J.M. Bonino).[2]

Whatever they disagree over, and that is a great deal, Christian radicals are one in their opposition to capitalism. So unequivocal is their antagonism that their hope is in the transformation of society rather than its reform. There is only one political expression of discipleship: in Paul Tillich's words, 'Any serious Christian must be a socialist.'[3] It is profoundly a way of life that now exerts, as liberation theology, a great influence over the majority of Third World Christians and Churches, and the international ecumenical movement. Yet its origins lie deep in Western capitalist histories with the emergence of Christian socialism in the mid-nineteenth century in Britain and France. Taken as one great movement it may come to rank in significance with the Reformation because of its radical effects on church life and theology. It could be regarded, with some justification, as the most palpable and decisive Christian response to the market economy.

However, to begin the task of defining and elaborating it is, on closer examination, much more problematic. It is certainly at least as complex as the conservative response, and more difficult to name. For example, socialism itself has numerous definitions,[4] and a great variety of individuals and groups have claimed to be Christian socialists – from hard-line Marxists within liberation theology to the reformist social democrats of Western

Europe. However, the dominant position of the liberationist strand suggests, if not requires, a refinement of the definition of Christian socialism by discarding its social democratic wing. This can be located more accurately in the following mainstream liberal response. Recent events in Europe, along with the historical need to distinguish between social reformism and socialism, combine with liberation theology to suggest a reformulation of social democracy and consequently of socialism. These developments allow socialism to be defined as the rejection of capitalism and the promotion of 'a system featuring public and co-operative ownership of the major means of production' (the Frankfurt Declaration of the Socialist International, 1951).[5] Such a definition does not rule out the use of the market mechanism as well as government planning in making production decisions. But that would be a decision subordinate to the central role of social ownership and the pursuit of greater justice and equality, particularly with regard to the more disadvantaged. This fits with the understanding of Kenneth Leech, one of the few (and possibly the leading one) Christian socialists in Britain. He defines it as 'a form of society in which the productive process is controlled by the workers'.[6] All these clarifications enable the concept of Christian socialism to symbolize the Christian commitment to radical and fundamental change in the social order. The conflict between capitalism and socialism becomes, in Segundo's words, the 'Crux Theologica'.[7]

However, even with such a precise definition of Christian socialism, it includes the two very different agendas of the more Western-oriented democratic socialism and the more Marxist-oriented Third World liberation theology. The latter is particularly important in providing the sharp cutting-edge of the contemporary radical response to the market economy, particularly given its international character, and the accelerating conflict between First and Third Worlds. In many ways it can be argued that it has revitalized the tired Christian socialism of Western Europe, particularly in its promotion of a radical change in theological method. Its emphasis on standing with the oppressed in their struggles is the indispensable prerequisite for theological reflection and discipleship, and has assured a wholeness in Christian response, linking praxis, theology and church witness. Living in apocalyptic contexts, its opposition to capitalism is implacable. For Bonino, as for them all, 'We are simply facing the normal and unavoidable consequences of the basic principles of capitalist production as they work themselves out in our global, technological time.'[8] From such a perspective, facing realities means the replacement of capitalism, not its reform.

The other major strand in the Christian socialist response is profoundly Western in origin and character. At first sight, its plurality does not compare well with the coherence of the liberationist strand, but it gains authority as a reminder of the continuing challenge of democracy and the limited value of the market mechanism. Essentially, it represents the natural convergence of a number of movements including:

1. The political theology of Jürgen Moltmann, with its recognition that breaking the vicious circle of poverty can only be achieved through 'economic co-determination and control of economic power by the producers'.[9]

2. The religious socialism developed through the works of the early Tillich, and still asserting in 1952 that, 'If the prophetic message is true, there is nothing "beyond religious socialism".'[10]

3. The tradition of British Christian socialism, so splendidly illustrated by the life of R.H. Tawney, continues through the contributions of theological activists like Kenneth Leech.

4. In North America, young theologians like Gary Dorrien are reaffirming the democratic socialism of predecessors like Walter Rauschenbusch as a natural link with the liberationists of South America.

Standing between these two major strands are a number of radical liberationist movements including the ecological, black and feminist. Both Dorrien and Leech regard an engagement with them as central to the future of the Christian socialist project. Running alongside these major perspectives are a variety of organizations in Britain, like Christian CND, Church Action on Poverty, and the West European Network, which act as centres of resistance and certainly stand in a correlative relationship to Christian socialism. In a period of rapid change, the overlap between them should be taken into account by any discussion of the contemporary radical response to the market economy.

The problem, of course, is how to organize such diverse material into a coherent response. The definition of Christian socialism began the process, but the choice of a representative figure focuses the discussion even further. Ulrich Duchrow has been selected for such a role for a variety of reasons. Representing the major church tradition of German Lutheranism, he stands firmly in the Western context. However, his work in South America, and his major involvement with the World Council of Churches, allows him to straddle the two strands of Christian socialism, even from the vantage-point of Western Europe. His powerful recognition of the economic question as central to the contemporary economic task proved decisive in the selection process.

Elaborating the historical context of the response follows the format established in the conservative response in Chapter 4, with the important difference that locating the response in the British community of memory is done through the work of R.H. Tawney. Its implications for church life and theological method are particularly noteworthy.

Characteristics of the response

The fundamental character of the radical response emerges from its repudiation of capitalism and its consequences for people and communities.[11] Its historical origins reflect that rejectionist accent, as does its contemporary style. What arouses Brian Griffiths's sense of injustice concerning nineteenth-century Britain is precisely what motivates Third World theologians now, but with much greater cause. The presence of large-scale deprivation in the West similarly motivates the European tradition of Christian socialism:

> The emergence of Communism as a world force . . . is not merely the result of the plotting of a few evil men; it is the inevitable offshoot of a materialistic world, in which the poor were despised. . . . It is not for those, who have been satisfied with a world in which power and riches have ruled . . .[12]

It is therefore a total response to an unacceptable context. So although it is a reaction to the market economy, it is not as economically oriented as the response that affirms the market. Partly this is because in rejecting capitalism it can disregard the fundamental economic problems faced by basic economics. Its frequent use of Marxist analysis only confirms that basic neglect of economics. By attempting to use Marxism as Aquinas used Aristotle, liberation theology asserts its commitment to what it regards as the best politics and economics at our disposal. In doing so, it reduces its capacity to deal with basic modern economic problems and, conversely, increases the dominant role of politics in its programme. Much of this is qualified in the Western strand, in that it accords a limited role to the market as mechanism and so recognizes basic economic problems and the role of prices in facing them. Similarly, it modifies the tendency to an omnicompetent politics and state by emphasizing political democracy. Both strands stress the values of justice and equality, and obviously neglect the role of values as a resource for the better functioning of the market. There is a clear presumption in favour of the public or social ownership of the means of production, even though the Western tradition increasingly modifies this by encouraging plural forms of ownership in medium-sized or smaller enterprises.

From this brief survey it can be seen that the response's character is derived largely from its rejection of the market economy and its social consequences. Its understanding of an alternative system of political economy emerges from this basic perspective. Arising as it does out of such human concern ensures that involvement in society becomes primary both as providing an understanding of the present predicament and as the struggle for feasible alternatives. The emphasis on praxis is powerful in both strands, but especially in liberation theology which raises it to a fine art.

So clear are these beliefs, and held with such conviction, that they become a matter of faith. Capitalism and all its works are treated as idols. By despiritualizing the natural order so that it can be reduced to commodities, they become things 'in the oppressive process of a limitless industrial economy'.[13] They degenerate into situations that Christians have to reject unequivocally because 'capital gains take priority over the lives of women and men as a form of idolatry'.[14] The task becomes identifying capitalism as idolatry; it is raised to the level of an act of faith, a confessional issue, a declaration of heresy.

Engaging in a life or death struggle becomes profoundly a matter of faith-commitment, of idealism. It becomes the business, despite all odds, of belief in 'the energy of God realizing itself in human life'.[15] It becomes an inspiration for, and shape of, Christian social vision, and the source of a renewed interest in the place of utopias in Christian thought and practice. For Kenneth Leech, although 'the Kingdom of God is not a purely otherworldly hope', it 'stands as a challenge to contemporary socialism with its conspicuous lack of vision'.[16]

As a matter of belief, such faith-ideals are then presented to the world 'regardless of the consequences'.[17] It was to result in R.H. Tawney, like F.D. Maurice before him, choosing the 'way of co-operation' even if it did not yield the expected economic advantages.[18] It comes to reflect a faith that 'hopes in things not yet seen'. It represents the symbiosis of Christianity and socialism, of vision and programme, each needing the other.[19]

The price of such radical idealism is considerable in that its emphasis on criticism appears to be at the expense of its ability to construct a detailed feasible alternative to capitalism. This is particularly the case with liberation theologians. They are so aware of the existing abuses in the capitalist system that they never foresee 'the abuses that would inevitably follow from the action they recommended'.[20]

The response's understanding of economic and political life follows these distinctive emphases and their related deficiencies. So, in the case of economics, the use of the more pejorative concept 'capitalism' is always preferred to 'market economy'. The choice reflects accurately the historical and international contexts of socialism, and its refusal to accommodate to the later socialization of the market and the failure of Marxist economies. Faith-commitment and idealism capitalize on such understandings by promoting a liberationist biblical economics even when it conflicts with traditional basic economics.

Always dominating economic questions like the co-ordination of supply and demand, and incentives for producers and consumers, are ownership and participation questions. The social ownership of the means of production still plays a prominent part in the thinking of liberation theology, even though Christian socialists in the West have increasingly accepted the need for more plural forms of ownership and the limited use of the market mechanism. The latter strand has complemented this modification with a much greater emphasis on economic democracy, on the 'democratization of the workplace'.[21]

Differences between the two strands in the field of economics is understandable given their different historical and contemporary contexts. The same reasons account for the dissimilarity of approach with regard to explanations of Third World poverty. Given the character of the response, both are clearly deeply disturbed by it. Once again, however, the over-reliance by liberation theology on Marxist theory, in this case dependency theory, is qualified by the West's suspicion of unicausal explanations. Without in any way detracting from the major contribution to international poverty by the Western economic system and multinationals, some Western Christian socialists do not regard the poverty of the Third World as simply the result of Western prosperity.

The major difference between the two strands is in the political field. With the Marxist liberation theology, the dominance of politics over economics is consistent with the experience of command economies. Yet even in the Western strand, this political priority is reflected in the recognition given to political above economic life in the works, for example, of Kenneth Leech. Where the conflict between them occurs, it relates to the recognition of economic and political democracy. For example, Moltmann's political theology is committed to democratic socialism, including as the preferred form of post-revolutionary government for Latin America. To liberation theologians, however, this is yet another example of 'bourgeois religious progressivism'. For Juan Luis Segundo, all social–democratic strategies (for such he regards political and economic democracy) are within the capitalist camp. The eschatological reserve of Western theologians like Moltmann and Tillich, with their recognition that all political systems fall short of the Christian hope, only confirms the suspicions of many liberation theologians like Segundo, who essentially baptize and absolutize political revolutions.[22] Only if these deep divisions are evaded by focusing attention elsewhere can the radical response present a united and coherent response to the modern market economy. Some Western Christian socialists, like Moltmann, Dorrien and Tawney, would not accept that as a price worth paying. Their commitment to political democracy, and to basic civil and political liberties, are intrinsic to the Christian socialist project.

Ulrich Duchrow: the global economist

Brought up in what was West Germany, Duchrow's life and career followed a very normal route. The Lutheran Church, including the Confessing Church tradition, has a deeply conservative character despite its noble history of protest under Hitler. To be ordained, and to pursue an academic career in theology, is even more restrictive. Yet even then, Duchrow's work on the great Lutheran doctrine of the two kingdoms emerged as both reinterpretation and challenge. Not for him was the separation of secular life from the Church a justification for non-interference in the social order.

But then it all changed with a visit to Brazil. It was here that he experienced what can only be described as a Damascus road conversion. For Brazil exhibited the characteristics of a dual society of the most dramatic and awful kind. Cheek-by-jowl with the obvious manifestations of modernization, in terms of city life and advanced technology, were some of the world's poorest regions and peoples. As the former small minority became richer, the latter, as the vast majority, became poorer and more oppressed. What could his traditional theology and churchmanship make of that? It was a question that other radicals like Maurice, Gore, Rauschenbusch and Niebuhr had faced years before him. In seeking the answer, there began a transformation of his life and theology which continues to this day. Along the way he was helped by many people and groups, but in particular he was influenced by his contact with the German economist–theologian Franz Hinkelammert from the Ecumenical Department of Investigation in Costa Rica. The deep polarization experienced within Brazil seemed to be bound inextricably with the great gulf between First and Third Worlds. The neo-Marxist dependency theory, powerfully expounded by Hinkelammert, provided the tool of analysis that explained such divisions. Mechanisms of national and international capitalism were ensuring that the rich at the centre got richer at the expense of the poor at the margins getting poorer.

Returning to Germany, he began the labour of re-ordering his understanding and re-working his material in the light of his Brazilian experience. At the centre of that task was the economic question of what he called the global economy. Although not an economist, and always a theologian, he moved into economics precisely because of what it did to people and their communities in countries such as Brazil. It is the simple explanation of why he writes as he does.

As the results of his rethinking began to emerge, he became a focus of radical church protest against the involvement of the Western Churches in the capitalist economy – what Hinkelammert called 'the ideological weapons of death'.[23] Always leading from the front because of his passionate concern, his charismatic speaking and personality have exercised a growing influence on church protest organizations and networks in Europe. He has become a leading Western exponent of the radical Christian criticism of capitalism.

The power of his argument depends much on his use of case examples drawn from the Third World and his vivid detailed use of the Scriptures. His recent translation of the secret strategic papers of the North American and Latin American secret services and military, *Total War Against the Poor*, is a vivid and stark reminder of the ruthless violence used against radical activists among the poor, and all in the Churches who side with them.[24]

His activities in the Church reflect this commitment and style. Working essentially with radical groups, particularly with what he calls 'discipleship groups', his influence percolates from such bases through a whole series of networks. Developing the economic literacy of local congregations as part of their practical social witness informs most of his work. That he is able to do so to such good effect is the result, to no small extent, of the way he has structured his work. Combining two jobs, as Professor of Theology at the University of Heidelberg and as secretary for mission and ecumenical relations in the Baden region of the Evangelical Church, he is able to bring together his theology and church advocacy. Partly because of his radical views and campaigning style, he is not a major influence in the German Lutheran Church.

All these involvements have gained immeasurably from his work for the World Council of Churches, particularly as consultant to its proposal, following the Vancouver Assembly (1983), for a conciliar process of mutual commitment to Justice, Peace and the Integrity of Creation. Working through the Commission on the Churches' Participation in Development (CCPD), his influence has extended to the recent Assembly at Canberra (1991). Through these contacts and networks he has been able to maintain his contact with Third World Christians in their struggles against oppression, and develop his work on the global economy.

Holding these involvements together is a deep personal commitment reflected in his own costly lifestyle. In a remarkable way, he therefore brings together many of the major features of the contemporary market economy, from its base in the advanced society of (West) Germany to the ecumenical movements standing alongside the oppressed of the Third World. Yet he does so as a radical critique of the market economy as his reading of the signs of our context.

For Duchrow, the contemporary Christian task is crystal clear; its overriding concern must be to accept the universal challenge of the global economy, for that is where God is.[25] And God is there precisely because that is where his people, the poor of the world, are suffering most. For every year, according to Duchrow, more than 40 million deaths are caused by starvation. The sheer mind-blowing misery, which we but glimpse through our sanitized television screens, is 'the direct result of the workings of the present global economic system'.[26] The much-heralded economic growth of the West, through its market economies, is part of an international capitalist system, and gained at the terrible expense of the vast majority of the world's population.

Transnational corporations, Western governments, international trade agreements like GATT (the General Agreement on Tariffs and Trade), the International Monetary Fund and the banks are all part of the system. The latter particularly are enmeshed in the desperate oppression of international debt which so cripples Third World countries, and is paid for by the death and suffering of innocent men and women in their millions. The 'mechanism of interest again bearing interest' is 'the gas chambers of today', buttressed by 'transnational total security strategies'.[27] World poverty, caused by the global market economy, is on the same level of moral opprobium as the holocaust, nuclear warfare, and apartheid.

It is within such a context that the great changes in East,-
ern Europe in 1989 are considered. For in espousing Western
lifestyles, the East only sees 'the glamorous shop windows of
the West and not the blood, sweat, tears and death of two-thirds
of humanity with which their surplus is paid for'.[28] They are
throwing away limited social progress for consumer satisfaction.
They are submitting to the Western disease of accumulation for
its own sake and for the rich, at the expense of the many poor
and the planet's resources.

With such a global market economy, and with such devastating
consequences that show no signs of abating (indeed, rather of
accelerating), we are clearly in the midst of apocalyptic times. At
the very heart of these disturbances lies the capitalist free market
economy. Because of the scale of the catastrophe, and capitalism's
direct role in it, it needs to be regarded not just as an economic
system, but as demonic, as a 'monstrous form of idolatry'. That
false worship is best exemplified by the role played by money in
the market system. Pursued and accumulated for its own sake,
in the end it enslaves man. It becomes, in Marx's words, the
fetishism of capital.[29]

The market economy is such an idol writ large, dominating
society as the harsh determinist ideology of Hayek and Nozick.
Their claim that the market cannot itself exploit anyone only
hides the reality and confirms the charge of idolatry. For to 'turn
money into a fetish is also to turn all human, social and political
relationships into a fetish. In other words, we are faced with a
clear choice.'[30]

The demonic nature of the economic system presents the
Churches and theology with a choice: following false gods and
obedience to the living God. For it is that God of the Bible who
always leads the poor to freedom, and challenges all, including
economic systems, who unjustly use them. This is how closely
linked idolatry and the treatment of the poor are.[31] Choosing
to stand for or against the global market economy becomes a
matter of faith itself, affecting the very centre of the Church's
life and theology. The latter is particularly important for this
argument. For since we are dealing with a credal business, it
cannot be handled by the reasoned moderation of mainstream
Christian social ethics, with its arguments for a responsible society
at Evanston in 1954 and 'Economic Justice for All' in 1986.[32]

Both assume the present holders of power can be reasoned into relinquishing it by a theological method that seeks to mediate between the Bible and economics to promote a 'basic morality in the world'. Yet confronting a demonic global market economy, wielding unparalleled power, can be achieved only through the self-revealing God of the Bible in a direct unencumbered way. It is this 'perspective rediscovered by liberation theology' that gives 'a much more realistic perspective on the modern and present systems of political economy than a position harmonising from the beginning existing institutions and their "reason" and the self-revelation of the liberating God of the Bible'.[33]

It is thus the appeal to harsh realism and biblical faith in the face of a demonic system that drives Duchrow to regard the global economy as a matter of confessional status (*status confessionis*), as a matter of faith itself. He therefore places it alongside the Jewish question in the 1930s (the Barmen Declaration, 1934), apartheid (declared by the Lutheran World Federation in 1977), and weapons of mass destruction (first declared in 1980). Not surprisingly, like so many of his views, the proposal has aroused much controversy. For many in the West do not regard complex economic matters as an appropriate issue for such unequivocal pronouncements. Yet his experience and analysis of the Third World, when combined with his theological tradition in the Confessing Church, mean that, like Martin Luther, he can do no other. For that Church, through the Barmen Declaration in 1934, had stood out heroically against Hitler and his puppet German Christians. In contrast, the latter regarded the Jewish problem, like other secular matters, as secondary to questions of faith. Dietrich Bonhoeffer opposed them with all his might, arguing that matters of politics, economics and the family (the three estates) could be of credal status. Certainly he felt that the attack on the Jews was such a *status confessionis*, and for two reasons; first, because the state was interfering too much in the life of the Church, by seeking to permeate it with the Nazi ideology; and secondly, because the state had failed to fulfil its mandate to protect all its citizens, including the Jews.

Using these two reasons, Duchrow justifies treating the global market economy as a *status confessionis*. For the state has clearly failed to meet the most basic needs of people – with 40 million deaths a year occurring through starvation while others grow rich.

Just as distressing is the behaviour of Churches and Christians, particularly in the wealthy West, who appeal to Christ in support of the market economy. The use of Christian arguments for such a cause, by what Luther called plutologians, is essentially heresy. He justifies this charge against most Western Christians and theologians because, on the one hand, they condone the exploitation of the Third World by condoning the market economy. This they do by failing to take proper note of such explanations of international poverty as the dependency theory, and by ignoring the evidence of a system of 'global interconnected fascism'.[34]

On the other hand, the heresy charge is made because such arguments give credence to Christians who actively support the forces of oppression in the Third World, from the churches of the word in Guatemala (evangelicals encouraging political persecution) to their allies the American Institute for Religion and Democracy, supported by Novak and Neuhaus.[35] All are guilty because by backing the free market economy they promote, in Barmen's words, 'the false doctrine that the church is permitted to form its own message or its order according to its own desire or according to prevailing philosophy or political convictions'.[36] The Church can never countenance systems of mass destruction. To do so is both heresy and idolatry.

It could be argued, of course, that such arguments are exclusive to a particular Christian denomination. Duchrow is certainly aware of this problem. Yet he is also clear that tradition or communities of memory are essential for Christian assurance and guidance. It was in this belief that he devoted so much of his earlier life to a disciplined reflection on his own Lutheran tradition of the two kingdoms. This, in turn, has proved to be an important resource for his later rejection of attempts to treat economics and the market as autonomous realities independent of Christian moral judgements.

In the light of this experience, each of us is urged to search our own denominational traditions for direction. It is in this spirit that he enters into dialogue with other Christians to stimulate them to develop equivalent arguments, out of their traditions, for treating social issues as a *status confessionis*. Thus at the Vancouver Assembly in 1983 he discovered that the

Orthodox and the American Baptists had examples in their history when the very being of the Church was at stake over a social issue.[37]

Complementing this consensus of denominational traditions is Duchrow's commitment to work with the World Council of Churches in the proposed conciliar process of mutual commitment by the Churches to Justice, Peace and the Integrity of Creation. It has provided major support for his involvement in the confessional process by enabling him to hear at first hand Third World Christian experiences of the pain caused by the global economy. Equally, it has given him another tool for rejecting the market economy on the basis of its gross injustices in production and distribution for present and future needs, its lack of people-participation in structural decision-making, and its failure to treat the earth's resources responsibly. The commitment to 'the overarching perspective' of Justice, Peace and the Integrity of Creation leads inevitably, for Duchrow, to a Church in solidarity with the poor and in opposition to the global market economy. It represents the end of the Constantinian era, one of the significant breakthroughs in the history of the Church.[38] No wonder it is being accompanied by much conflict, as those in power in Church and theology are challenged by such confessional Christianity. Duchrow fully understands this in his theology, as already noted, and in his view of the Church. Although he accepts that the Church consists of a number of levels, his radical stance means that he gravitates far more towards the grassroots local congregation – and particularly towards what he calls 'discipleship groups'. Recognizing that the regional Church has to relate to the state, and therefore enter into compromises, the weight of moving towards a truly confessional Church on the global economy has to be carried by the discipleship groups. Their calling is to lead the Church's resistance to the contemporary political economy by acting as both prophetic critic of, and alternative to, the prevailing economic systems. His works are full of tested practical strategies to achieve the end of keeping 'the church in faithful discipleship of its Lord'.[39]

Within the general framework of the confessional rejection of the global market economy, Duchrow develops his views on economics and the market economy, and then on the politics of feasible alternatives.

Although not an economist, and clearly subordinating economics to his theological convictions, he does have some understanding of the classical economic mechanism and systems. Each are appraised from the basic presupposition that the market economy is a proven 'mechanism of the god of capital growth' which leads to over 40 million deaths a year.[40]

His fundamental criticism is of the market's claim to be autonomous, particularly of moral–theological demands. Recognizing its theoretical origins in the late eighteenth century as a natural mechanism, he sees how this linked to the misuse of the two-kingdoms doctrine and its assertion of the autonomy of the secular realm. The result was the classical and neo-classical view of the 'supposed autonomy of the market'. All these claims are rejected by Duchrow both in principle (no secular arena can be independent of God's sovereignty) and because they do not fulfil the God-given mandate to meet basic human needs.[41]

From this basic conviction about economics, Duchrow develops his approach to three further economic issues. First, he rejects classical economics' view of people as an abstraction, as 'economic man'. Obviously, he understands the value of theoretical models in an academic discipline, but he notes its tendency to absolutize abstractions. The Christian doctrine of man is always about concrete humanity.[42] Secondly, he registers a deep unease over economics' tendency to narrow its field of enquiry: for example, by assuming that rational individuals have choice when clearly they do not in the Third World, and by assuming individual self-interest takes priority over communal needs.[43] Thirdly, he questions the commitment to exchange value rather than production to meet concrete human needs.[44] Similarly, the division of labour is regarded not as a means to economic growth, but as a way to keep workers in subjection.[45] There is no serious discussion of the price mechanism or of the fundamental economic problem of scarcity.

Underlying all these views is a basic stance that is essentially Aristotelian. For Duchrow, his analysis is 'brilliant', and he recognizes its convergence with Aquinas, Luther and Marx. Each is deeply suspicious of capital, interest on productive loans, and the treatment of money as of value in its own right, as a fetish. It is a static, household, view of the economy, with use value predominating over exchange value. Economic growth is therefore an 'idolatrous increase in the wealth of the few at the cost of the life of the majority and of the world itself'.[46] Some have suggested Luther represented the end of such thinking, the last of the medieval schoolmen. Others have claimed the honour for Marx. It would be easy to give the position to Duchrow. That would be clever but unwise. He is yet another in the long line of schoolmen. There is no end to the tendency.

Given the confessional analysis of economics, he then identifies three stages in the development of the market system: first, as raw *laissez-faire* capitalism, secondly as welfare capitalism, and thirdly as national defence capitalism. The second stage includes the emergence of capitalism as the social market economy. Even though the latter was developed by Erhardt in West Germany, with an impressive social framework, its intrinsic properties always meant growth at the expense of the Third World and the earth's resources. There is always the tendency to develop into the third stage of national defence capitalism with its erosion of the welfare state. Mrs Thatcher, President Reagan, and President Pinochet of Chile all illustrate the propensity of the market economy to exploit fellow citizens, the Third World, and the created order. That, in its essence, is what global market economies and economics are about.[47]

What of Duchrow's politics of feasible alternatives? Consistent with his confessional theology, he begins to elaborate what he calls 'God's political economy', particularly following his detailed interpretation of the biblical witness.[48] The task is to seek a transformation from being operatives in the capitalist system to being co-operators with God (*Co-operatores Dei*).[49] Not surprisingly, given his rejection of much modern economics and the market economy, his biblical view confirms his presumption that Christian witness is not about adapting to the world's political and economic structures. Rather, the God of Israel is seen as 'essentially in opposition to a political and economic system that concentrates power and wealth . . . while excluding and exploiting others'.[50]

The alternative he begins to construct is a confessional – conservationist model of political economy.[51] He develops it according to what he describes as basic principles for 'a new orientation', including:

1. analysis of critiques and aims must occur 'from below';
2. the alternative must be within the limits of 'creature based creation';
3. one area must not develop at the expense of others;
4. participation in basic economic decisions;
5. the division of labour must not be used for capital accumulation, but to achieve a 'human life-standard for all';
6. the dominating addiction of unlimited needs must be replaced by basic needs criteria.

What this adds up to, for Third and First Worlds, is 'a new independent, decentralized, ecologically sympathetic system of self-provision (subsistence economy) in order to satisfy basic needs'.[52] It would be an 'economy of the enough', reflecting the Dutch neo-Calvinist Goudzwaard's 'enough of the too much, and enough of the too little'.[53] It would certainly require radical new ways of allocating scarce resources, of production, distribution and exchange. It would represent the contextualizing of biblical-schoolmen economics in a world increasingly influenced by the twin, related challenges and constraints of massive international poverty and a threatened environment.

Yet facing the question of feasibility reduces the clarity of Duchrow's vision, if not its practicality. For he still talks in places of the reform of the market economy through institutional economics (following Galbraith, who clearly accepts the price mechanism and basic market economy), and he recognizes occasionally the value of the market mechanism. How to reconcile these views with his analysis of economics and his 'new orientation' is never developed. The confusion is increased by his support of the Chinese and Cuban economies because they meet basic needs. The alarming abuse of human rights that command economies entail is regarded as 'needless', and not endemic. There is no facing up to the problem of, on the one hand, the politicization of economics by command economies and by his confessional-conservationism. There is no major analysis of the value of the relative autonomy of economic life. On the other hand, there is also no recognition of the constraints of the practice of politics on democracy, and the problem of majority rule. How do you persuade people in democracies, including the West, to adopt causes in conflict with their immediate interests? That involves a long and complex yet feasible road, as does the reform of economics and market economies. Reading the signs of the times as apocalyptic, and so requiring confessional stances, is not conducive to such journeys. And yet his support of countermovements, or 'countervailing forces' – including trade unions, women's groups, Third World groups, co-operatives, and discipleship groups – do contain the seeds of practical politics in a democratic society. However, such tensions and qualifications are always subordinate to his overriding concern to confront the evils of the global market economy. He remains, in the end, a classic example of the radical Christian rejection of the market economy.

'The Banner of Christ in the Hands of the Socialists':[54] R.H. Tawney and the English tradition of Christian socialism

Searching for his vocation in 1903, Tawney decided to live and work in the desperate conditions of the East End of London. The choice had been put before him by Caird, the great Master of Balliol College, Oxford. According to William Beveridge, Tawney's future brother-in-law, Caird's suggestion was that they should go to Poplar 'to discover why with so much wealth, there was also so much poverty in London'.[55] It was in pursuit of an answer to this profoundly moral question about 'the condition of England' that Tawney was to dedicate the rest of his long life, until his death in 1962. Once again, like Duchrow and many other Christian radicals, it was to be a journey initiated by a Damascus-road conversion. From a privileged upper-middle-class family, and education at Rugby School (where he began a life-long friendship with William Temple) and Oxford, he moved to the East End of London. He then taught textile workers in Workers' Education Association classes in Rochdale where he began what he regarded as his real education. For it was in these areas and with such groups that he discovered some of the major issues influencing the lives of ordinary men and women. Why was there so much poverty, low pay, bad housing and ill health? Why did so few own so much and exercise such power, and yet appeared to do so little for the good of society as a whole? Tawney's answer was to develop a radical challenge to the existing social order. Selecting key issues like education, the labour movement (trade unions, co-operatives, and the Labour Party), democracy and low pay, he constructed a major moral critique of capitalism and a major feasible alternative. In doing so, he made important contributions in each of these fields, including to Christian social thought and practice.

Selecting a bridge between the contemporary Christian radical-ism of Ulrich Duchrow, and the English tradition of Christian socialism which relates most closely to it, was a difficult personal choice for me. The emerging definition of Christian socialism ruled out much of what is normally (and I believe mistakenly) regarded as Christian socialism. Individuals like F.D. Maurice and William Temple, and organizations like the Christian Socialist Movement (1848–54) and the Christian Social Union (1889–1918), were not socialist in the radical economic and political meaning of the word. They should be described more accurately as Christian social reformers. The confusion of the two strands has led to the unwarranted elevation of Temple to a position of unchallenged eminence in British Christian social thought, and to the undervaluing of a much more radical challenge to capitalism.

To choose a strong representative of the latter able to stand alongside Duchrow almost compelled my selection of Tawney. Although dead for thirty years, he still exerts an influence in the labour movement. Sadly, no one else stands out in today's Christian Left in Britain with a well-developed response to the market economy. Fortunately, Tawney's death in 1962 brings him almost into the present. His long life also enables him to be an obvious introduction to the tradition of Christian socialism, because he knew most of its leaders and was a member of most of the organizations and conferences concerned.

To capture the style and content of Tawney's epic challenge to capitalism in a few pages is not easy. It is made more difficult because by their very nature radical responses do not follow the format used by traditional economics and neo-conservatives. For example, basic economics does not occupy a prominent place in the radical response because it challenges many of its assumptions. It also broadens the Christian response to include a more comprehensive understanding of society firmly rooted in Christian values. The task of rejecting capitalism and rebuilding society on such a basis involved, not surprisingly, a total response encompassing practice, theory and theology, church life, and personal lifestyle. Tawney epitomizes all these characteristics, and thus illustrating them needs to begin with the underlying character of the response before noting its implications for economics and politics.

Engaging capitalism to develop a criticism and alternative required a total effort that Tawney could only describe as a way of life. Under the influence of Charles Gore, this centred on his belief that Christianity certainly involved theology, but 'it is first of all a life, a life for the individual soul, and a social life – the life of a brotherhood, the Church.'[56] It was the primacy of involvement, of what the liberation theologians now call praxis, that dominated Tawney's Christian response. Implementing it in society in pursuit of an answer to Caird's question meant a major involvement in a number of related fields. It resulted in his life-long practical commitment to adult working-class education, principally through the Workers' Education Association (WEA), the labour movement, particularly through the Labour Party, the co-operative movement and the trade unions, the struggle for economic as well as political democracy, and work for the economically marginalized. In each, he regarded his involvement as a way of life encompassing practice, theory, and personal conviction. Informing them was a commitment to Christianity and biblical teachings, which regarded their influence as of direct relevance to contemporary life. Following the example of Gore's *Sermon on the Mount* (1896), and the constitutions of the Christian socialist organizations to which he belonged, he regarded the laws discernible in the Bible as the governing principles for economic and political life. His attempt to use Temple's more indirect mediating principles never took firm hold. It was from such a basis that he developed his moral rejection of capitalism, his feasible alternatives, and his understanding of the history of Christian social thought.

Reflecting this grasp of commitment and Christianity was his prophetic denunciation of systems and positions that blatantly contradicted God's declared purposes for human living. It is in this spirit of prophecy that he recounts Bishop Latimer's comments after one of his sermons condemning enclosures for oppressing the landless poor: 'Ther is a certaine man that shortly after my fyrst sermon, beynge asked if he had bene at the sermon that day, answered, yea. I praye you, said he, how lyked you hym? Mary, sayed he, even as I lyked him always – a sedicious fellow.'[57] For Tawney, the Christian denunciation of capitalism stood in that tradition because it contradicted basic Christian values and promoted values like greed and self-interest which profoundly damaged the common good. It was essentially not just irreligious, but anti-religious. It was heresy.[58]

The basis for his rejection of capitalism and committed way of living was a profoundly moral understanding of life, derived principally from his Christian faith.[59] His recognition of the supreme importance of each person, including their relationships, and of the values associated 'with the Christian conception of the dignity of man',[60] led him to apply these understandings to complex social affairs. Whether dealing with equality or property in a modern society,[61] or with the origins of capitalism, he always emphasized the primacy of moral values in economic and political issues. Consequently, he rejected the secular autonomy of economics or politics, asserting his ideals without compromise and thereby gravitating towards utopianism. It was this spirit that Titmuss saw as under threat today in the new edition of Tawney's *Equality*. He regretted that 'everything becomes a matter of compromise between power groups in society', and assumed no one cared about politics as 'a radically different order'.[62]

The rejection of secular autonomies by asserting the primacy of moral values had two important consequences. On the one hand, it led Tawney to misinterpret the history of Christian social thought. He did this by overemphasizing the value of the medieval hegemony of Church and theology over economic life, by rejecting Christian contributions to the growing independence of economics and politics in the eighteenth and early nineteenth centuries, and by an unbalanced affirmation of the appearance of Christian socialism in the mid-nineteenth century. He therefore failed to come to terms with the emergence of disciplines like economics with their high degree of relative autonomy, and persisted in promoting a pre-modern view of the relationship between moral values and economics.

On the other hand, the promotion of such values did allow him to engage key social issues in a secular world without continual recourse to explicit Christian insights. His Christian morality was highly implicit in all his work on the labour movement and education, and in books like *Equality*.[63] This allowed him to collaborate with non-Christians in promoting similar values.[64]

Relating to this way of life, prophecy and moral values were a high doctrine of the Church. As a promoter of Christian values and as opponent of capitalism, the Church had a clear programme for a Christian society, and unequivocal rules for membership. It had a duty to enforce its discipline, and 'to reject those of its members who habitually and wilfully disregard its moral standards'.[65] His hope for the Church was profoundly pre-Constantinian, and resonates strongly with Duchrow's 'discipleship groups'. It is important to note that this sectarian view of the Church links with his preference for a direct theological method, and his understanding of the history of Christian social thought.

Despite a narrow view of the Church, Tawney contributed much to the official Church in the decade after 1918, beginning with his formative involvement in the report of the Fifth Committee, *Christianity and Industrial Problems*. Arguing for a 'fundamental change in the spirit of the system' of industry, it developed into the most comprehensive statement of the Church on economic affairs.[66] George Lansbury, a future leader of the Labour Party, and fellow member of the Committee, later commented that:

> Nobody denied capitalism and landlordism were of the devil, but all except Tawney jibbed at Socialism. So we compromised by declaring the first charge on industry was the decent, adequate maintenance of the workers, and their dependants. Events proved that this is unattainable within the capitalist system.[67]

Other conferences in which Tawney played an important part included the Conference on Politics, Economics and Citizenship (COPEC, 1924) and the International Missionary Conference in Jerusalem in 1928. The latter, along with his visit to China, developed his understanding of the international character and problems of capitalism. By the great Oxford Conference of

1937, he was increasingly impatient with the Churches for prevaricating over capitalism's profoundly unchristian nature. The emergence of the balanced responses of mainstream Christian social ethics at Oxford only confirmed this suspicion: 'I have almost ceased to expect that the contribution will come from men or institutions described as Christian.'[68] The conference was partly redeemed by a Welsh archdeacon who, according to Tawney, talked interminably about the Trinity, but passed the test by concluding that the mines should be nationalized!

Only within such a framework does Tawney develop his understanding of two central features of the modern market economy: the economy itself, and politics. Like Duchrow, the ambience of his approach to economics is revealed by his use of the concept 'capitalism' rather than market economy. Following in the footsteps of Carlyle and Ruskin, nineteenth-century *laissez-faire* capitalism was rejected decisively: 'Capitalism corrupts human relations by permitting the use of man by man for pecuniary gain'.[69] By treating people as means, and regarding the economic mechanism as beyond man's control, the market was fundamentally irreligious. He had little, if any, understanding of the relative autonomy of economics as discipline and system, even though he had been assistant to the Professor of Political Economy at Glasgow University in 1907. He had no views on the essential role of the price mechanism, and did not regard the conflict between producers and consumers as inevitable. These fundamental rejections of the bases of modern economics and economy were confirmed in his *Acquisitive Society* by powerful arguments for restricting private property in favour of what he called a functional society.

Relating to this strong commitment to social purpose and a functional society was a high estimate of politics in general, and democracy in particular. The latter's effectiveness depended on both mechanisms and supporting values and habits, what he called 'social tissue'.[70] This consisted of basic civil and political liberties, a concern for the 'ordinary decencies of human intercourse',[71] and values like toleration and compromise. All had to be manifested in a democratic way of life. He was adamant that the gains of political democracy, including civil and political liberties, should never be sacrificed for a supposedly higher good. Like Malthus, he believed that the ladder should never be thrown down. Arguing for a new social framework in 1945, he acknowledged that 'a new social synthesis . . . may do justice both to the value of the liberal era, and also to the equally important aspects of life to which that era was too often blind'.[72]

Despite concern for the preservation of political democracy, he was equally clear that its survival and flourishing depended on extending 'the application of the principles of democracy from the political sphere, where they are now accepted, to industrial organisations and economic life, where they are still received with suspicion'.[73] He was therefore a strong supporter of the public ownership of the principal means of production, distribution and exchange, and of guild socialism, with its worker–guild control of industries. Complementing this emphasis, and at times in conflict with it, was a high doctrine of the state, expressing his commitment to collectivism and to positive as well as negative freedoms. Yet even this strong support for the modern state in its relations with economics was qualified by his greater commitment to the democratic control of the state. Tawney was a supporter of 'Henry Dubb', the common man, above all else: The 'estimate of the value to be put on the muddled soul of Henry Dubb' was the ultimate moral criterion against which all societies and ideologies were measured.[74]

Somebody once said to William Temple: 'What we need are more men like Tawney.' Temple's reply was straight and to the point: 'There are no men like Tawney.'[75] A telling story can often catch the character of a person or the mood of a period better than empirical data, but it is not always as accurate. So it is with Temple's story of Tawney. For a brief survey of the history of Christian socialism reveals a number of impressive pioneers, supported by organizations, whose importance Tawney would have been the first to acknowledge. They combine to illuminate further the characteristics, strengths and limitations of the radical Christian response, and help to locate it firmly in the British context. Tawney can be seen as its embodiment, not least because he knew many of the individuals concerned and belonged to many of the organizations. He acts as a graphic link between the community of memory and the contemporary radical response to the market economy.

F.D. Maurice

Any consideration of modern critical Christian social thought has to begin with Maurice. Both the radical and liberal responses can trace their origins to him and the fragile little group collected around him from 1848 to 1854. Of course, some will argue that his passionate commitment to the monarchy and aristocracy identify him too closely with the *ancien régime* and sever his relationship with radicalism. Contemporary opinion would not have agreed. Many felt that he was rightly removed from the chair of divinity at King's College, London, in 1853. With his fellow Christian socialists he was accused of propagating Chartism, Red Republicanism and communism, and therefore of supporting anarchy, infidelity and immorality.[76] Maurice was indeed an extremely complex thinker with a multi-faceted theology capable of inspiring very different movements. It is not difficult therefore to discover in his life and writings substantial sources for the radical Christian socialist response. It was a debt explicitly recognized by many of its leaders, from Stewart Headlam to Conrad Noel.

Maurice's choice of issues for involvement in the struggle against *laissez-faire* capitalism eerily prefigure Tawney's. His commitment to producer co-operatives and to adult working-class education reflect the moralist's continuing selection of strategic pressure points for the criticism of society and its reconstruction. Unlike Tawney, though, Maurice was first and foremost a theologian putting into practice what his beliefs demanded. For him, 'The truth is that every man is in Christ; the condemnation of every man is that he will not own the truth.'[77] From that truth as the divine constitution of humanity, the Kingdom of Christ,[78] arose both his distinctive commitment to practical experiments like the co-operatives, and his non-sectarian commitment to work with anyone sharing such purposes. It led to Norman's acknowledgement of his contribution to the 'humanizing' of society, to what was in effect the socializing of the market.[79] It reflected a fundamentally important transformation in church life, and therefore in society, from stressing the atonement to focusing on the incarnation.

Given such emphases in his beliefs, the choice of producer co-operatives as the entry point into the great question of political economy assumes a symbolic as well as practical importance. It was to be a recurring and dominant theme throughout the history of the radical response, and so warrants further elaboration.

For Maurice and his colleagues, co-operatives expressed the divine principle that every man was in Christ, and stood in opposition to the principle of selfish individualism and its corollary of competition: 'the remedy for the evils of competition lies in the brotherly and Christian principle of co-operation – that is, of joint work, with shared or common profits'.[80] It was a project that so expressed the deepest Christian beliefs about God's purposes for human living, that it was promoted, according to the Webbs, 'with an almost apostolic fervour', even though it held 'no great promise for the future'.[81] Again, it was commitment to the divine ideal that dominated the approach to the ordering of production. So, for Charles Kingsley:

> The failure of a hundred schemes would not alter my conviction that they are attempts in the right direction. . . . For it is my conviction that not self-interest, but self-sacrifice, is the only law upon which human society can be grounded with any hope of prosperity and permanence.[82]

Yet behind the moral commitment to 'the principle of association' lay a potentially radical criticism of capitalism and the seeds of a radical alternative. The task, in an economically practical way, was to help the poor not in their poverty, but out of it, ensuring the workers received the fruits of their labour rather than the capitalists. It included a rejection of the wage system as a profoundly defective expression of the relationship between people.[83] However, even this serious critique was based on a theological ideal, divorced from economic relationships and asserting that, 'Consumption is the merely human element in life; production is the divine. God is the Eternal Producer.'[84] Production and producer co-operatives were therefore greatly preferred to consumption and consumer co-operatives, with their use of wage payments and condoning of the market. They reflected God's order which, for Maurice, 'seems to me more than ever the antagonist of man's systems; Christian Socialism is in my mind the assertion of God's order'.[85]

The promotion of producer co-operatives, and the religious principles that this expressed, struck at the heart of the capitalist system. According to Maurice, and enunciating one of the great persisting themes of Christian socialism, 'Competition is put forth as the law of the universe. That is a lie. The time is come for us to declare that it is a lie by word and deed.'[86] Indeed, so vehement was the rejection of the economic principle of competition that it came to express the Christian opposition to the market, and to the power of self-interest within it. Yet even then, Maurice was arguing for the spiritual principle governing human relationships, and that was quite compatible with his concern to affirm political economy against its misuse by utilitarians: 'We are not setting at naught the principles of political economy, but are vindicating them from a mean and dishonourable perversion of them.'[87] It was in this essentially conservative spirit that Maurice strongly opposed the movement for political democracy as a threat to the existing underlying social order: 'The sovereignty of the people, in any sense or form, is at once the silliest and most blasphemous of all contradictions.'[88] A contemporary interpreter of Maurice's thinking, J. Llewelyn Davies, assumed this same commitment to God's ordering of society would have allowed Maurice to come to terms with the power of the modern state in a most positive way, as 'a sacred and divine institution bearing a witness for law and justice . . .'[89]

It will be evident that Maurice's theology ensured the domination of moral values over economic realities, in stark contrast to the views of the Christian political economists who asserted the importance of the relative autonomy of the economic discipline. The conflict was to be of supreme importance for Christian social thought because it led both combatants to promote one-sided views of political economy, and to ignore each other's valuable insights. A splendid story illustrates this. In 1836 Maurice agreed to contend the election to the great Drummond chair of political economy at Oxford. He was urged to do so by support of the High Church party, dominant then in Oxford life. Maurice's *Subscription No Bondage* of 1835 had greatly appealed to them, and led them to believe they could make economics subject to 'their own High Church scheme of

Christian Ethics'. His opponent was Merivale, and it was he who triumphed in the elections principally because the High Church deserted Maurice's cause because of his 'unsound opinions on the matter of infant baptism'. 'This of course sealed his fate as a Political Economist'! (Merivale.) What is even more interesting, and alarming, is Maurice's reasons for proceeding with the election: 'finding there was no one else ready to come forward on this ground, that political economy is not the foundation of morals and politics, but must have them for its foundation or be worth nothing, I have consented to be proposed'. Then came the astonishing rider: 'I shall of course endeavour to master the details of the subject . . .'![90] It was to be a fatal deceit, and one that continues to infect Christian socialism: fatal because it prevented a serious conversation with modern economics, and deceitful because, in John Stuart Mill's words, his great abilities 'served him not for putting something better into the place of the worthless heap of received opinions . . . , but for proving to his own mind that the Church of England had known everything from the first . . .'[91]

The emphasis on Christian values did, of course, have a positive effect, by encouraging the criticism of the free market, and urging its restraint. That is the great value of the radical response. Yet it also allowed a growing recognition of the importance of implicit Christianity, expressed through values shared with others. Like Neale, another founder of Christian socialism and deeply involved in consumer co-operatives, Maurice preferred not to use Christian language in his secular involvement. The validity of the divine constitution of humankind was not dependent on human naming. It was important, too, not to obstruct collaboration with non-Christian recognizers of the Kingdom.[92]

Like other Christian socialists, Maurice was also concerned to reform the Church to be a more fitting instrument of God's humanizing purposes. Socializing the Church was just as important as Christianizing socialism. The task was always to connect 'the Church Reformation with the Social Reformation'.[93] The message of the radical response has always aspired to a totality embracing radical change in the Church as well as society, in institutions as well as individuals.

John Ludlow

John Ludlow has been described as 'arguably the most important of the Christian Socialist leaders' of the nineteenth century[94] on the basis of his grasp of socialism as a political and economic counterforce to capitalism. His influence was heightened, too, by his longevity, encompassing the French Revolution of 1848 and the Pan Anglican Congress of 1908. The two events symbolized his commitment to socialism, including much learned from Proudhon, Blanc, and Buchez, and to the Church, the complementary parts of his very practical involvement in society. In this sense, he differed from the more theoretical Maurice, as well as in his recognition that Christian socialism required the overthrow of the existing social order. It was no longer a matter of palliatives, but of rooting out a diseased system. And for that task, radical politics was indispensable. Yet for such socialism to be effective meant acknowledging Christianity as 'the only foundation of Socialism'. That, in its turn, meant that 'No man can be a true Radical who is not a Christian.'[95] Arising out of his fundamental commitment to the co-operative principle, the content of that radicalism was clearly socialist, verging on a planned economy, and replacing the supply and demand of market forces and the wage system. However, like Tawney later, these powerful forces were always related to a commitment to democracy as 'the necessary accompaniment of socialism'.[96]

In all these ways, he developed Christian socialism in more radical directions and more closely related to the secular political movement. It should be no surprise, therefore, that the differences with Maurice also revealed themselves in a conflicting approach to theology. Maurice was committed to the theological task as digging to uncover the underlying divine order of reality. Constructing human systems contradicted such an approach. Yet Ludlow, more in touch with the desperate need for change, was convinced that rebuilding society was an urgent obligation. It was a difficult decision to take because of his deep appreciation of Maurice's theological gifts. Yet in the end Ludlow had to come to terms with the difference:

> If I am true to my own faith, build I must . . . digging, as he [Maurice] tells me; a very healthy exercise no doubt, but as yet it seems to me, a little out of date for those who know that the

foundation-stone is laid . . . and who see around them crowds of poor wretches wanting a roof to stand under . . .[97]

Stewart Headlam

In the years after 1870 the British suffered all the social upheavals of a deep economic depression. It was a time of great unrest, of demonstrations even in the affluent heart of London's clubland, culminating in the death of a demonstrator on Bloody Sunday, 13 November 1887. It was such stirring events that provoked Hancock into preaching his sermon on the 'banner of Christ in the hands of the socialists'. Of much greater impact was the appearance of Stewart Headlam at the head of the demonstrator's funeral procession. For it was Headlam who, ten years previously, had founded the Guild of St Matthew and become the centre of a much more radical and politicized Christian socialism. Like his hero Maurice, the heart of Headlam's political commitment was his Christian belief and theology, based on the great formula that, 'The Church exists to bear witness to men that they are brothers, that God is now and for ever, here and everywhere, the Father of all men.' (The Fatherhood of God, FOG, leading to the Brotherhood of Man, BOM.)[98] Like the liberation theologians after him, the service of the poor was inspiration for and expression of belief.[99]

Although regarding himself as Maurice's disciple, it was Ludlow's Christian socialism that Headlam developed in two important ways. First, he saw much more clearly the need to work for a radical change in the social order through collaboration with secular socialists. He therefore reinterpreted Christianity to relate to socialism, rather than choose a variety of socialism to fit conventional Christianity.[100] And it was a socialism committed to the redistribution of wealth, a minimum wage, the reform of the land, and secular education for all. All these reforms were dependent on a high view of the state.

Secondly, he complemented his commitment to socialism by the use of a key contemporary tool of social analysis and reconstruction, in much the same way as liberation theology has used Marxism. Headlam's chosen method was the Single Tax of Henry George, the great American social reformer. George's views were expounded in his *Progress and Poverty* (1879), and concerned the progressive increase of the taxation of land values as the means for the radical reform of society through state action (it assumed that land was the basis of social injustice in England). In Headlam's hands it became the key to open all doors. 'By easy transitions, he connected prostitution and drunkenness with the absence of a tax on land values.'[101] It was to be a key recurring feature of Christian socialism, stretching from the use of producer co-operatives by Maurice, the dependency theory of J.A. Hobson (1902), the guild socialism of Maurice Reckitt and R.H. Tawney, to the social credit theory of Major Douglas and the Christendom Group in the 1930s. The use of Marxism by contemporary liberation theologians arguably stands in this tradition. In each case, using Reckitt's appraisal of national guilds, they were promoted as 'the essential standard by which all social change is tested'.[102] It was to prove, without exception, a profoundly defective contribution to Christian social thought.

It was not just individuals who formed the tradition of Christian socialism. Almost as important was the influence of Christian socialist organizations. Following the pioneering role of the Guild of St Matthew came the Church Socialist League in 1906, the first Anglican society dedicated to the propagation of socialism. Operating under the slogan of F.L. Donaldson – 'Christianity is the religion of which Socialism is the practice'[103] – it accepted, through its first full-time organizer, Conrad Noel, that it had to be 'fully socialist in the ordinary sense understood by the secular socialist bodies'.[104] R.H. Tawney was a member.

The subsequent story of the Christian socialist response to capitalism was characterized by the Left's search for pure socialism. The result was the splintering of the movement into groups like the communist Catholic Crusade of Conrad Noel and the League of the Kingdom of God. They became increasingly abstruse and marginalized from mainstream political and religious life. It was not until 1960 that their remnants came together to form the existing Christian Socialist Movement. The inaugural meeting took place in Donald Soper's church in London, and R.H. Tawney was on the platform. I know this because I was there! By advocating the common ownership of the major resources of the world, it continued the tradition that socialism, in contrast to capitalism, was 'the political expression of the quest for the Kingdom of God on earth'. Its election 'manifesto' for 1964 could have been written by any of the pioneers, or by its contemporary exponents like Tawney and Duchrow:

> Capitalism is based on the motive of avarice and the finance of usury. . . . Christians must see industry as a service, to be run by the community to meet men's needs. . . . That is socialism; the application of Christian principles to industrial life. In the modern world there is no Christian alternative.[105]

Thus were the historic accents of the radical Christian socialist response to the market economy continued into the present context.

Addendum on Church and theology

There is a strong rationale supporting the radical response's high view of the Church and its function in society. The unequivocal condemnation of capitalism and the equally decisive promotion of an alternative godly commonwealth are part of a vision for the Church in the achievement of radical change. It is essentially a role, using Luther's concept, of co-operators with God in promoting his purposes for the world. It therefore involves collaborating with people, movements and ideologies that appear to share similar social goals.

The radical character of the Christian social vision, epitomized in its demand for the overthrow of existing capitalist systems, inevitably influences the response's understanding of the Church's organization. Although accepting the institutional and official Church (Duchrow's 'regional' Church), its involvement in compromise, because of its necessary relationship with existing structures, reduces the possibility of a major role in the pursuit of radical change. The movement to the Left of official Churches, like the Roman Catholics at Medellín in South America (1968) and the report *Economic Justice for All* of the Roman Catholic bishops of the United States (1986), has not been decisive or continuous enough to change this judgement. Consequently, there is a continuous concern to change the Church, to socialize it in Maurice's terms, so that it reflects the radical Christian social vision. For many exponents of the response this leads to a highly sectarian view of the Church, using its discipline to enforce its principles on its members. So Duchrow, following in the tradition of Martin Luther, argues that Holy Communion should be refused to persistent flouters of the radical critique of apartheid, nuclear weapons, multinationals and the global market economy.

The failure, as yet, to capture the official Church for this collection of radical policies has two consequences. On the one hand, it leads to a struggle against the conservative Church, and in particular against those parts that support reactionary policies and persecute radical Christians. Charges of apostasy with regard to the Church of England in the eighteenth and early nineteenth century were common in the circles of radical Christian social thought. They are consistent with treating capitalism as idolatry. Duchrow extends this judgement to the present day with regard to Novak's Institute of Religion and Democracy, and its rejection of *Economic Justice For All* and support for extreme Right-wing Christian groups in South America.

On the other hand, the inability to capture the official Church also leads to a natural support for a form of the Church that is more amenable to conversion as a tool of radical change. Duchrow's discipleship groups are a classic example, as were the Christian socialist organizations in Britain. There has been a long history of small mutual support groups in radical Christian life – from Maurice's Bible study fraternity, and Gore's 'Holy Party', to Rauschenbusch's 'Brotherhood of the Kingdom' in the USA. The base communities of South America are liberation theology's equivalent, and indeed Segundo goes much further and argues explicitly for the sectarian Church. Duchrow's use of a *status confessionis* connects with such advocacy, although Western churches are traditionally reluctant to support sectarianism in any form. Recent developments in the USA in post-liberal theology have, however, modified this position, with Hauerwas and others arguing for a distinctive story. For them:

> The church's social task is first of all its willingness to be a community formed by a language the world does not share . . . the church's social ethics is not first of all to be found in the statements by which it tries to influence the ethos of those in power, but rather . . . is first and foremost found in its ability to sustain a people who are not at home in the liberal presumptions of our civilisation and society.[106]

Despite the high place given to the Church in the radical project, its nature is such as to encourage collaboration with non-Christians who work for radical change. Duchrow's fifth type of Church – obedient non-recognizers of the Kingdom, and Tawney's implicit Christianity – are two strands that support this view. Both lead to an encouragement of socialist parties and pressure groups in the field of the Third World, the environment, anti-racism and feminism. It includes the (old) East German Churches' critical, but none the less constructive, co-operation with the state socialist regime.

The importance of the contemporary context for Christian social thought is emphasized particularly by radical Christians. Liberation theology emerged as a rejection of Western capitalist dominated theology on the grounds that it was singularly inappropriate for the South American context. The theological task was rather to reconstruct an indigenous theology from the ground, and that meant with and for the poor. Practical involvement, or praxis, with the struggle for liberation was the primary Christian task, and theological reflection on it was purely secondary. The challenge that this constitutes to Western theology is enormous because traditional theology is regarded as a top-down, theoretical imposition on realities, generally supportive and reflective of the oppressive status quo. Yet the challenge is not so different from the way-of-life commitment of R.H. Tawney.

The claim to be context-centred is, however, no longer so dominant. Commitment to the poor in the Third World includes invariably a rejection of capitalism, especially in its international form. Consequently, there is a growing tendency to seek to impose a similar theological model on the Western Churches given their entanglement with capitalism. *The Road to Damascus* document is now regarded, by its Third World authors, as 'liberation theology for the first world, liberation theology for you'.[107] It is an argument remarkably similar to the neo-conservatives' recommendation of the free market to the Third World, but in the opposite direction. The form of Church and theology are once again closely connected.

The moral character of the rejection of capitalism on the basis of experiencing its effects on the marginalized provides a basis for theological reflection for First and Third World strands of the radical response. Yet it does more than that for it leads invariably to a theology that promotes a direct relationship not just between experience and theology, but also, in consequence, between theological sources like the Bible, and experience. Duchrow's powerful hands-on exposition of the Old Testament as a reflection on the task of liberation, and support for it, is a fine example of this trend. It leads to what John Bennett has described as the Christian policies type of theology; in other words, directly identifying particular Christian insights with particular policies.[108]

The employment of the Scriptures and theology in support of, and as inspired by, the liberation movement is reinforced by an equal willingness to use secular tools in the task of liberation and theology. The use of Marxist religion stands alongside the use of the Bible as a shared stance with the poor. Yet it goes further than that, because the commitment to secular analysis normally involves concentration on one major tool to the exclusion of others. The reliance on Marxism is but one link in a chain going back to Maurice's producer co-operatives, Headlam's single tax, Reckitt's guild socialism, and the Christendom Group's social credit.

The theological character of the response's rejection of capitalism has another consequence for theological method, for it moves away from the traditional dependence of Christian social thought on Christian social ethics to a more dogmatic biblical theology. This movement is supported by a number of factors. First, liberation theology's pursuit of a theology of revolution rather than of order leads to a rejection of such classic formulations of Christian social ethics as 'the responsible society', and its accommodation to democracy and the market economy. There is no common basis of morality when confronted with such divisions in such apocalyptic times. There is deep unease, too, with the use of reason to mediate unduly between scriptural imperatives and the demands of the situation. The sin of dilution is just as harmful as that of petrifaction. Secondly, the rejection of capitalism as a *status confessionis* is regarded as a matter of Christian doctrine and heresy. The use by Christian social ethics of levels of judgement on complex matters like economics is seen as quite inappropriate for matters demanding unequivocal condemnation. Thirdly, the comprehensive nature of the market economy is regarded as requiring an equally comprehensive theological response, beyond the narrow confines of Christian social ethics, and linking doctrine, contemplation and action.

It is in this intimacy and consistency of relationship between involvement in rejection and rebuilding theology, Church witness and personal discipleship that the radical response is given such power. It has enabled it to exist for much of the long history of the market economy, and sustained it through a variety of forms. It has ensured its survival and development as one of the great styles of Christian involvement in the modern world.

Notes

1 R.H. Tawney, *Religion and the Rise of Capitalism* (Penguin 1966 edn), p. 280.

2 J.M. Bonino, *Christians and Marxists: The Mutual Challenge to Revolution* (Hodder & Stoughton 1976), p. 114.

3 Quoted in M. Novak, *The Spirit of Democratic Capitalism* (American Enterprise Institute/Simon & Schuster 1982), p. 242.

4 Ronald Preston refers to thirty-nine definitions by Rappoport in 1924, and four major tendencies in Berki in 1975: see R. Preston, *Church and Society in the Late Twentieth Century* (SCM Press 1983), p. 13.

5 G.J. Dorrien, *Reconstructing the Common Good: Theology and the Social Order* (New York, Orbis, 1990), pp. 3–4.

6 K. Leech, *The Radical Anglo-Catholic Social Vision* (Discussion Paper 2, Centre for Theology and Public Issues, New College, Edinburgh 1989), p. 6.

7 The title of one of his most famous essays: 'Capitalism Versus Socialism: Crux Theologica', in Dorrien, p. 112.

8 In Dorrien, p. 143.

9 In Dorrien, p. 87.

10 In Dorrien, p. 71.

11 D. Hay, *Economics Today: A Christian Critique* (Apollos 1989), p. 177: 'Each variety of socialism starts at the same point, a fundamental dislike of capitalism and its effects'.

12 J.P. Wogaman, *Christians and the Great Economic Debate* (SCM Press 1977), p. 64, quoting D.L. Munby.

13 Paul Tillich, quoted in Dorrien, p. 57.

14 The Sao Paulo statement, 'Call for Obedient Discipleship', in *Economics: A Matter of Faith*, (WCC CCPD Documents, July 1988, no. 11), p. 9.

15 Walter Rauschenbusch, whose idealism inspired Martin Luther King, quoted in Dorrien, p. 42.

16 Leech, p. 14.

17 Dorrien, p. 72.

18 R.H. Tawney, *The Radical Tradition* (Penguin 1966 edn), pp. 174 and 176.

19 Leech, p. 7, agrees with the black theologian Cornel West that, 'an alliance between prophetic Christianity and progressive Marxism offers the last humane hope for mankind'.

20 Munby's criticism of socialism in general is very applicable to liberation

theology. See D.L. Munby, *Christianity and Economic Problems* (Macmillan 1956), pp. 77–8.

21 M. Douglas Meeks, *God the Economist: The Doctrine of God and Political Economy* (Fortress Press 1989), p. 155.

22 Dorrien, p. 122.

23 F.J. Hinkelammert, *The Ideological Weapons of Death: A Theological Critique of Capitalism* (Orbis Books 1986).

24 U. Duchrow, G. Eisenburger, and J. Heppler, *Totaler Krieg gegen die Armen* (Munchen 1989).

25 U. Duchrow, *Global Economy: A Confessional Issue for the Churches?* (WCC Publications 1987), p. 26.

26 Duchrow, p. 92.

27 U. Duchrow, 'Political and Economic Wellbeing and Justice: A Global View', in R. Franklin, ed., *Studies in Christian Ethics* (vol. 3, no. 1, T & T Clark 1990), p. 80–1, quoting Walter Altmann.

28 Duchrow, 'Political and Economic Wellbeing', p. 92.

29 Duchrow, *Global Economy*, quoting Hinkelammert, pp. 172–4.

30 Duchrow, *Global Economy*, p. 175.

31 Also argued by D.E. Jenkins in *God, Politics and the Future* (SCM Press 1988), pp. 45f.

32 The World Council of Churches began the process of 'the responsible society' at its first Assembly in Amsterdam 1948, but majored on it at its second, in Evanston. In 1986 the Roman Catholic Bishops of the USA produced their Pastoral Letter entitled *Economic Justice For All*.

33 Duchrow, 'Political and Economic Wellbeing', p. 86.

34 Duchrow, *Global Economy*, p. 115. For evidence of such organized world-wide oppression, see note 24 above.

35 Duchrow, *Global Economy*, pp. 117f.

36 Duchrow, *Global Economy*, p. 97.

37 Duchrow, in *Economics: A Matter of Faith*, pp. 15–16.

38 Duchrow, *Global Economy*, pp. 72–3.

39 Duchrow, *Global Economy*, p. 63.

40 Duchrow, 'Political and Economic Wellbeing', p. 69.

41 Duchrow, *Global Economy*, p. 149.

42 Duchrow, *Global Economy*, p. 151.

43 Duchrow, *Global Economy*, p. 152.

44 Duchrow, *Global Economy*, p. 153.

45 Duchrow, *Global Economy*, p. 156.

46 Duchrow, in *Poverty and Polarisation: A Call to Commitment* (Report of the WEN Consultation, William Temple Foundation 1988), p. 30.

47 Duchrow, *Global Economy*, pp. 145–6.

48 Duchrow, 'Political and Economic Wellbeing,' pp. 61–2.

49 Duchrow, *Global Economy*, p. 58, quoting Martin Luther.

50 Duchrow, *Global Economy*, p. 67.

51 Resurrecting Wogaman's final economic type, the conservationist, in *Christians and the Great Economic Debate*.

52 Duchrow, in *Poverty and Polarisation*, pp. 33–4.

53 Duchrow, 'Political and Economic Wellbeing,' p. 82.

54 A title of one of Thomas Hancock's sermons during the unrest of 1886–7. See C. Binyon, *The Christian Socialist Movement in England: An Introduction to the Study of its History* (SPCK 1931), p. 132.

55 J. Atherton, 'R.H. Tawney as a Christian Social Moralist', Ph.D. thesis (University of Manchester 1979), p. 34.

56 C. Gore, *Christianity Applied to the Life of Men and of Nations* (Murray 1940), p. 31.

57 *Seven Sermons before King Edward VI*, Bishop Latimer, quoted in Tawney, *Religion and the Rise of Capitalism*, p. 271.

58 R.H. Tawney, *Religion and the Rise of Capitalism*, p. 280. Recognized by R. Preston, in *Religion and the Persistence of Capitalism* (SCM Press 1979), p. 104.

59 The importance of his faith for his life is revealed in J.M. Winter and D.M. Joslin, eds, *R.H. Tawney's Commonplace Book* (CUP 1972).

60 R.H. Tawney, *The Radical Tradition*, p. 166.

61 R.H. Tawney, *The Acquisitive Society* (Bell 1921), *Equality* (Allen & Unwin 1931); revised with new chapter, 4th edn 1952; 1964 edn – introduction by R.M. Titmuss.

62 R.H. Tawney, *Equality*, p. 14, quoted in Preston, *Religion and the Persistence of Capitalism*, p. 108.

63 D.B. Forrester, *Beliefs, Values and Policies: Conviction Politics in a Secular Age* (Clarendon Press, 1989), p. 88.

64 Compare Duchrow's fifth type of church – of non-Christians who do God's will.

65 Quoted in Atherton, p. 232.

66 M.B. Reckitt, *Maurice to Temple: A Century of the Social Movement in the Church of England* (Faber 1947), p. 163.

67 D.O. Wagner, *The Church of England and Social Reform Since 1854* (Columbia University Press 1930), p. 298.

68 Memorandum of the Oxford Conference, quoted in Preston, *Religion and the Persistence of Capitalism*, p. 86.

69 Tawney, *The Radical Tradition*, p. 168.

70 *The Highway* (January 1945), p. 47.

71 R.H. Tawney, *The Attack and Other Papers* (Allen & Unwin 1953), p. 73.

72 Tawney's LSE papers, quoted in Atherton, p. 263.

73 Tawney's LSE papers, quoted in Atherton, p. 330.

74 Tawney, *The Attack and Other Papers*, p. 163.

75 Quoted in Preston, *Religion and the Persistence of Capitalism*, p. 88.

76 *The Quarterly Review* vol. LXXXIX, September. 1851, pp. 491–543. Quoted in T. Christensen, *Origin and History of Christian Socialism* (Aarhus 1962), p. 207.

77 Quoted in E.R. Norman, *The Victorian Christian Socialists* (CUP 1987), p. 7.

78 The title of possibly his greatest book, published in 1838.

79 Norman, p. 1.

80 *Tracts on Christian Socialism*, no. 2, p. 5. Quoted in Christensen, pp. 131–2.

81 S. and B. Webb, *The History of Trade Unionism*, p. 325, quoted in S. Mayor, *The Churches and the Labour Movement*, (Independent Press 1967), p. 168.
82 C. Kingsley, quoted in Reckitt, p. 73.
83 Maurice to Kingsley, January 1850, quoted in Reckitt, pp. 88f.
84 Quoted in Reckitt, p. 89.
85 Quoted in Christensen, p. 145.
86 Maurice, *Life of F.D. Maurice*, vol. 2, p. 32.
87 Norman, p. 16, quoting F.D. Maurice, *Reasons for Co-operation* (John W. Parker 1851).
88 Norman, p. 22.
89 Maurice's eight letters to *The Daily News* (September 1868), in J.Llewelyn Davies, *Social Questions from the Point of View of Christian Theology* (Macmillan 1886), p. 249.
90 The story is told in B. Hilton, *The Age of Atonement: The Influence of Evangelicalism on Social and Economic Thought, 1785–1865* (Clarendon Press 1988), pp. 47–8.
91 J.S. Mill, *Autobiography*, pp. 107–8, in Christensen, p. 27.
92 Christensen, p. 167.
93 Christensen, p. 105, quoting Maurice to Ludlow, 25 August 1849.
94 Norman, p. 62.
95 Christensen, pp. 79 and 136.
96 Norman, p. 69.
97 Christensen, p. 307.
98 Quoted in Norman, p. 102.
99 Quoted in Norman, p. 119.
100 Norman, p. 107.
101 Wagner, p. 193.
102 Quoted in Wagner, p. 281.
103 Reckitt, p. 151.
104 P. d'A. Jones, *The Christian Socialist Revival, 1877–1914: Religion, Class and Social Conscience in Late Victorian England* (Princeton University Press 1968), p. 247.
105 Mayor, pp. 374–5.
106 Quoted in D.F. Ford, ed., *The Modern Theologians: An Introduction to Christian Theology in the Twentieth Century*, vol. 2 (Basil Blackwell 1989), pp. 122–3.
107 Father Smangaliso Mkhatshawa, the first black secretary of the South African Roman Catholic Bishops, quoted by P. Hebblethwaite in *The Guardian* (3 August 1989).
108 J.C. Bennett, *Christian Ethics and Social Policy* (New York, Charles Scribner's Sons 1946), pp. 46–51.

Six

The Liberal Response
Subordinating the Market:
The Mainstream Liberal Tradition

In sum, the miraculous market mechanism may be a good servant, but it is almost certainly a bad master.[1]

The last response for consideration is under the same pressure as the final candidate at an interview. It is difficult to give careful consideration at the end of a long process. A response that stands between two extremes makes the task even more difficult. The voice of moderation in Christian social thought invariably finds itself competing with the conviction politics and theology of Right and Left. To be unequivocal in difficult times, and encountering a complex reality like the market economy, always possesses an attraction that the more balanced position lacks. Facing such a challenge understandably leads people to associate the liberal response with 'a little of this and a little of that adding up to not much of either'.[2]

Although there is truth in these judgements, they do no justice to the historic and contemporary significance of this Christian response. The cumulative effect of the quality of its insights and impact on Church and society in modern market economies mark it out as arguably the most influential and pervasive of the three responses. For standing between the ends of the spectrum of *laissez-faire* capitalism and communist command economies has allowed it to combine the insights of each into a coherent whole, into what, in political terms, it refers to as the mixed economies of the West. Supporting this stance, and indeed inspiring it to a considerable degree, has been a complementary theological development. This combined a deep commitment to Christian tradition with the need to interpret it in the light of the changing modern context. The emergence of progressive orthodoxy in the USA or liberal catholicism in Britain influenced as well as reflected that changing context.

It is not surprising that the combination began to exert a major influence on the Churches' response to Western industrialization and urbanization. From the mid-nineteenth century the emergence of Christian socialism and social reform in Britain, and the social gospel in the USA, began to establish a decisive hold on the official Churches in their social witness in the early part of this century. Through the pioneering work of figures like Maurice, Westcott and Gore in England, and Washington Gladden, Shailer Mathews and Walter Rauschenbusch in the USA, the goal of socializing the Churches began to be achieved. From such a strong base it was almost inevitable that the response attained a dominant voice in the early ecumenical movement within the two countries and internationally. The latter was achieved initially through the Life and Work Conferences of Stockholm (1925) and Oxford (1937), and then through their successor, the World Council of Churches. Again, the contributions of key exponents of the tradition like Reinhold Niebuhr and John Bennett in the USA, and William Temple and Joe Oldham in Britain, were formative in the development. Only after the Geneva Conference of 1966 did Third World Churches and liberation theology begin to dislodge the hold of the liberals on the World Council of Churches.

Within the USA and Britain, though, the response still continues to dominate the mainstream Churches. It is the contemporary heirs of the tradition – Christian social ethicists like J. Philip Wogaman and Charles Curran in the USA and Ronald Preston in Britain – who continue to exert its influence on the official Churches in their social witness. Interestingly, the quality and quantity of their pronouncements has been increased to a notable extent by the challenge of neo-conservatism in the 1980s, producing such major reports as the Roman Catholic *Economic Justice For All* in the USA and *Faith in the City* in Britain. Yet such examples, important as they are, do not convey the extent of the response's influence, for the 'official Churches' in Britain can be divided into three parts. First, the governing bodies of the Churches have produced major statements and reports on economic affairs, particularly in terms of their social consequences. Examples in Britain include *Faith in the City* (Church of England), *Mission Alongside the Poor* (Methodists), and *The Ethics of Investment and Banking* (Church of Scotland). Secondly, the Churches' social action curias, through their Social Responsibility departments at national level, have generated reports and debates in the field of political economy, including *Perspectives on Economics* (1984), *Not Just for the Poor* (1986), and *Just Sharing* (1988). Thirdly, the leaders of the major Churches have pronounced on economic affairs: from the Archbishop of Canterbury, the Presidents of the Methodist Conference, and the Archbishop of Westminster, to the Moderator of the General Assembly of the Church of Scotland.[3] It is the cumulative effect of these interventions that reveals a consistency and coherence suggestive of a shared tradition and an 'ethics establishment'.[4] Because these are clearly related to the liberal response, its contribution to the debate about market economies will be illuminated through the work of one of its principal and most accomplished exponents, J. Philip Wogaman. Locating the tradition in its British historical context will be done through the writings of another leading Christian social ethicist, Ronald H. Preston. Together, they certainly stand on a par with the representatives of the other responses.

Despite such evidence to the contrary, doubts still arise over the appropriateness of the concept of 'mainstream liberal tradition'. For example, the word 'liberal' is closely associated with libertarian economics and ideologies – whether of *laissez-faire* in the nineteenth century or its modern equivalent of Friedman, Hayek and Nozick. The word 'mainstream' too can be misleading when it is restricted to the major denominations in their official capacities. In no way can the liberal response be said to represent the views of grassroots' Christians and congregations. However, after much deliberation, and with the above provisos, the concept is worth staying with. Following the lead of the great philosopher Martin Buber, who stood in the Jewish equivalent of the mainstream liberal tradition and faced a similar struggle, there are no better alternatives. When asking the question of whether to continue to use the concept 'God' to describe the Divine, given its persistent misuse, Buber decided in the end that he 'could not give it up'.[5]

Characteristics of the response

Like the other responses, theological convictions inform its centre of value, yet because of their character and style they have very different consequences for Christian involvement in society. These relate to, if not reflect, its general ethos: maintaining a balance between extremes. Indeed, it is because of this that many holding the Left and Right responses charge it with a lack of theology. However, from its theological considerations there emerge its understandings of change, and the roles of the state, politics and economics. All are reflected in its influence on the mainline Churches.

At the heart of the response's theological convictions is an understanding of God and his purposes for the world. Elaborated as the great acts of God through creation, incarnation, redemption, Church and last things, the emphasis is particularly on their social consequences. The classic formula of faith in the Fatherhood of God as leading to a commitment to the brotherhood of man runs deep through its history. Wogaman tells the story of Nelson Rockefeller's campaigns for New York governor and US vice-president. When he came to a certain point in his speeches the reporters simply wrote 'BOM-FOG'. It came to indicate his 'somewhat less than precise political objectives for the long run'.[6] Yet it also revealed the consequentialist nature of his strongly held faith. For belief in a God acting in and through history is intimately related to a belief in the Christian obligation to share in that involvement. And that co-operation involves promoting in society what are understood to be his purposes and, concomitantly, struggling against all that impedes them.

Influencing such Christian involvement is a recognition of finitude and sin which affects profoundly its approach to politics and economics. As Wogaman observes, the resulting theological realism leads, on the one hand, to an acceptance that all human projects are intrinsically provisional. There will be no Kingdom of God established by them on earth, and the moral judgements in the social arena are invariably profoundly relative. They are rarely of an 'either-or kind' and are far more likely to be 'both-and'.

On the other hand, theological realism also leads to a distancing from the tendency to divide the world into good forces and bad. The unequivocal condemnation of the market by the Left, and of communism and socialism by the Right, is regarded as inaccurate empirically and theologically. It is worth noting, however, that the liberal establishment in ethics and Church also has a tendency to intolerance levelled at both Left and Right, and those who reject some of its sacred cows. Denys Munby found this out when he attacked its defective economics in contemporary church statements and the revered history of Christian socialism.[7] It is the cumulative effect of these beliefs and insights that are as important for how political economy is approached as for the content of its moral judgements.

For example, the liberal response has an understanding of change that distinguishes it from the other responses, particularly when taken in conjunction with its views on the state, politics and the economy. So its emphasis on process arises out of a belief in relative judgements and theological realism as instrumental for progress towards Christian social goals. The result is a strong commitment to reform as the principal means of affecting social change. At this point, radicals accuse liberals of a piecemeal reformism which makes little difference to the fundamentally unjust social order. Yet that is to confuse gradualness with dilatoriness. It is certainly not achieving change through 'a cumulative series of partial steps', as proposed by the American evangelical liberal, Mott.[8] Neither is it the purposeful gradualness of the Fabians.[9] For liberal involvement has contributed to radical changes in capitalist societies, in relation to the Welfare State in Britain and the liberation of black people in the USA. They continue to be engaged in a whole series of pressure groups.

Springing from this 'reforming mind-set', and indeed contributing to it, is the liberal approach to the state, politics and economics. Indeed, the latter can only be viewed in the social context provided by the other two. Since the late nineteenth and early twentieth centuries, the tradition has placed a high value on the modern state. It has regarded the state as a dyke against sin, but much more as the principal means for achieving social change. Through its agency, the harmful effects of the free market began to be corrected by regulating the forces of injustice and of redistributing the basic resources needed for meaningful participation in society. In Britain, this meant strong support for Beveridge's proposals for the Welfare State and Keynes's macroeconomic programmes to manage the economy at near full employment. Indeed, so deep has been the commitment of the official Churches that they fought, and continue to do so, against neo-conservative attacks on both programmes. Debates in the General Synod on the reports *Perspectives on Economics* and

Not Just for the Poor attacked government monetarist policies and reforms of the Welfare State. At times, these church commitments have come close to underwriting the corporate state of the 1960s and 1970s, and even gave a qualified support to the closed shop.[10] There is a way in which the official Churches and leading theologians of the liberal tradition are still bound up with these views, despite gestures to the greatly changed context of the 1980s. It suggests a 'mental-set' inhibiting them 'from anticipating the upheavals' of the late 1970s and 1980s.[11]

Despite the tendency to corporatism, the liberal response is safeguarded from its excesses because it gives priority in its social framework to the practice of politics in general, and of democracy in particular. To date, the latter is regarded as the closest approximation of a political order to basic Christian insights into human nature. Reinhold Niebuhr's famous aphorism best catches this high theological estimate of democracy: 'Man's capacity for justice makes democracy possible; but man's inclination to injustice makes democracy necessary.'[12] It is a valuation never accorded the market, even as mechanism, by the tradition. Niebuhr of course is not alone in this approval, because it is shared by most Western theologians, including Barth and Brunner, and certainly by those in the liberal response like Temple, Wogaman and Preston. Indeed, the latter would argue further, for the extension of democracy from political life into the economy. They justify their programme because of the concentration of unaccountable power in the modern market economy, and the importance of broadening participation in economic decision-making. *Economic Justice For All* illustrates this tendency very clearly.[13]

It is in relation to this concern for democracy in the widest sense that the commitment to democratic socialism can best be understood. Although recognizing the legitimacy of the social market, there is a clear preference for what the principal exponents of the response call democratic socialism. Benne referred to it as 'a religious consensus on the prima facie appeal of socialism'.[14] However, by this is almost invariably meant the politics of a moderate British Labour Party, a market socialism, and not the socialism of the liberation theologians and the radical response.

It is only within this framework, subordinated to democratic politics and a strong state, that the economy itself is located and considered. The market is therefore valued but only as a mechanism, probably essential for, yet subordinate to, more significant social purposes. Like economic growth, it is necessary, but not at all sufficient, for the good life.[15] For Wogaman, it is a servant;[16] for Preston, a serviceable drudge.[17] Both understand the nature and value of the profit motive, incentives, competition and the price mechanism. They recognize too, especially Preston, the constraints imposed by basic economic problems.

However, this acceptance of economics, and the market as mechanism, is rarely understood or shared by most others in the tradition, and certainly not by official church statements. Indeed, Munby, who himself has strong relationships with it, regards it as fatally flawed.[18] He makes this judgement because it has not grasped basic economics, and the value of the market mechanism and economy. That verdict is supported by the early history of the tradition, which was shaped totally by the strong reaction against the excesses of the free market and its awful social consequences. Dominated by these social constraints, it never understood the lessons of classic economics, nor acknowledged the influence of the basic economic problem of the allocation of scarce resources. As a result, the response has continued to concentrate on the issue of wealth distribution at the expense of the necessity and problems of its creation; it has focused on the social consequences of economic change and the market economy, and not on the necessity of the latter. From Reinhold Niebuhr to *Economic Justice For All* to *Faith in the City*, all suffer from this fatal defect.[19] Accepting the necessity and constraints of economics and the market is like the alcoholic exalting, in passing, the virtues of abstinence.

All these presumptions are confirmed (indeed, partly determined) by a social framework and its theological expression as the common good and interdependence. It is because this commitment is so strong that it overrides regularly 'the legitimate claims of self-interest, as expressing the inalienable rights and value of the individual personality'.[20] When joined to the overriding priority of social consequences, the result is inevitably a subordinationist – if not minimalist – view of market economics.

The reluctant acceptance of the market mechanism and the much higher estimate given to social and political goals has resulted in two related judgements. First, it has ensured a commitment to 'mixed economies', with a major role for the state as overall planner and limited producer, undergirded by a strong Welfare State.[21] Appropriately, the place of private property is accepted, but firmly located within limits: 'all human property rights are relative and contingent only'.[22] Secondly, the subordination of the market to political life is often associated with a harsher judgement on the New Right than on socialist or communist societies. In the 1970s the Chinese, Tanzanian and Cuban experiments were observed with interest, while Thatcherism and Reaganomics in the 1980s were almost unreservedly condemned. There was little recognition that the success of the latter was due significantly to the failure of the corporate and socialist states of the 1970s. There is almost an intrinsic sympathy for socialist experiments.

The approach to gradual change, the state, politics and economics combine to produce a coherent programme for progressive change. It is this that has become so influential in the mainstream Churches, and in their pronouncements on political and economic affairs. The remarkable resonance between the statements of governing bodies, social responsibility functions and leaders, both in the USA and Britain, has been noted already. It is the main indication of the central role of the mainstream liberal tradition. That influence is also partly the result of the tradition's commitment to the positive function of the Church in modern society. Emerging out of the Western Churches, including through their influence on the early ecumenical movement, it advocates a leadership role for the Church in society. Unlike the radical response, it therefore assumes no discontinuity between Church and society in market economies. Its task is to support the laity and citizens in the exercise of their civic responsibilities. Supporting this understanding of the Church, operating in relation to such a framework, is a theological method. Taking theological insights seriously, it also seeks to come to terms with the empirical realities of a changing context. Out of this relationship, guidelines are developed which reflect the ability of Christian beliefs to listen to society. They provide guidance for Christians in their involvement in movements and programmes. Again, it all adds up to a comprehensive and consistent Christian response to the market economy.

J. Philip Wogaman: the Christian social ethicist on economic affairs

It is always a temptation to regard a conversion experience in adulthood as a prerequisite for effective discipleship. It is certainly the case with Christian social witness. Many neo-conservatives, including Griffiths and Novak, moved dramatically from a strong socialist commitment to a belief in the free market. Others, like Duchrow, experiencing the apocalyptic conditions of Third World poverty, transformed their theology and lifestyles from traditional to liberationist. Yet radical experiences do not delegitimize ordinary routine experiences. William Temple was always thankful for the graces of being a once-born Christian. Not, of course, that such a journey is without experiences that disclose new understandings of faith and life. However, they tend to inspire a progressive development rather than a radical change of direction.

So it is with Philip Wogaman. Brought up in a Methodist manse in the desert region of Arizona in the USA, he saw at first hand the exploitation of migrant workers and the operating of a racist society. Guided by a sensitive father, these formative years of the 1940s showed him the importance of economic life and its disturbing effects on the vulnerable. It was from such foundations that he developed into one of the foremost Christian social ethicists in the USA.

To reach such a position required much more than formative life experiences; they needed to be complemented, as they were, by an academic life. His first book, *Guaranteed Annual Income* (1968),[23] brought together experience and theology, enabling him to relate Christian ethics, economics and poverty. It provided the means for sharpening his teeth on some of the key ingredients for effective Christian social thought. In contrast, the 1970s represented a period of theological consolidation. From his base as Professor of Christian Social Ethics at Wesley Theological Seminary, Washington DC, he set out his theological method[24] and elaborated it through economic issues.[25] A major development occurred in the 1970s when he was appointed Chairman of the United Methodist Task Force as part of the Churches' involvement in the Nestlé controversy. (This concerned the high-pressured selling of baby-milk products by multinationals to Third World countries.)

After a successful international boycott, the international authorities developed a framework for acceptable marketing behaviour. Until its end, in 1991, he was involved in the government commission to monitor its implementation.

It was such experiences that illustrated key themes in his life as an ethicist. For example, it reflected his commitment to work with his official church structure and the National Council of Churches. It also continued his supportive but discerning relationship with decision-makers in secular life, including the US Senate. The Centre for Theology and Public Policy, a think-tank based in his seminary, also reflected these concerns. Just as influential was his growing experience of and commitment to international poverty through the Nestlé enquiry, which took him to Third World countries.

In terms of his extensive contribution to Christian social ethics, it is difficult to think of anyone better equipped to represent the mainstream liberal tradition. His magisterial *Christian Perspectives on Politics*[26] is arguably the best book in the tradition published for decades. He is familiar, and equally highly regarded, in Britain and the USA. Despite the studied moderation of many of his ideas, and his gentle persuasive manner, it is worth recalling that his views represent a strong challenge in the conservative American context. Remember that it was Tillich, exponent of religious socialism under Hitler, and whose books were burned publicly in 1933, who found it difficult even to mention socialism in his new adopted country of the USA. He never overcame his feeling 'that there was something unseemly about advocating socialism in the United States, the colossal bastion of capitalism'.[27] Wogaman has no such inhibitions! He has nailed his flag to the mast of democratic socialism.

A way of beginning to understand this response is by recognizing the important part played in it by Christian social ethicists like Wogaman. Indeed, so intimate is the relationship in terms of the character and history of the response, that it is difficult to decide cause and effect. What can be done is to acknowledge that its reformist and progressive nature lends itself to the discerning moral judgements of Christian social ethics. Avoiding unequivocal statements reflects the latter's understanding of the complexity of contemporary economic and political affairs. It also means avoiding a theological method that moves directly from Scriptures or doctrine to unambiguous pronouncements on detailed policies. This in turn connects with a view of the Church's role in the market economy as critical solidarity with great institutions, based on discerning moral judgements.

The connection between Christian social ethics and liberal response did not arise by chance. The development of the Church's reaction to market societies in the late nineteenth and early twentieth centuries was closely associated with the emergence of Christian social ethics as an academic discipline, particularly in the USA. Indeed, it became a significant part of the Churches' response. Its principal exponents came to exercise great influence on church policies in the USA and Britain, and then in the early ecumenical movement. They included such figures as Reinhold Niebuhr, John Bennett, Joe Oldham, to Ronald Preston and Philip Wogaman in the present. The choice of the latter therefore illustrates the character of the response in important ways.

Such a decision means that beginning with the theological basis of Wogaman's contribution does not simply reflect the priorities in his thinking, but also the relationship between Christian social ethics and the liberal response. For he, more than anyone else, has elaborated the theological basis of his judgements and his theological method. So when confronted with economic issues he is aware immediately of the theological and moral questions they raise. Economics, like politics, is an 'inescapable aspect of human existence, with direct relevance to the divine-human encounter'.[28] How we handle economics invariably reflects our 'centre of value'.

From among the great insights of Christian belief, how do we choose and understand the core meanings that illuminate contemporary economics? To do this, Wogaman uses 'theological entry points' which highlight particular Christian understandings from the perspective of economics. For example, one of the great theological entry points is a recognition of 'physical existence as God's Creation'. This in turn commits theology to 'a basically positive attitude toward economic life and material well-being'.[29] More controversial, but equally revealing of his theological stance, is his choice of 'the priority of grace over works' as an entry point. For this profoundly challenges contemporary economic realities like the market economy. Allocating rewards according to what people 'deserve' contradicts the biblical belief that God's acceptance is not dependent on our effort at all.

What emerges out of the interaction between faith and economics are Christian 'presumptions' as a basis for moral judgement and action in economics. Adopted provisionally, they should only be set aside when Christian and empirical evidence suggests otherwise. Running through all his work, in a much more explicit way than Preston, there is a continual testing of theological entry points and moral presumptions with regard to general economic problems and detailed policy discussions. From the conflict between production and the environment to particular proposals for guaranteed incomes, his theological method is brought to bear in a consistent and substantial manner.

An equally important part of this theological approach concerns his use of ethical surveys. As typologies, they have become a classic tool for Christian social ethics by illuminating the different ways major issues are approached. In the light of their strengths and limitations, a more adequate response is then developed.[30] Thus in *Christians and the Great Economic Debate* Wogaman identifies five economic types. From *laissez-faire* capitalism at one end of the spectrum to Marxism at the other, he examines in between them social market capitalism, democratic socialism, and economic conservationism. Like Richard Niebuhr's classic typology in *Christ and Culture*, the social ethicist invariably rejects the two extremes, although learning much from them, and settles on those that hold the balance between them. So Wogaman dismisses *laissez-faire* capitalism and Marxism because of their intrinsic claims to be hard determinist ideologies. His choice narrows to social market capitalism or democratic socialism, with his preference in the end being the latter. The reasons for his judgement emerge in his development of a social framework within which economics can best be addressed.

It is through a consideration of social priorities that we can see Wogaman's understanding of a social framework for Christian guidance. Appropriately, he draws on one of the major proposals of the early ecumenical movement for his governing concept. Originating at the First Assembly of the World Council of Churches at Amsterdam in 1948, and dominating the Second Assembly at Evanston in 1954, the responsible society exercised the same influence on Christian social ethics as Justice, Peace and the Integrity of Creation has on the liberationist movement; it was defined as a society where 'those who hold political authority or economic power are responsible for its exercise to God and the people whose welfare is affected by it'.[31] Within such a social vision Wogaman is able to develop various social priorities that indicate the main directions for social progress; they include adequate production, equity and security, employment and educational opportunity, conservation, and a new world order.[32]

Just as important though, this enables him to address the problems of implementing social priorities. To begin with, listing priorities should never be regarded as a 'lexical' ordering of objectives; it is always necessary to recognize the effect of priorities on one another. So the priority of adequate production is influenced by the priority of conservation, in terms of *how* we produce as much as *what* is produced. Similarly, the priority of a new world order acknowledges the pervasive consequences of international realities, including the gap between rich and poor, the contribution of multinationals, and disarmament. He also understands that finitude inevitably implies that saying yes to one priority means saying no to another. It reflects the fundamental economic problem that wants outstrip resources, and so choices have to be made; the cost of a choice always includes the forgoing of the opportunities lost through not choosing other priorities. To raise the living standards of the world's poor to a significant degree will inevitably put enormous pressures on the earth's resources. There is a clear way in which economic questions run through all attempts to implement social priorities.

Although the ethical character of the responsible society is revealed by the interaction of social priorities and the constraints of implementation, there is a strong sense in which a concern for the vulnerable acts as focal point and supreme test of Christian commitment. Four of his five priorities address social matters, partly from the perspective of the poor, whereas economic affairs are expressed directly only in the priority of adequate production. Although this should be seen as illustrating the historical and dominant concern of the liberal response with the social consequences of an economy, Wogaman is too much of an ethicist and realist not to address also the economic problems of such a concern. The priority of equity and security therefore accepts the need for income security for all citizens, and yet recognizes the need to so structure it – but not at the expense of incentives. Despite these qualifications, the poor always remain the most important test of all priorities, because of the nature of Christian concern for the weakest link in the chain. The Christian involvement in Third World poverty, and the marginalization of a growing minority in First World countries, percolates all his priorities as a moral commitment, in the same way that economics does as the need to face up to realities. It is the balancing of the two, to serve the social purposes of the responsible society, that best reveals the skill of the social ethicist.

Although social priorities fill out the content of the responsible society, it is the practice of politics that becomes the dominant means for achieving them. For Wogaman that is predominantly a matter of democratic politics, rather than economics: 'for either capitalism or socialism to warrant the label "democratic", the economic order must finally be accountable to the political order, and the political order must be democratic'.[33] More than most contemporary theologians, he has recognized the supreme importance of political democracy for human living and Christian discipleship. Like Walter Rauschenbusch, and most Western theologians, he accepts democracy as more in accordance with Christian principles than any other political system known to us: 'The fundamental redemption of the state took place when special privilege was thrust out of the constitution and theory of our government and it was based on the principle of personal liberty and equal rights.'[34] It is in this Christian support of democratic life that he sees the vital role of the 'habits of the heart'. Virtues like prudence, justice, compromise and toleration combine to dispose us to co-operate for the common good. Yet, in the tradition of theological realism, Wogaman always understands that 'neither personal virtue nor sincere piety are any guarantee of social wisdom'.[35] The role of appropriate mechanisms will always be indispensable for the sustaining of democracy.

On such a basis, he is able to confront the liberationist's marginalization of political democracy by bringing it back into the centre of Christian discipleship. In a carefully reasoned argument he therefore accepts that Third World countries might have to postpone the implementation of democracy. Yet it can never be more than a temporary delay. The Christian presumption must always be in favour of democracy: 'Governmental systems that are less than democratic should be required to face a continuing burden of proof to show that it is not yet possible to be democratic.'[36] Similarly, he attacks free market libertarians seeking to remove economics from political interference. Yet even then it is never a simple assertion of political control over the economy. The growth of the market economy in the nineteenth century established the value of a freely operating economy as the most effective way of ordering it for the prosperity of all. 'Government, to some extent, has been on the defensive ever since.'[37] The dangers of an undue interference in economic affairs are well understood by Wogaman. Yet he is also aware of the necessary growth of government involvement in the overall management of the economy, supported by particular interventions varying from regulating financial practices to ensuring open competition. His conclusion recognizes the need both for political control of the economy and for its relative autonomy: 'in the final analysis we should face the truth that neither politics nor economics is simply reducible to the other'.[38]

It is the combination of a responsible society constituted by social priorities and democratic politics that drives Wogaman into a personal commitment to a democratic socialism of a Western social democratic kind. Profound social questions are raised by Christian commitments to a society in which all can participate properly, to a new world order, and to the conservation of the earth's resources. They push the balance away from social market capitalism in favour of democratic socialism: 'My own inclination, over the long run, is more toward democratic socialism than toward the other. . . . I would at least agree with John Bennett that we live at a time when the socialist question needs to be pressed. I take it this means that, up to a point, other alternatives are forced to bear a burden of proof.'[39] Values, in the end, take priority over basic economics, but never at their total expense.

It is within such a framework and ordering that Wogaman's views on economics must be located and considered. Yet in many ways a simple subordinationist view of economics does not do justice to his grasp of economics and his recognition of its central importance in contemporary life. His judgement that economics and the market are good servants but bad masters certainly summarizes his position. However, within his wider social framework he accepts the indispensable contribution of economics to human welfare. He is therefore concerned not to reduce economics to a simple instrument of social purposes.[40] Consequently, he recognizes its character as a social science and elaborates the contribution to economic life of the price mechanism, competition, the profit motive, and necessary inequalities. Yet his wider commitment to a responsible society and his work on economics means that he is well aware of the defects of the market economy, including its tendency to cyclical unemployment, concentrations of wealth and power, and threats to the environment. It is this critical appraisal of market economies that reinforces his judgement that: 'In sum, the miraculous market mechanism may be a good servant, but it is almost certainly a bad master.'[41] The market is essentially a mechanism to be used only within, and subordinate to, a wider social framework. His theological analysis of economics therefore drives him to support mixed economies, as defined earlier by Munby, with their combinations of public and private ownership, and planning and the price mechanism. They reflect, in other words, an 'empirical approach that ignores the dogmas of the extreme right and left'.[42] Despite the problems they encountered in the 1970s with stagflation, Wogaman is convinced that mixed economies are likely to be the best way forward for the foreseeable future.[43] The debate between socialism and capitalism, between social questions and economic realities, has not yet been decided, as far as Wogaman is concerned.

It is this ambivalence that reflects the balancing act so typical of Christian social ethics, and the liberal response's inability to face up to the fundamental contradictions of socialism. Running through Wogaman's views, particularly in the 1970s and early 1980s, is a tendency to give command economies at least the benefit of the doubt. China under Mao, and Cuba, were seen as possibly working towards a new human type,[44] and the Soviet economy was still seen as capable of being as successful as market economies: 'There is plenty of evidence that production can occur successfully under state auspices just as that it can be stimulated by a private enterprise system.'[45] The collapse of command economies in Eastern Europe and the Soviet Union has overtaken these balanced judgements. It suggests the need for a major reappraisal of the liberal response to market economies and, conversely, to command economies. Its understanding of the market as servant-mechanism subordinated to a wider social and political framework does not necessarily ensure that this reappraisal will happen. The liberal response may be as dogmatically restricted as the responses of Left and Right.

Incarnationalists in the market: 'the liberal tendency', or Christian social reform from Richmond to Preston

It is always difficult to grasp the comprehensive nature of change in the modern world. In less than 150 years, the extent and depth of change has exceeded by almost an incalculable amount whatever went before it in human history. Because it is so recent a development, and is likely to become a permanent condition, it is never easy to appreciate. Being in the midst of a phenomenon erodes the possibility of detached appraisal. Yet it need not be so; indeed, it may well be that the permanence of rapid change provides an understanding of historical tradition as part of present judgements.

A reflection on the current liberal response to market economies suggests such a judgement. For in it, contemporary engagement and historical tradition are bound together in a seemingly inextricable fashion. The reason is not hard to find. The emergence of industrialization in the mid-nineteenth century, particularly in the USA and Britain, was associated with the development of modern economics and Christian social ethics. Consequently, it should not be a matter of surprise that their key exponents, blessed with longevity, should have experienced personally many of the changes and known many of the principal exponents. They became major contributors to contemporary schools of thought, but also living entry points into supportive traditions and communities of memory. So it is with the economist J.K. Galbraith, and with the Christian social ethicist Ronald H. Preston.

R.H. Preston

Preston is first and foremost the leading Christian social ethicist in Britain. Indeed, he is the only one to stand comparison with the likes of Duchrow, Wogaman and Novak. He is renowned for the judicious nature of his Christian comment on current affairs in advanced economies. The content of his moral judgements has focused especially on industrial, economic, political, and social policy matters. Since the 1970s, a number of books and articles have flowed from his pen, including *Perspectives on Strikes* (editor 1975), *Religion and the Persistence of Capitalism* (1979), *Church and Society in the Late Twentieth Century: The Economic and Political Task* (1983), and *The Future of Christian Ethics* (1987). They represent Christian moral reasoning of 'the liberal tendency' at its best, a combination of practical wisdom and unobtrusive moral theology. The latter has reflected his long-standing commitment to moral judgements which stand in between the general claims of Christian belief and the particular demands of empirical situations. This is complemented by an equally decisive rejection of any attempt to move directly from biblical and doctrinal insights to detailed pronouncements on complex contemporary affairs.

It is in this combination of Christian beliefs and secular analysis that forms his contribution to Christian social ethics and reflects his background. Trained in economics at the London School of Economics in the early 1930s, he became Industrial Secretary of the Student Christian Movement (SCM). From that basis, he read theology at Oxford and then served a three-year curacy in Sheffield until 1943. Those were the years that saw the beginnings of one of the great unheralded episcopates, when Lesley Hunter was Bishop of Sheffield. A whole host of future liberal leaders of the Church, and major organizations like Industrial Mission, emerged from that context in the 1940s. After five years as Study Secretary of the SCM, when he was involved in the social witness of the ecumenical movement, he moved to Manchester and taught Christian Social Ethics at Manchester University from 1949 until his retirement in 1980.

His commitment to modern social ethics has always reflected his loyalty to the Church. It has nourished his Christian moral judgement, and provided an important vehicle for its expression. From his early SCM days he has been committed to, and often deeply involved in, the ecumenical movement. He has worked tirelessly to develop ecumenical social ethics as a firm foundation for the pronouncements of the World Council of Churches on world affairs. His six months in Geneva resulted in *Technology and Social Justice* (1971), a symposium on the social and economic teaching of the World Council of Churches from 1966 to 1968. Complementing his ecumenical social witness has been a series of contributions to his own Church of England's pronouncements on economic and social matters, including *Not Just for the Poor* (1986) and *Changing Britain* (1987). His has been a powerful confirmation and resourcing of the connection between the liberal tendency and the mainstream Churches, which stands on a level with any other exponent of the tradition, including Wogaman.

The part played by longevity in the development of a Christian social ethicist should never be underestimated. It has certainly contributed to the growing maturity of Preston's social judgements. Just as important, however, it allows him to be a particularly fine entry point into the tradition of Christian social thought that relates most closely to the liberal response in Britain. For the majority of its major exponents have been, or are, known to him personally. Thus he knew Temple, Oldham and Reinhold Niebuhr; he has continued to keep in close touch with Paul Abrecht, who ran the Church and Society department of the World Council of Churches for over thirty years; and he is regarded as a colleague by John Bennett, the American social ethicist, who was scribe at the Oxford Conference and at the Amsterdam and Evanston Assemblies of the World Council of Churches, Preston provides an intimate link with the liberal response in Britain and internationally.

Since his contribution to Christian social ethics is so substantial, it warrants elaboration as a complement to Wogaman's thought, but also as an introduction to liberal Christian social thinking in Britain. For, in particular, he has a clear understanding of belonging to such a tradition. Interpreting modern Christian social ethics as a response to capitalism, he traces its 'origin' to 1848 and the work of F.D. Maurice. This he regards as essentially 'a recovery of a theological critique of the assumptions behind the social order which had died out with the collapse of traditional Anglican and Puritan moral theology at the end of the seventeenth century'.[46] What he approves in Maurice is the theological rejection of any attempt to elevate competition and possessive individualism into an overall philosophy of life, into laws of God. Conversely, what he disapproves of in the work of the Christian political economists is their uncritical encouragement of the autonomy of economics and the free market.[47]

It is here that an important problem arises for the liberal tradition. For although Preston accepts the contribution of Maurice

and his successors, despite grave defects in their economic understanding, he does not balance this with a complementary approval
of the contributions of Christian political economy to the Christian
understanding of economics, despite their limitations. Nor does
he subject the pre-modern tradition of theology's domination of
economics to a consistent and vigorous criticism as a basis for any
'recovery' of a balanced theological critique of the social order.
His beloved Baxter somehow remains less touched by his acerbic
judgement, maybe for the same reasons Tawney does.[48] It remains
one of the great blind spots of the liberal tradition. For correcting
it would do more than restore greater accuracy to its historical
judgements, an important requirement for the continuation of
a healthy tradition; it would also give greater coherence and
consistency to the development of guidelines for Christian social
thought when facing the contemporary context. For Preston's
criteria include a concern for the poor, equality, participation
in decision-making, and a positive as well as negative view of
the state.[49] The addition of a concern for economic goals and
realities, and their critical interaction with the other more socially
oriented criteria, would be more consistent with major features
in his work. It would add more force to his continuing criticism
of the 'over-dramatic' language[50] of the ecumenical movement for
similar inconsistencies and defects.

Preston's understanding of theological method supports this
potential for greater consistency and coherence in Christian social
thought. The balanced nature of his judgements on contemporary
affairs reflects a theological method that seeks to bring into a
reciprocal relationship understandings of Christian doctrine and
the Scriptures, and diagnoses of what is going on in today's
world. The development of both perspectives is consistent with
the liberal tendency; the insights into Christian belief reflect the
dialogue between tradition and modern intellectual developments,
like historical criticism and evolution. It led to what was known
in England as the liberal catholicism of Gore, and the progressive
orthodoxy of American evangelicals in the social gospel tradition.
The other perspective – the recognition of the contemporary
context through its empirical analysis – went some way towards
accepting at least the relative autonomy of secular disciplines
like economics. Preston's emphasis on eschatology brings both
together, so that no economic or political scheme can ever

correspond to Christian hopes. The uncertainties appropriate to each perspective rule that out.

The implications of such a theological method are enormous. It has led Preston to continue to advocate middle axioms as the classic way of developing provisional guidelines, through the collaboration of theological and secular experts, for Christian discipleship in the modern world.[51] Equally, it has produced a severe rejection of any attempt to move directly from the Scriptures, doctrine or natural law to detailed ethical prescriptions for contemporary living.[52] In this regard, he indicts both neo-conservatives and radicals. There can be no *status confessionis* on complex economic affairs for him. The search is always for a shared moral basis of operating in society, between Christians, and with non-Christians; the objective is the common good of all. It is never a distinctively Christian social order.[53] It is always compatible with his character as a reflective commentator on contemporary affairs from a Christian basis.

The acknowledgement of the relative autonomy of secular disciplines is reflected in his understanding of economics.[54] In this, he has the unusual advantage of a training in economics. Almost uniquely in contemporary Christian social thought, the results are books pervaded by clear understandings of modern economics stretching way beyond the traditional limitation of Christian theological comments on economic systems. For Preston is clear that any Christian attempt to address economic questions has to begin with the basic economic problem facing any economic system – namely, 'how to allocate scarce resources which can enter into the economic system and which have alternative uses'.[55] Within this fundamental problem are the subsidiary ones of: how to register demands for goods and services, how to ensure production matches demand, how to distribute rewards for production, and how to allocate resources between present and future consumption.[56]

Only when these basics are acknowledged is it then wise to take note of the two existing ways of addressing them: the two ideal types of the free market and the planned economy. Both are inevitably profoundly defective in practice. However, his deepest theological as well as economic criticisms are reserved for the former, whether as nineteenth-century *laissez-faire* capitalism or the libertarian ideology of the New Right. The routine defects of the free market certainly arouse his judgement, with its tendency to monopolies, unemployment, inequalities, harmful effects on the environment, the pressure on positional goods, and the inability to deliver basic social goods such as housing.[57] What agitates him most, however, like F.D. Maurice before him, is the free market's intrinsic tendency to encourage possessive individualism. Such individualism he regards as 'fundamentally false', a contradiction of the Christian view of the human.[58] Because of this fatal flaw, the elevation of capitalism and individualism into an overall philosophy rouses his unremitting hostility.

Conversely, the other ideal type, the planned economy, gets off more lightly. As a means of allocating scarce resources, central state planning is clearly deficient, and he has always acknowledged this. Yet even in the late 1970s he was able to produce the classic balanced judgement of the liberal Christian social ethicist: that the planned economies of the Eastern bloc were 'neither more nor less successful' than market economies;[59] and that there was 'no evolutionary tendency at work to produce either the collapse of capitalism or the advent or collapse of socialism'.[60]

In the end, concurring with Wogaman, he reasons for a strong social framework with the practice of politics central to it (although he does not argue for political democracy to the extent of Wogaman or Novak). For one of his major criticisms of the New Right concerns its denigration of politics and overestimate of economics. Yet even then, he regards the practice of politics as penultimate: it should never be raised to the level of an ultimate in the way he argues Duchrow does. It is in this discerning spirit that he questions the current tendency among democratic socialists to advocate decentralized politics. There will always be a need for national and international levels of political activity; the local will never possess the wider knowledge needed for decision-making in a post-industrial society, and is less able to balance irreconcilable demands.[61] Given such qualifications, economics is generally subordinated to political oversight, including the key decision as to what is and is not delegated to it. What he is arguing for essentially is a mixed economy, combining planning and market mechanism, and with a strong Welfare State. It would be under the political control of his theological commitment to a wider social framework. His tendency therefore, like Wogaman, is to support democratic socialism, even though he is not aware of any working model to support his commitment. Like others in a similar predicament, he falls back on the Swedish example. His historic belief in equality as the distinguishing feature of socialism, and in fellowship, produce his affinity to socialism.[62] Yet his economic sense probably means that, like Sweden, he will be unlikely to move beyond a radical social democratic position on an essentially market economy base.

It is within such a framework that he can locate the market as a mechanism. It then becomes the best chance for solving fundamental economic problems, 'one of mankind's most useful devices for deciding a basic problem in any society, the allocation of relatively scarce resources between alternative uses'.[63] Yet it can only be that if it is treated as 'a servant and not a master'. Valuable as it is, it can never be more than a 'serviceable drudge' for Christian opinion.[64] It is a predominantly liberal and reformist view that characterizes the eminently reasonable belief in the market as a mechanism in the service of wider social goals. It extends even to his belief that such 'wise policies' could break the 'sound barrier' of absolute poverty in most of the Third World by the year AD 2000.[65]

The year 1889 was a momentous one, another *annus mirabilis*. It was the year of the great dock strike, one of the most important conflicts in our industrial history. Helped by the mediation of Cardinal Manning, its settlement facilitated the emergence of the general worker unions. It was also a year that signalled the coming of age of the Fabian Society, with the publication of the first *Fabian Essays*. The English tradition of evolutionary socialism and social reform,[66] based on research and practical proposals for change, was the political complement of English Christian social reform.

It was in such a context of economic change and social reform that the liberal response took important steps which connected with equivalent secular developments. The publication of *Lux Mundi*, and the founding of the Christian Social Union (CSU), paralleled the *Fabian Essays* and the Fabian Society. They were also symptomatic of wider changes in Christian social thought and practice. So important were these developments that they constitute a convincing argument for regarding the events of 1889 as a more valid starting-point for modern Christian social thought, especially of the mainstream liberal tradition. In appraising

Christian responses to market economies, it is important to correct the traditional overemphasis on 1848 and F.D. Maurice, just as it is to acknowledge the superiority of Ronald Preston over William Temple's contribution to Christian social ethics. It was, in other words, the year 1889 that began to see the emergence of modern liberal Christian social thought, through publications, organizations and major individuals.

Lux Mundi

Lux Mundi: a series of studies in the Religion of the Incarnation was edited by Charles Gore, and sought 'to put the Catholic Faith in its right relation to modern intellectual and moral problems'.[67] Although a collection of twelve uncompromisingly scholarly essays, it aroused enormous interest, going through ten editions in twelve months. It was the *Honest to God* of the late nineteenth century, because it sought to engage the modern context by reinterpreting the faith in relation to the profound intellectual and social transformations of the times. The great themes of historical criticism and the Scriptures, evolution and Christian doctrine, and the communitarian nature of the human are all played out in its pages. Indeed, so strong was the latter, particularly through the influence of Gore and Scott Holland, that it is difficult to separate *Lux Mundi* from the principal Christian organization for social reform, the CSU.

Equally important, however, was *Lux Mundi*'s commitment to reinterpret faith through modern categories of thought, while remaining firmly wedded to the core of Christian beliefs. This was achieved through an understanding of the incarnation, which became the principal doctrinal entry point into interpreting contemporary life and acting on it. It reflected the dramatic change, in the nineteenth century, from soteriology to incarnation; it was with the latter that social Christianity 'desired to see the laws of political economy brought into contact'.[68] It came to characterize the liberal response to contemporary change, whether as liberal catholicism or progressive orthodoxy. Along with the contributions of Gore, Richmond, Scott Holland, Westcott and Temple, 'the patterns of thought they formed became the core assumptions of "Christian social ethics" for most of the [next] century, and gradually penetrated the convictions of the majority of

Westerners'.[69] *Lux Mundi* was as important for social Christianity as the *Fabian Essays* were for socialism.[70]

So marked, prevalent and continuing have been these characteristics, combining modern intellectual and social needs, that they should be regarded as a major type of Christian response to society. Some have called it a 'liberal tendency', defining it as 'an outlook sympathetic to progress, tolerant of the social control of economic life, and conscious of the human factors involved'.[71] Others talk of 'social-unionism' (after the CSU)[72] or, in the USA, 'Christian sociology'.[73] It may be more helpful to collect these various conceptions into the organizing concept of 'Christian social reform', representing intellectual and practical commitments to progressive gradual change.

CSU

It was progressive gradual change that was promoted by the CSU, with its conviction 'to claim for the Christian Law the ultimate authority to rule social practice';[74] this was intended to be an explicit challenge to the pretensions of *laissez-faire*, and its concern to exempt economics from that universal principle. The CSU therefore came to manifest many of the strengths and limitations of Christian social reform, including the liberal tendency in Christian social ethics. For example, it represented the emerging domination of official opinion in the Church by the mainstream liberal tradition. Compared to the 'shock troop' tactics of the Guild of St Matthew, the CSU exemplified 'the army of occupation',[75] 'an informal committee of the English Church upon social questions'.[76] Its commendable modesty probably sprang from its commitment to study the facts of the social situation before bringing Christian beliefs to bear on it. Complementing the moral criticism of the defects of the market was a growing realism related to this rise of 'Christian sociology' as taking the context seriously. In the case of the CSU, it led to numerous campaigns directed against sweated industries. It was this attention to detail, joined to a breadth of church membership, which ensured the CSU was never captured by any one issue – like, for example, the Single Tax or guild socialism. Yet there were costs attached to these characteristics. Its very reasonableness led many to accuse it of 'death by a thousand qualifications'. Donaldson, a leader of the

Church Socialist League, cruelly parodied it as the organization of 'Here's a social evil; let's read a paper on it.'[77]

When Maurice argued for the need to socialize Christianity to complement the Christianizing of socialism, the task must have appeared utopian in the extreme. In 1853 Frederic Harrison regarded the Church as a 'selfish sect', so estranged from the poor majority of the population that 'this Church cannot last a generation'. Yet by turn of the century Maurice's dream had become a reality. For, in 1911, Harrison wrote of the 'immense rally of the Established Church' as a 'moral as well as a great social revival of Church power, mainly in the towns, and largely designed as a political experiment'.[78]

These great inroads into the establishment were made particularly through the CSU. For example, regarding the leadership of the Church, between 1889 and 1913 fourteen out of the fifty-three bishops appointed were CSU members. By 1900 'Christian socialism' was fashionable in church circles, and official church bodies engaged regularly with major contemporary social questions and often in a critical manner. The report of the Committee of Convocation, *The Moral Witness of the Church on Economic Subjects* (1907), was chaired by Gore, and represented the apogee of liberal achievement as an official church critique of the market economy. In its conclusion it used church principles to reject orthodox classical liberalism and capitalist economics, and argued for a just distribution of resources.[79] In noting this dramatic capture of the Church by the cause of Christian social reform, it is important to recognize that official Church of England bodies emerged virtually parallel to the growth of Christian social reform: the Church Congress began in 1861, the Lambeth Conference in 1867, and the Convocations of Canterbury and York occurred in 1847 and 1859. Their combined emergence ensured that the official Church began, and has continued to this day, a tradition of criticism of the excesses of the market and its intrinsic virtues – such as competition and profit. By 1923 the National Assembly of the Church of England had appointed a Social and Industrial Committee, enlarged into a Commission in 1924.[80] It was the successors of these bodies that became the bane of the Thatcher government's life in the 1980s. No wonder Raymond Plant compared Gore's report of 1907 with *Faith in the City*.[81]

Wilfrid Richmond

The socializing of the Church was always the achievement of individuals as well as organizations, and the end of the nineteenth century had more than its fair share of the former, with some more well known than others. For example, in the latter category, a sadly underrated contribution to Christian social reform was made by Wilfrid Richmond, organiser of PESEK (a group concerned with politics, economics, socialism, ethics and Christianity).[82] This misjudgement of Richmond was not made by his contemporaries in the USA, who held him in high regard. Yet even in Britain, Gore was inspired to found the CSU after attending his lectures in 1889 on Economic Morals.[83] Described as one of the 'incarnationalist economists',[84] Richmond's task was 'to enforce the principle that economic conduct is a matter of duty, and therefore part of the province of conscience and of morals'.[85] Yet he was clear that this could not be achieved by a wholesale rejection of *laissez-faire*, based on basic misunderstandings of economics. Through his contact with the great economist Alfred Marshall, he realized that Christian social thought had to analyse economic systems, and accept the contribution of the division of labour and competition to economic growth. He understood well the need to distinguish between economics as a valued means for achieving preferred social goals, and the elaboration of those wider social purposes. Economics could never therefore be proclaimed as the laws of God, determining purposes as well as means. The skill of discernment, so essential to modern Christian social ethics, had begun to emerge. 'Ends and means are two different things, but they are different in idea rather than distinct in fact. If men are to be led to seek real wealth, we must see what is the wealth they do seek' . . . and we thus need 'to know what are the methods by which it is produced.'[86]

Brooke Foss Westcott

If Richmond was an inspiration for the founding of the CSU, and an early contributor to the development of Christian social ethics, Brooke Foss Westcott was the national leader who gave Christian social reform 'respectability'.[87] As one of the great scholar Bishops of Durham, he understood the implications of the rediscovery of eschatology for Christian socialism, as the relativizer of social ideals. He was a great exponent, too, of the Fatherhood of God requiring the Brotherhood of man.[88] Like Maurice before him, the contemporary context was the source of theological and religious inspiration. As Bishop of Durham, it was therefore not surprising to find Westcott mediating in the miners' strike of 1892. But it was his conviction that 'behind every social question there lies not only a moral but a religious question' that led him to accept the presidency of the CSU. The emphasis by classical economics on competition, individualism and economic autonomy was inevitably unacceptable. The only alternative seemed to be what he called socialism, but by which he meant social reform:

> Individualism and Socialism correspond with opposite views of humanity. Individualism regards humanity as made up of disconnected or warring atoms; Socialism regards it as an organic whole, a vital unity formed by the combination of contributory members mutually interdependent. It follows that Socialism differs from Individualism both in method and in aim. The method of Socialism is co-operation, the method of Individualism is competition . . . The aim of Socialism is the fulfilment of service, the aim of Individualism is the attainment of some personal advantage . . .[89]

It has been a confusion of socialism and social reform that has bedevilled English criticism of the market economy to this day, just as Westcott's misunderstanding of economics has likewise continued to exercise an undue influence on Christian social reform. It has become an hereditary disease of church leaders and official church bodies. The problem has been best summed up by Henry Scott Holland. After listening to Westcott's great speech on socialism (quoted above), delivered to the Church Congress meeting at Hull in 1890, Scott Holland commented that everyone was deeply moved, but couldn't remember a word on leaving the hall!

Charles Gore and Henry Scott Holland

The two moving spirits behind the CSU and *Lux Mundi*, Charles Gore and Henry Scott Holland, contributed to Christian social reform a growing commitment to a strong, positive view of the state. Emerging with democracy as the centre of a strong social framework, it was soon regarded as the only way to make the market acceptable to Christian opinion. It therefore came to symbolize the need to regulate the market's tendency to abuse people and communities, and its complement: the need to promote civic virtue. Yet by 1900 the signs of an active modern state were becoming more and more visible, and a cause of great alarm. When Gore was accused of encouraging such 'grandmotherly legislation', his reply was 'Everyman his own grandmother.'[90]

Scott Holland was even more convinced of the importance and value of the state in a market economy:[91]

> The state must take up our task of neighbourly responsibility or it can never be taken up at all. But this is Socialism, you cry. Exactly . . . Socialism, in emphasising the moral significance of the state, has got hold of the real trend of things, under which we are all mentally and rationally moving.[92]

The belief in a physical apostolic succession – that is, that bishops descended in an unbroken line from the apostles – was still held by many, even in the 1960s. Most scholars now question that belief. What is incontrovertible is the 'apostolic succession' of Christian social reform, stretching in a continuous line from Maurice, who taught Westcott, who taught Gore, who taught Temple and Tawney, who taught Preston. That is precisely where William Temple should be located: one in a long chain, albeit a vital link in that chain.

William Temple

Developments in Christian social ethics since William Temple's death confirm that judgement. It is the argument of this book that he should be placed in between the first nexus of Christian social reform at the end of the nineteenth century, focused around *Lux Mundi* and the CSU, and the work of Ronald Preston today. Only in that sense can Mayor's judgement be accepted: that Temple is 'the logical conclusion of the Christian Socialist Movement began by Maurice and organised by the CSU'.[93] What must be rejected is Peck's intemperate eulogy of Temple, that: 'His valiant attempts to reach a statement of Christian social doctrine will doubtless prove to have been amongst the most significant intellectual labours of our epoch.'[94]

Like Westcott and Gore before him, Temple's early years were informed by a deep rejection of *laissez-faire* capitalism and the espousal of what he assumed to be the virtuous opposite. Competition, the insignia of capitalism, was 'inherently a principle of selfishness, and, indeed, of hatred. . . . The alternative stands before us – Socialism or Heresy, we are involved in one or the other.'[95] It was these early convictions that led him to extend the remit of Christian social reform to include the management of the economy for wider social purposes, particularly for the sake of the poor. In the achievement of such goals, the state became the principal means, and indeed, as the Welfare State (a term that he coined), became a goal in itself as part of the corporate state. Declaring even for limited nationalization, he was more and more convinced that 'the Christian is called on to assent to great steps in the direction of collectivism'.[96]

The publication in 1942 of his *Christianity and Social Order* soon became one of the small classics of Christian social reform. Bringing his life's work to a coherent and persuasive conclusion, it set out Christian reasons why the Church should interfere in the social order, and the principles on which it should do so. On their basis, in the Appendix, he elaborates a personal programme for social reform that is still relevant. *Faith in the City* and *Not Just for the Poor*, major church reports in the 1980s, reflect many of his conclusions.

However, the significance of his contribution to church life also affected a wider arena. It reflects the development of the liberal tendency to flow from national Churches into the emerging ecumenical movement. His involvement in COPEC (1924), leading into the first international Life and Work Conference at Stockholm (1925), reached a climax at the Oxford Conference in 1937. Its four criticisms of the assumptions of capitalism are still valid – namely, that it encourages acquisitiveness, inequalities, irresponsible economic power, and the frustration of Christian vocation.[97] After his untimely death in 1944, the establishment of the World Council of Churches in 1948 persisted with what was now the classic balanced critique of *laissez-faire* capitalism and communism, even though by then the former no longer existed in practice. It was a confusion extended into the Evanston Assembly of 1954, with its arguments for mixed economies between the two extremes.

Although the liberal tradition developed into the ecumenical movement, it still persists as the principal strand in Christian social ethics in Britain and the USA, through the work of Wogaman and Preston. Both confirm the dominant influence of the response on their official Churches, and their relationship with market economies. They are no longer influential in the liberationist-oriented World Council of Churches. Yet despite the careful theological and economic analysis of Wogaman and Preston, it is still a perspective over-influenced by its early reaction against the market as *laissez-faire* capitalism. The spirit of Oxford still stalks many official church corridors:

> When the necessary work of society is so organized as to make the acquisition of wealth the chief criterion of success, it encourages a feverish scramble for money, and a false respect for the victors in the struggle, which is as fatal in its moral consequences as any other form of idolatry.[98]

It is the combination of the two perspectives, Oxford with the measured judgements of Wogaman and Preston, that produces the view of the market as mere mechanism, subordinate to wider social purposes.

Addendum on Church and theology

A detailed analysis of the liberal response has revealed a close relationship between its main features and its understanding of the Church and theology. Indeed, the connection is so close that separating them for the sake of discussion becomes more artificial than normal. The mainstream liberal tradition, its character and history, determines more than most its linkage with church social witness and the theological understanding deployed to support it. So much of the relevant material to support this claim is therefore necessarily included in the main text itself.

What does emerge to attract further comment are the implications for the understanding of Church and theology of a relationship with market economies that is essentially reformist.

Within that context, the Church is seen as having a supportive but also critical role. For example, Wogaman and Preston do allow for the operation of a radical function in the Church. Thus the prophetic role of small groups is recognized as a legitimate contribution to Christian life. However, their presumption is always to work constructively with complex matters, like economics, in what they regard as a mixed economy context. Such issues can never be reduced to an apocalyptic either-or, a darkness in which all cats are grey.[99] The task is always to work on the assumption that it is possible to achieve gradual but purposeful change on the basis of discerning judgements and practice. This necessarily includes a supportive as well as critical role.

The model used to advocate such positive but discerning involvement in market economies has been called 'critical solidarity'.[100] It is a term that accurately describes the relationship of Church and state in practice. However, it does not remove the unease felt in most church bodies over an open commitment to liberal democracy and the market economy, and particularly to the latter. It is this reluctance or ambivalence to face up to issues of basic economics and the market that Preston tries to capture when he argues that critical and solidarity must be given equal weight. Yet, in practice, the official Churches accept the established orderings, including the market economy, not least for strong financial reasons. They have made no serious attempt to promote a radical alternative. Their task is always to affirm and increase the use of the market as mechanism for wider social purposes.

Even their commitment to the vulnerable does not simply reflect the priority of moral progress over economic means. Some commentators have also interpreted this bias to the poor as an expression of a coinciding of the interests of the emerging middle class of professionals and bureaucrats, reflected also in the growth of the official Church, and a growing underclass. Both are committed to a strong corporate state operating in a paternalist and redistributory manner.[101] It indicates the presence of a strong element of self-concern in the most obvious moral purposes, including the Church's.

It is this fundamental ambivalence over the role of the Church which leads many in the mainstream liberal tradition to accept the existing establishment of the Churches of England and Scotland. Even those who support greater reform still argue for the Church's role in promoting civic religion and a common morality. The fundamental ambivalences of a reformist view of the Church add up to yet another reason why the mainstream liberal tradition of the Western Churches is regarded as being so out of touch with the World Council of Churches and Third World Churches in their stand against the market economy.

It is the same spirit of purposeful compromise that pervades the theology of the liberal response. The result is a major contribution to Christian social ethics which still occupies a dominant place in Western Christian social thought. Much of its strength derives from its ability to take account of changing trends and motifs, while remaining securely in the mainstream Christian tradition. It was well described as progressive orthodoxy and liberal catholicism; it is concerned essentially with the reform of tradition and not its overturn.

The development of theological method reflects a similar character, of working from traditional Christian beliefs to what to do in and with the context. Engagement with the latter clearly contributes to the emerging moral judgements. There is consequently no direct imposition of beliefs on a situation, taking no serious account of the realities of life. The beliefs are mediated through the context, and so are influenced by it. It is such emerging moral guidelines that can be said to mediate between beliefs and situation.

However, the use of concepts like 'mediating', 'educational', 'interactive' and 'indirect' do not describe with sufficient accuracy this procedure for developing moral judgements according to the character of reformed tradition. They detract from what is essentially movement from beliefs to a situation, and the moral judgements made in it. For the mainstream liberal tradition consistently describes its theological method as bringing *to bear* the religion of the incarnation on the social and economic life of man;[102] Preston refers to drawing 'broad considerations from Christian faith' in the light of which New Right economics can then be appraised.[103] Of course, creating such moral judgements depends upon a careful study of the 'facts' of the situation using the relevant experts, preferably in a collaborative effort. In this sense there is a 'dialogue' between implications of belief and the context. It is an important reason why such judgements or guidelines are regarded as provisional and not definitive for all times and all situations. Yet in the end Christian beliefs are the core value. This must always be ultimately decisive in the formation of the wider social framework, and the policies necessary to support it. Economics in general, and the market mechanism in particular, must be subordinate to those greater social and moral purposes. Theological method and the Christian estimate of the market form a consistent and coherent part of the liberal tradition. It is essentially the way of reform, in an ultimately subordinationist framework and ethos.

Notes

1 J.P. Wogaman, *Christians and the Great Economic Debate* (SCM Press 1977), p. 97.
2 J. Atherton, *Faith in the Nation: A Christian Vision for Britain* (SPCK 1988), p. 140.
3 J. Atherton, 'The Limits of the Market', in M. Alison and D.L. Edwards, eds, *Christianity and Conservatism: Are Christianity and Conservatism Compatible?* (Hodder & Stoughton 1990), pp. 266–7.
4 R. Benne, *The Ethic of Democratic Capitalism: A Moral Reassessment* (Philadelphia, Fortress Press, 1981), p. 5.
5 M. Buber, *The Eclipse of God: Studies in The Relation Between Religion and Philosophy* (New York, Harper & Row, 1952), p. 8.
6 J.P. Wogaman, *Christian Perspectives on Politics* (SCM Press 1988), p. 90. The concept 'mainstream liberal tradition' is Wogaman's.
7 A.M.C. Waterman, 'Denys Munby on Economics and Christianity', *Theology* (March–April 1990, vol. XCIII, no. 752), p. 109. Waterman comments that Munby's devastating criticisms of Mairet's *The National Church and the Social Order* (1957) were received 'cooly, not to say frigidly' by his fellow Anglicans. The Methodist Board of Social Responsibility recently rejected a fine report on wealth creation, presumably because it did not condemn unequivocally the market system.
8 Quoted in Wogaman, *Christian Perspectives on Politics*, p. 95.
9 See J. Atherton, 'R.H. Tawney as a Christian Social Moralist', Ph.D thesis (University of Manchester 1979), p. 362.
10 *Understanding Closed Shops: A Christian Enquiry into Compulsory Trade Union Membership* (Church Information Office 1977).
11 J.C.D. Clark, in *Revolution and Rebellion* (Cambridge University Press 1986), p. 20, describes the problems of the Keynesians and Fabians of the post-war generation.
12 R. Niebuhr, *The Children of Light and the Children of Darkness* (Nisbet 1945), p. xi.
13 *Economic Justice For All*, Origins, NC Documentary Services, 10 October 1985, vol. 15, no. 17, para. 283f.
14 R. Benne, *The Ethic of Democratic Capitalism*, p. 9.

15 Ronald Preston in D.L. Munby, ed., *Economic Growth in World Perspective* (SCM Press 1966), p. 111.
16 Wogaman, *Christians and the Great Economic Debate*, p. 97.
17 R. Preston, *The Future of Christian Ethics* (SCM Press 1987), p. 154. A Tawney concept in his *The Radical Tradition*, ed. R. Hinden (Allen & Unwin 1964), p. 168.
18 Waterman's appraisal of Munby, p. 110 (see note 7).
19 On Niebuhr and Rawls, see Benne, p. 17.
20 J. Sleeman, *Basic Economic Problems: A Christian Approach* (SCM Press 1953), p. 147.
21 For a definition of such a mixed economy, see D.L. Munby, *Christianity and Economic Problems* (Macmillan 1956), p. 235.
22 Munby, *Christianity and Economic Problems*, p. 98.
23 J.P. Wogaman, *Guaranteed Annual Income: The Moral Issues* (Nashville, Abingdon, 1968).
24 J.P. Wogaman, *A Christian Method of Moral Judgement* (SCM Press 1976).
25 J.P. Wogaman, *Christians and the Great Economic Debate* (SCM Press 1977).
26 (SCM Press 1988).
27 G. Dorrien, *Reconstructing the Common Good: Theology and the Social Order* (New York, Orbis, 1990), p. 71.
28 Wogaman, *Christian Perspectives on Politics*, p. 3.
29 J.P. Wogaman, *Economics and Ethics: A Christian Enquiry* (SCM Press 1986), pp. 33–5.
30 F.D. Maurice began to develop such a method in his *Kingdom of Christ* in 1838. Henry Clarke, another American Professor of Christian Social Ethics, in his review of Wogaman's *Christian Perspectives on Politics*, commented very positively on this skill: 'it is a first-rate example of the kind of scholarship in which Wogaman excels, namely, a clear presentation of significant issues and of the way in which these issues are addressed by opposing thinkers' (*Crucible* (January–March 1989), p. 39).
31 Quoted in Wogaman, *Economics and Ethics*, p. 27.
32 Wogaman, *Economics and Ethics*. With regard to poverty, he discusses briefly the dependency theory, but rejects it (*Christians and the Great Economic Debate*, p. 22). He gives a much fuller treatment to multinationals in both *Christians and the Great Economic Debate*, pp. 114–19, and *Economics and Ethics*, pp. 122–4. Essentially he accepts their contribution, providing they are subject to better regulation.
33 Wogaman, *Economics and Ethics*, p. 29.
34 Wogaman, *Christian Perspectives on Politics*, p. 162, quoting Rauschenbusch.
35 Wogaman, *Christian Perspectives on Politics*, p. 172.
36 Wogaman, *Christian Perspectives on Politics*, p. 163–4.
37 Wogaman, *Christian Perspectives on Politics*, p. 211.
38 Wogaman, *Christian Perspectives on Politics*, p. 229.
39 Wogaman, *Christians and the Great Economic Debate*, p. 158.
40 Wogaman, *Christians and the Great Economic Debate*, pp. 44–5.
41 Wogaman, *Christians and the Great Economic Debate*, p. 97.

42 Quoting Munby, Wogaman, *Christians and the Great Economic Debate*, p. 101.
43 Wogaman, *Christian Perspectives on Politics*, p. 229.
44 Wogaman, *Christians and the Great Economic Debate*, p. 161.
45 Wogaman, *Economics and Ethics*, p. 61.
46 R.H. Preston, *Church and Society in the Late Twentieth Century* (SCM Press 1983), p. 15.
47 Preston, *Church and Society in the Late Twentieth Century* (SCM Press 1983), p. 56–7.
48 Tawney's wife, Jeannette, edited selections from Baxter's *A Christian Directory*.
49 Preston, *Religion and the Persistence of Capitalism* (SCM Press 1979), p. 49. To these criteria should be added his reflections on the World Council of Churches' slogan of Justice, Participation and Sustainability, pp. 51–5.
50 Preston, *Religion and the Persistence of Capitalism*, p. 56.
51 His best exposition of middle axioms is in *Church and Society*, appendix 2, pp. 141–56.
52 For example, in *Religion and the Persistence of Capitalism*, p. 8.
53 In contrast to other groups and theologians, for example in the Christendom Group; see Preston, *Church and Society*, p. 24.
54 See Preston, *Religion and the Persistence of Capitalism*, pp. 8f.
55 Preston, *Religion and the Persistence of Capitalism*, p. 24.
56 Preston, *Religion and the Persistence of Capitalism*, p. 25.
57 For Hirsch's arguments, see Preston, *Religion and the Persistence of Capitalism*, pp. 34–5.
58 Preston, *Religion and the Persistence of Capitalism*, p. 73.
59 Preston, *Religion and the Persistence of Capitalism*, p. 141.
60 Preston, *Religion and the Persistence of Capitalism*, p. 38.
61 Preston, *Religion and the Persistence of Capitalism*, p. 132.
62 Preston, *Religion and the Persistence of Capitalism*, pp. 4–5.
63 Preston, *Church and Society*, pp. 31–2.
64 Preston, *Church and Society*, pp. 115 and 117.
65 Preston, *Church and Society*, p. 55.
66 The distinction between them was very unclear in this period (and it still is).
67 P. d'A.Jones, *The Christian Socialist Revival, 1877–1914: Religion, Class and Social Conscience in late Victorian England* (Princeton University Press 1968), p. 171.
68 H. Scott Holland, preface to Wilfrid Richmond's *Economic Morals*, 1890. In B. Hilton, *The Age of Atonement: The Influence of Evangelicalism on Social and Economic Thought 1785–1865* (Clarendon Press 1988), p. 6.
69 M.L. Stackhouse, *Public Theology and Political Economy* (Grand Rapids, MI, Eerdmans, 1987), p. 50, discussing the social gospel in the USA.
70 G.C. Binyon, *The Christian Socialist Movement in England* (SPCK 1931), pp. 155–6. Wogaman mistakenly associates the Fabian Society with the more radical type of socialists.
71 S. Mayor, *The Churches and the Labour Movement* (Independent Press 1967), p. 345.

72 d'A. Jones, p. 177.
73 Stackhouse.
74 d'A. Jones, quoting the constitution of the CSU, p. 177.
75 d'A. Jones, p. 164.
76 d'A. Jones, p. 185, quoting P. Dearmer, *Beginnings of the CSU* (Commonwealth Press 1912).
77 d'A. Jones, p. 220.
78 F. Harrison, *Autobiographic Memoirs*, vol. 1, pp. 143 and 147, quoted in D.O. Wagner, *The Church of England and Social Reform Since 1854* (New York, Columbia University Press, 1930), p. 103.
79 Wagner, pp. 243f.
80 Wagner, p. 309.
81 Plant in J.C.D. Clark, ed., *Ideas and Politics in Modern Britain* (Macmillan 1990), p. 122.
82 d'A. Jones, p. 175.
83 See Richmond's *Christian Economics* (1888) and *Economic Morals* (1890).
84 Hilton, p. 6.
85 W. Richmond, *Christian Economics* (Rivingtons 1888), preface.
86 Richmond, *Christian Economics*, p. 35.
87 E.R. Norman's judgement in *The Victorian Christian Socialists* (Cambridge University Press 1987), ch. 9.
88 See his *Social Aspects of Christianity* (Macmillan 1887), quoted in Wagner, p. 205.
89 B.F. Westcott, 'Socialism', a paper read to the Church Congress, Hull, 1890 (The Guild of St Matthew 1890), p. 4.
90 Mayor, p. 202.
91 Preston, in *Church and Society*, pp. 75f, sees Scott Holland as a member of the 'old left'. This is not consistent with the argument and definitions pursued in this book.
92 Wagner, p. 217; Reckitt, p. 153.
93 Mayor, p. 372.
94 Quoted in M. Reckitt, *Maurice to Temple: A Century of the Social Movement in the Church of England* (Faber 1947), p. 186.
95 Quoted in Wagner, p. 270.
96 Quoted in Mayor, p. 227.
97 Munby, p. 97.
98 Quoted in M. Novak, *The Spirit of Democratic Capitalism* (American Enterprise Institute/Simon & Schuster 1982), p. 35.
99 A saying used by Preston and Tawney (and before them by Nietzsche).
100 Developed by G.S. Ecclestone in *The Church of England and Politics* (CIO Publishing 1981), a report he produced while Secretary of the Board for Social Responsibility of the Church of England. He has sadly since died.
101 P. Berger, *The Capitalist Revolution: Fifty Propositions about Prosperity, Equality and Liberty* (Wildwood House 1987), p. 70.
102 The aim of the Scott Holland Lectures, to which Lindsay, Demant and Preston have contributed.
103 In *The New Right: A Theological Assessment* (Occasional Paper 5, 1985).

Conclusion to Part Two
Learning from the Responses

*Among Christians who have seriously and thoughtfully faced
the historical situation with which we are dealing there is, as
I have proved by testing, an observable convergence.*[1]

The three responses to market economies are important because
they represent a substantial cross-section of Christian and secular
opinion. They indicate wide agreement on the central significance
of the global market economy in today's world. However, the
convergences also include a shared inadequacy in the face of the
contemporary context. Given the understanding of the market
economy beginning to develop in this argument, and of the grave
challenges to it, each response has serious limitations as a sole basis
for discipleship. The power of the relationship between market
and challenges is such as to suggest that the traditional ways
of responding are no longer adequate for contemporary social
witness, and are even more unlikely to be so for the future.

Surveying the strengths and limitations of the responses also
begins to suggest some of the main features for a framework for
supporting a more adequate response to market economies for the
foreseeable future. In this sense, William Temple's understanding
of convergences in Christian social thought, noted at the beginning of this section, provides the material for both rejecting
existing stances and developing more adequate replacements.

The conservative response teaches the importance of the market and economics for life in the contemporary context

1. It is committed profoundly to the market economy, and
recognizes that its continued effectiveness depends to a very
significant degree on the relatively unfettered operation of the

market system. By this is meant the price system, competition, profit, incentives, self-interest, inequalities and private ownership. The presumption is always to promote the free operating of the market system because of its proven economic superiority to other systems, and because of its association with the survival of civil and political liberties.

2. Despite the clear preference for the free market, interference in it is justified. On the one hand, it is necessary for a more effective operating of the market – for example, by challenging the tendency to monopoly. On the other hand, it is important for the protection of the environment and people (through the Welfare State) against the harmful social consequences of the market.

3. There is a firm acknowledgement that certain matters external to the market, and which improve its operating, are of great importance in their own right. Values like truth and trust have been consistently regarded as essential for the survival of the market. Their close association with Christian belief and lifestyles is part of a wider concern to locate the market in a Christian framework. Complementing these commitments is an equally strong criticism of many secular values and insights, particularly if regarded as a product of the Enlightenment. This is part and parcel of a more general search for a distinctively Christian response to the contemporary context.

4. The market system, although highly valued, is never regarded as a law of God or a natural construct. Consequently, there is a clear distancing from the ideological libertarian understanding of the market of Hayek and Friedman. This frees the dynamic nature of the market from the restraints of religious and ideological legalism.

At this point, a profound unresolved ambiguity has begun to emerge. On the one hand, priority is given to Christian beliefs as framework and values; on the other hand, there is a seemingly equal commitment, in practice certainly, to the central importance of the market and economics. In discussion it is normally the former that is dominant, suggesting an ultimately subordinationist view of the market and economics. The rejection of Enlightenment views, so inextricably connected to the market and modern economics, supports this conclusion. The response is not intrinsically sympathetic to the way of interaction between 'facts' and values.

5. This interpretation is supported by the response's understanding of the challenges to the market. In so strongly affirming the market system, it assumes that its great challenges can be dealt with in that framework. There is no recognition that the challenges possess an autonomy in their own right, as well as a value from their impinging on the market. Consequently, the profound questions raised by them are to be solved within the market economy. They are ultimately subordinated to the market in a way opposite to the radical response's subjugation of the market to the challenges.

6. Because of these constraints, the conservative commitment to reform is never sufficient to overcome many of the disturbing consequences of a more freely operating market. These are matters raised substantially by the challenges, particularly as poverty, participation and environment. There is at best inadequate evidence that such questions can be addressed effectively by modest internal adjustments to the market. The arguments of Benne, Novak and Griffiths place an undue reliance on justice or democracy to retrieve the moral case for the market. The comprehensive challenge of the relatively autonomous questions, both individually and collectively, cannot be dispensed with by such insufficient means.

7. The contribution of conservatives to theological method, and through history, reflects these strengths and limitations. Theologically, Christian principles derived from Scripture and wider Christian tradition are used to support the commitment to modest reform within a general support for the market. Historically, the Christian political economists pioneered the need to take seriously modern economics and the market economy. Their weakness was to fail to give the challenges a similar autonomy. Conservatives have never been able to respond sufficiently to a changing context and the persistence of the challenges, even by major adjustments to the market system. They have never generated a Keynes or a Galbraith, and so never warranted the serious title of Christian reformers. Theirs is the way of an essential accommodation to the market economy, sensitive to the great challenges, but only from within that market framework.

The radical response teaches the importance of the great challenges to the market economy in the contemporary context

1. The commitment to people, and the poor in particular, militates in favour of a presumption for the human and the values most closely associated with it. The values arise from an acknowledgement of the supreme significance of each person, especially in and through their relationships; this leads into the preference for equality and solidarity (as co-operation and fraternity). It is this propensity to recognize the priority of human need over material, class and economic realities that has led many to sympathize with the radical response. So it was John Bennett, a classic social democrat, who argued for the need 'to press the socialistic questions even though we do not accept ready-made socialistic answers'.[2]

2. The commitment to human values is complemented by, and indeed leads to, a profound rejection of the market system. A deep concern over the grievous social consequences of *laissez-faire* capitalism, particularly as they affected the poor and their communities, provided both the motivation and content of social involvement. So deep-seated was the reaction that it led to a rejection of many of the central features of the market economy and modern economics. Individualism, self-interest, competition and profit were all treated with at least disdain. It is precisely at this point that the strength of theological humanism becomes equated with an equally profound deficiency. For the commitment to people-centred values, including a rejection of market economies, results in an unequivocal undervaluing of economics and the market mechanism.

3. These priorities are reflected in the response's approach to theological method and history. Theologically, the depth of commitment to the challenges, including as a rejection of the market, is such as to lead to a direct theology, moving from specific insights in Scripture to equally specific condemnations of contemporary economies. There is little room for the carefully discriminating judgements associated with complex modern realities like politics and economics in advanced democratic societies. This dogmatic decisiveness is linked with a refusal to seek to come to terms with the autonomies of modern secular and plural societies. There is

little understanding that such autonomies are invariably relative and rarely, if ever, absolute. The commitment to Scripture and doctrine is of such a kind as to impose Christian values on secular autonomies and disciplines. Similarly, tradition becomes the means for interpreting history in the sense of approving the origin and development of radical views and organizations, and disapproving of more conservative or liberal understandings. The importance of the work of the Christian political economists is either rejected or ignored. The contribution of F.D. Maurice and the later Christian socialists is regarded as the bed-rock of revived Christian social tradition.

4. The strong acknowledgement of human values and its close connection to the great challenges becomes a means for avoiding the complacency of a relatively undiscerning support of the market economy. The success of the latter, in association with liberal democracies, has meant that the events of 1989, and the collapse of command economies, has increased the temptation to regard market democracies as the near-completion of the human project. The great challenges are a constant reminder that such satisfaction can never be justified on theological or empirical grounds.

5. The commitment of the radical response to the challenges and to stand against the market leads to the presumption that the challenges can be made the basis of a radically restructured needs-based economy. This leads to a number of grave errors. On the one hand, it leads to the use of Marx or ecology as the basis of an alternative economics. This confuses the economic and political task, and invariably results in the hegemony of the latter over the former. There is no evidence that challenges can perform satisfactorily a function quite different to that of a countermovement. On the other hand, there are powerful arguments against writing-off modern economics and the market economy. There are strong technical reasons for not adopting such a stance (how do you actually allocate relatively scarce resources?), and equally strong moral reasons. To choose an alternative system because it is morally preferable but much less efficient is quite likely to produce more disturbing consequences for human living than an opposite formula. There are convincing arguments, theological as well as economic, for supporting a system proven to be the least harmful known to us as yet in the human journey. The

existence of alternatives with significantly worse records confirms that judgement. One does not throw away the ladder once a few rungs have been climbed.

The liberal response teaches the possibility of balanced judgements and reform in the contemporary context, from the perspective of the challenges but with some sensitivity to the market

1. Like the radical response, this one emerges from a deep reaction against *laissez-faire* capitalism. Pastoral contact with the harmful social consequences of industrial capitalism, when coupled with a theological conviction about the brotherhood of man, produced a continuing rejection of intrinsic features of the market system. Competition, the profit-motive and self-interest were contradictions of Christian beliefs and a needs-based economic sanity. However, unlike the radical response, the discerning nature of its stance against the free market meant that it was never able to develop a clear radical alternative, even though it has argued consistently that it has.

2. It therefore works in practice on the basis that the free market can be reformed into what it presumes to be a radical alternative, but which, in effect, is a form of the market economy, varying from democratic social market capitalism to a democratic socialist market. The recognition of the possibility of reform, and its achievement through gradual but purposeful change, is a major 'discovery' for Christian social thought and practice. Social market systems increasingly dominate the market economy, and justify much of the arguments for the response of liberal reform.

3. There are important proactive and negative implications flowing from such a conclusion. Positively, the response has developed a major alliance with the emergence of modern Christian social ethics, with an emphasis on discernment and balance. This was confirmed and developed through the early history of the ecumenical movement, culminating in the formulation of middle axioms and the responsible society. Some of its leading exponents, like Wogaman and Preston, continue to exercise a major influence on the theological discipline itself, and on the official Churches. Its language reflects the character of this approach to modern

economies; judgements on technology as a two-edged sword, or on economic growth as fundamentally ambiguous, abound. Negatively, the response's commitment to balanced judgements confirm its political and economic ambivalence. By reducing economic typologies to *laissez-faire* capitalism and command economies, it invariably moves to support the centrist position of 'mixed economies'. Yet this concept acts as a misnomer, disguising what is essentially and practically an involvement in market economies with a social democratic tendency.

4. Two important lessons flow from this finding. On the one hand, there is a need to acknowledge that the market economy is the dominant type, within which various models can and do exist. Talk of third ways and mixed economies produce more confusion than light. On the other hand, the profound ambiguities running through the response illustrate the danger of an inclination to moral subordinationism. This takes at least two forms. It involves giving an ultimate priority to politics and state over economics. The concepts of the responsible society and the common good reflect this emphasis and reduce its potential for dynamic change. One is left with the impression that it will never be possible or even desirable to move beyond a Welfare State society of the Swedish kind. The market, as a result, is reduced to the position of servant, mechanism and servile drudge. The response therefore has a propensity to corporatism, and judgements that are not sufficiently and decisively critical of command economies. Yet the subordinationism also emerges from an ultimate commitment to the priority of Christian beliefs and values over secular discoveries.

5. This emphasis is also reflected in the response's approach to theological method and history. Theologically, its commitment to a tradition of Christian social ethics that stresses discerning judgements has provided Christian social thought with indispensable tools for assessing complex contemporary situations, especially in advanced economies. Yet it moves essentially from Christian beliefs to judgements on society, although it recognizes that the facts of the situation have to play a major part in their formation. In proceeding from beliefs to judgements, it is not so far removed from the direct theology of the radical response, and the less direct theology of the conservative. The international character of the market economy, and the power of the great challenges, have

revealed the value of the liberal contribution, but also indicated its weaknesses in comparison with the other responses. It can be argued that the latter speak more clearly to those wider agendas. The way of Christian social ethics is no longer commensurate to the size of the task in the way it was in the 1950s with its use of the responsible society. Historically, the same subordinationism is reflected in the concentration on the challenge to the free market, beginning with Maurice and the rejection of the value of the attempts of the Christian political economists to come to terms with the emergence of the market and the associated modern discipline of economics.

Emerging from this brief survey is an important decision that has personal as well as wider implications. At the beginning of this research project, taking the market seriously meant a commitment to the realism of economics and the market, but within a framework of wider social purposes. It was a position well described by Reinhold Niebuhr, one of the great exponents of the mainstream liberal tradition. In an autobiographical essay he described his 'strong conviction that a realist conception of human nature should be made the servant of an ethic of progressive justice and should not be made into a bastion of conservatism, particularly a conservatism which defends unjust privileges'.[3] The project's task was therefore to reformulate the mainstream liberal position in the light of a new market-based realism.[4]

However, the enquiry into the three responses has now convinced me that such a thesis is no longer tenable. Each has important strengths and weaknesses to contribute to the development of Christian social thought. No one response stands out as sufficiently adequate to justify being the principal vehicle for the job of reformulation.[5] What is required is rather a listening to, while distancing from, all three responses. The fact that none of the responses recognizes sufficiently the relative autonomy of both market and challenges is only one reason why such a position of detached concern must be promoted. For without these autonomies, a developmental relationship between them of an interactive kind would be unlikely if not impossible. So the end of the dominance of the mainstream liberal tradition forces us to engage in an open interaction between market and challenges, between economics and theology. It frees the liberal response to play a more constructive role in relationship to, and on a par with, the conservative and radical responses. For that is all it is and should be.

Notes

1 W. Temple, Supplement to the Christian News-Letter 1944, in Maurice Reckitt, *Maurice to Temple: A Century of the Social Movement in the Church of England* (Faber 1947), p. 195.
2 J.C. Bennett, *The Radical Imperative: From Theology to Social Ethics* (Philadelphia, Westminster, 1975), p. 156.
3 R. Niebuhr, *Man's Nature and His Communities* (Bles 1966), p. 16.
4 As suggested in my 'The Limits of the Market' in M. Alison and D.L. Edwards, eds, *Christianity and Conservatism* (Hodder & Stoughton 1990), pp. 280f.
5 This is in contrast to J.P. Wogaman's verdict in *Christian Perspectives on Politics* (SCM Press), p. 102-3. He works from the mainstream liberal tradition, as would R.H. Preston.

Part Three

Questioning Economics:
The Development of Christian Social Thought

Talking about the events of our lives can affirm a sense of progress and wholeness. The value of reminiscence is that, even when what is being revealed relates to difficult times . . . it can help to maintain a sense of purpose or self-esteem. . . . The experiences of past and present are bridged. Thinking and talking about the future is made easier. What appears to be the uncertain residue of life can be transformed into a time of personal, spiritual growth and . . . religious conviction. . . . 'Christian faith, which relativises the past and the future, should be releasing people to speak realistically, respectfully and religiously about their . . . experience . . .'.[1]

It can be argued that a period of great change is not the time to rethink the response of Christianity to market economies. There are too many imponderables in a world that is too complex and moving too quickly. Holding on to a tradition in such circumstances is the way of good sense, especially if it seeks to accommodate some of the prevailing realities of life.

Yet that is the way of the second best. It always has been. In the changing world of the sixteenth and seventeenth centuries, commitment to traditional thought-forms became increasingly irrelevant even though some adaptation to a changing context was attempted. In the very different world of the late twentieth century, a predominantly conserving approach to the realities of our context will suffer the same fate. It will become even more marginalized in the public arena. The greatly increased pace and scale of economic change will see to that.

Accepting such a conclusion has driven some to engage in the task of reconstructing Christian social thought. I have argued recently for its reformulation.[2] It is to recognize that the context is changing to such an extent that the restatement of Christian tradition is no longer sufficient, even if it undergoes some amendment as a result. Facing up to the contemporary now seems to require the rebuilding of Christian social tradition in the light of contextual changes.

And yet, as the argument over the market economy has begun to evolve, I have become more and more uneasy with any suggestion of a return – even of a reformulation or a reconstruction. For we stand in no man's land. We are certain of the past, on the proven ground of the market economy, yet faced even there with the enormous challenges of Third World poverty and environmental disasters, to mention but two. The future is therefore profoundly uncertain, and yet there can never be any going back. Living in the interim is always about a very uncomfortable discipleship in a relatively unknown land; it is precisely the time and the place for developing and testing provisional frameworks for living. Part of that task is the halting search for new languages, for different concepts, commensurate with changing realities and new experiences. It is a mood and predicament beautifully captured by Matthew Arnold's assertion that we are:

> Wandering between two worlds, one dead.
> The other powerless to be born.[3]

In such a situation, even if we have not fashioned the new languages, we can at least declare a moratorium on those concepts that detract from the future by condoning a going back to the past. There is no place for a return to tradition, even in Wordsworth's sense of:

> What we have loved,
> Others will love, and we will teach them how.[4]

And yet within the task of facing up to an uncertain future, there is an important place for tradition. Communities of memory are surely part of our consideration of our present and future realities in the light of the past. They are an indispensable basis of knowledge and experience. Yet they can only be a part of the basis for response. However significant, they always include the dangers of a return to the past or the resistance to change in the present. We should always heed the warning that 'whereas tradition is the living faith of the dead, traditionalism is the dead faith of the living'. Tradition must never be the basis of automatic judgements. It must, at least, be always 'in a continuous process of reinterpretation and reappropriation'.[5] It can then become part of our conversation about the meaning and value of our common life in facing up to present and future realities. It becomes transformed into the task of *developing Christian social thought*.

It is an examination of that task which is the particular concern of this final part of the argument. It can only be attempted on the basis of what has been learned from the details, considered in Parts One and Two, of market economies and the principal Christian responses to them. Without both, there can be no satisfactory development of Christian social thought. They are an integral part of the Christian task. They provide the foundation for a consideration of the market economy and its great challenges (Chapters 7 and 8), through the interaction between them. This in turn suggests a framework and a dynamic for facing up to change (Chapter 9). The Postscript reflects a personal journey through such change.

Notes

1 *Ageing: Report of the Social Policy Committee of the Board for Social Responsibility* (Church House Publishing 1990), pp. 65–6.
2 J. Atherton, 'The Limits of the Market', in M. Alison and D.L. Edwards, eds, *Christianity and Conservatism* (Hodder & Stoughton 1990), pp. 281f.
3 Quoted in R.N. Bellah, ed., *Habits of the Heart* (New York, Harper & Row, 1986), p. 277.
4 Quoted in Bellah, ed., p. 293.
5 J. Pelikan, quoted in Bellah, ed., p. 140.

Seven

Developing the Market:
The Economics of Imperfection

*The pursuit of wealth . . . is, to the mass of mankind, the
great source of moral improvement* (Nassau Senior).

*One is taken by surprise on meeting with so very categorical
a contradiction of our Lord, St Chrysostom, St Leo, and all
Saints* (John Henry Newman).[1]

In 1825 Nassau Senior became the first incumbent of the
Drummond Chair of Political Economy at Oxford. As a Whig
and liberal Christian, he stood firmly in the tradition of *laissez-
faire* classical economics. He adopted a secular approach to the
discipline, possessing a mechanical view of society. In asserting
the scientific nature of economics, he defended it against the
accusation of amorality by arguing that the maximization of
wealth would banish 'economic insecurity and enable citizens
to develop feelings of benevolent sympathy with each other,
and a desire for each other's happiness'. Saving for future
use was the basis of 'moral improvement, sobriety, frugality
and law-abidingness'.[2] With his friend Richard Whateley, his
tutor and successor in the Drummond Chair, he illustrated the
development of modern economics as an independent discipline,
and its early relationship with moderate evangelical Christianity,
including its view of economics as a field of moral endeavour.

It was these sentiments, so clearly expressed in his inaugural
lecture, that John Henry Newman found so morally repugnant.
As one of the great leaders of the Anglican Oxford Movement, and
then of Roman Catholicism, he combined a willingness to listen to
modern intellectual developments with a deep sense of continuity
with early Christian thought and spirituality. Like F.D. Maurice,
he could never accept the implications of modern economics for
Christian thought and practice.

Yet the powerful conflict between economics and Christianity in the nineteenth century was no once-for-all historical episode. It continues in the life of contemporary Church and society. Thus, in the 1980s, Justin Dart, a member of President Reagan's 'Kitchen Cabinet', could declare with impunity that:

> I have never looked for a business that's going to render a service to mankind. I figure that if it employs a lot of people and makes a lot of money, it is in fact rendering a service to mankind. Greed is involved in everything we do. I find no fault with that.[3]

There is no recognition here of the unease with the pursuit of wealth creation that is so deeply rooted in Christian history. Denys Munby, while acknowledging the value of the market economy in achieving economic growth, is, unlike Dart, sensitive to the potential for evil of wealth accumulation. He sees it as 'the distraction that keeps men from thinking about God, the evils of a false dependence on the created order, and a would-be security that fails to take account of the inevitable fragility of human destiny on this earth'.[4] In both the nineteenth and the twentieth centuries, the relationship between the economic task and Christian belief has engendered conflict – and continues to.

Many arguments over the contribution to social purposes of economics and the market have concentrated on one of two approaches. They have argued either for their rejection on moral and spiritual grounds, or for their acceptance on economic and theological grounds. At first sight, proposing the market economy as the senior partner in an interactive process with the great challenges would seem to support the latter case. It appears that facing our contemporary context needs to include the market economy as an integral part of the framework and dynamic for the development of Christian social thought. A brief recapitulation of its strengths and weaknesses will confirm that judgement, particularly as it has led to the social market economy.

1. The market as the best available economy: a necessary basis for argument

If the challenges to the market economy are so grave, why

persist with a commitment to the market as a central part of the interactive process? The answer to that question rests ultimately on a recognition of the market's ability to address the basic problem of economics: namely how to allocate scarce resources in the light of their alternative uses and in relation to competing needs. Deriving from that core task flow a number of subordinate ones, including how to decide which goods and services to produce, how to measure and match their demand and supply, and how to allocate resources between present and future consumption. From problem and tasks there is no escape for those seeking to operate an effective economy in the modern world. The alternative is stagnation or worse, whatever the motive. The increasingly international character of the contemporary context has ensured that the days of utopian siege economies are well and truly numbered.

As the earlier survey revealed, many of the reasons for the market's ascendancy lie in its history, particularly its involvement with the development of modern economics. What is equally indisputable is that the market, and especially the price mechanism, is the prime allocatory system in all advanced economies. It has proved to be the most effective means for allocating resources to the most productive uses, particularly of land and capital, although less so for labour (as wages). The prices of resources therefore change to signal the most productive uses, and so resource movements follow the price changes. In other words, changes in the demand for commodities influence the changes in the demand for resources. It is in this ability to allocate resources between productive uses, and commodities between consuming individuals, that the market is more efficient than any other known system. This is particularly so when compared to the command economy, and when the relationship to political and civil liberties is also taken into consideration. The latter has played a convincing part in the market system being adopted in Eastern Europe and the Soviet Union. Separating and dispersing political and economic power appears to be essential as a defence against authoritarianism and support for varied initiatives.

However, despite proven advantages, there is a general recognition that the market system possesses major limitations. For example, even as a means for allocating scarce resources, the market has weaknesses in distributing purchasing power because this is linked to the existing distribution of resources. The greater the command over resources, the greater the influence over the functioning of the market. The possession of property as income and wealth, especially through accumulation and inheritance, becomes a key means of access to the market and, alternatively, a principal cause of exclusion. It therefore relates to the possession and exercise of power, providing an access to life but also a means for dominating others.[5] It is because these fundamental deficiencies produce what most regard as unacceptable differences in the distribution of resources and power, that the history of market economies has witnessed their gradual correction. Government policies on taxation, social security and incomes (including minimum wages) have played a major part in the necessary corrective and enhancing tasks. The commitment of liberal democracies and market economies to maintain important distinctions between politics and economics has thus been amended significantly with the development of the social priorities of the market economy and of macroeconomics in the discipline of economics. It is against these developments that libertarians like Hayek and Friedman have protested so vigorously. Yet their excessive anxiety over 'the coercive aspect of government action' quite underestimates the liberating achievements of government. In modern market economies, 'The state is often an instrument of freedom for large sections of the population. There are times when it is the only means of rescuing them from the tyranny of circumstances.'[6] It is the same tendency to increase the role of government in economic policy-making that has played such a central role in modifying the cyclical tendencies of market economies, with all their damaging consequences as unemployment.

Out of limitations at the heart of the distributory function, a spiral of other defects can be traced, each of which has to be addressed if advanced market economies are to maintain satisfactory relationships between economic and social priorities. For example, closely connected to the distributory weakness is the market's inclination, if left to its own devices, of developing 'powerful centripetal tendencies',[7] with resources following resources into more prosperous regions, like the South East of Britain, the 'golden triangle' of the European Community, and West coast of the United States. Similarly, the key 'virtue' of competition, with its intrinsic commitment to winners and losers, while benefiting the consumer, has resulted also in the growth of larger and larger companies, and the associated problem of oligopolies.

There are two other deficiencies always noted by economists, the issues of social goods and externalities. Both reveal the costs of the developing autonomy of markets and modern economics, with its exclusion of vital matters of human and environmental welfare. The reason for such a decision is that they do not conform to the intrinsic principles of the market and so are rejected as external to its operating. It can be argued that this is another example of misplaced concreteness, seeing that a proper organizing of social goods and externalities is so necessary for economic health. The significance of these factors is such that it warrants elaboration.

Social goods include those services that most people agree need to be provided if human living is to be effective in modern society. Yet, because they need supplying on a scale greater than most people will pay privately, they have been funded and often delivered through collective provision. Many local government services fall into this category, including roads, parks, lighting, along with education and training, and sometimes health care. There is a growing recognition that the shortage of reasonable housing for the more marginalized is a major weakness of the market system and needs more public intervention.

Externalities are an acknowledgement that market transactions have results not limited to those engaging in them, and so are omitted from the price calculus of these transactions. Pollution caused by industrial processes is one such externality. There has been a growing understanding in recent years that the market economy can be adapted to engage many of these problems through regulation and pricing systems. However, some aspects of non-renewable resources and pollution are so pervasive as to require at least major international efforts and possibly radical institutional change.[8]

Related to the concern for social goods and externalities, and reflecting their importance as signs and consequences of advanced economies, the late twentieth century has experienced an increasing criticism of economic growth. Connected to the evolution of the market economy, although not coterminous, economic growth became the basis of the dramatic social, economic and political changes of the last 200 years. Its acceleration in Western societies after the Second World War has resulted, among other things, in unease over many of the consequences of consumer sovereignty. Thus Mishan noted in 1967[9] that the satisfaction of more and more wants does not necessarily mean a proportionate advance in human welfare. The result has been so often not an increase in leisure, but of harder work under more pressure in order to obtain more sophisticated products. These do not necessarily bring a satisfaction commensurate with the human costs of providing them.[10]

It has been the arguments of Hirsch[11] that have taken the knowledge of the limitations of the market and economic growth to a new level of sophistication. Noting their neglect of social scarcity and bias towards commercialization, he observed that neither can be corrected in the way other externalities can. So, on the one hand, social scarcity represents the awareness that the amazing ability of the market to produce material goods begins to encounter the problem of positional goods. These are goods or services that are either absolutely or socially scarce – for example, access to relatively unspoiled countryside like the Lake District. The more affluent people become, the more they compete for such goods, with the result that 'if everyone stands on tiptoe no one sees better'.[12] A good's value depends on maintaining its relative scarcity. On the other hand, the propensity of the market is to commercialize more and more areas of human living, with contract replacing trust and mutual obligation, whether in health, education or family relationships. Many argue that the result will be the erosion of the traditional values on which the market has been so dependent.

Despite such criticism (and its gravity cannot be evaded by responsible opinion), its acceptance does not imply endorsement of non-market systems of allocation. Their record is one of greater inefficiency and inequality, and disastrous on externalities, as the world has learned from the lifting of the Iron Curtain. Arguments to abolish the market economy, based on these issues, therefore exhibit an intrinsic irresponsibility. Yet what they also reveal are 'plausible grounds for restrictions on the market'.[13] Nevertheless, caveats, however deep-seated, do not detract from the recognition across the spectrum of Western societies that the dominant place must continue to be given to free enterprise in economic life. Regardless of criticisms, among most people there is a perception that they are none-the-less better off in a market-organised society than in any other alternative. This view stems from the widespread belief that the market is more efficient than any other system of resource allocation, and hence that absolute standards of living are higher in a market-system than under any other resource-allocation system.[14]

What has begun to emerge from this brief survey of the market system could be described as an 'ambiguously positive' case. It is essentially positive in that it recognizes the primary importance of an effective and efficient economy for contemporary living. The first task of any economic order is 'to economize, to be as efficiently productive as possible'.[15] The post-war American enquiry into economic life rightly regarded economic progress as 'the most fundamental task of any economic system'.[16] Without that, so much becomes either unachievable or under grave threat. For example, cultural life, and political and social well-being, depend to an extent we often ignore on an economy's ability 'to establish margins of welfare beyond the satisfaction of primary needs',[17] to provide 'expanding possibilities for citizens'.[18] That cannot be attained by a disproportionate emphasis on justice, especially as distribution, because we are aware that the allocation system ensures that the production and distribution of resources are connected inextricably to each other. And production cannot be determined principally by the norm of justice.[19] For justice without efficiency is a moral lame duck in the contemporary context. Yet although efficiency is essential for social well-being, it is never sufficient in an advanced market economy. That is where justice, too, becomes essential. And that is where the operations of the market itself are inadequate, and require the complement of institutions and values. The case for the market is primarily positive, but inclusive of ambiguities.

It is in working through such arguments that one becomes aware of the fundamental inadequacy of traditional moral and theological discourse in relation to basic economic realities. Even Reinhold Niebuhr, one of the most accomplished of modern theologians, never really understood the functioning of modern economics in the way he understood political life. His judgements reveal a lack of familiarity with the fundamental details of economic life. It is as though so much of Christian thought needs to be 'brought to earth in terms of practical policies'.[20] Simplistic appeals to wealth creation and stewardship betray a similar refusal to engage economics on its own ground. The arguments of the World Council of Churches and Robert Benne – to replace equality with equity – are similarly inadequate.[21] They are so resonant of an insensitive theological colonization of a foreign land: what one economist has called the 'grandiose and presumptuous "Social Teaching"'. For nothing is served by 'ill-formed protest against the ineluctable', in the traditions, for example, of radical Christianity or modern church statements on economic affairs.[22]

Yet, as the argument has unravelled, another kind of theological discourse has begun to appear, one that works with and through the economic agenda. Allocation and efficiency then become central parts of the human project; not, as so often argued, as preconditions for a just society,[23] but as continuing co-partners with justice in that pursuit. Indeed, there will be many occasions when efficiency has priority over justice in the Christian task, or at least equivalent rank. For example, it can be argued with strong justification that a primary responsibility of a society is to maintain a strong economy. Subordinating that to the pursuit of wider responsibilities, as the World Council of Churches and Third World circles so often demand, would be likely to result in greater poverty and injustice. It is to ignore economic change as it relates to the framework and dynamic of modern economies. It is to go against the principle of not throwing down the ladder. Duchrow's use of an alternative Christian principle, of putting a spoke in the wheel of the market to bring it to a halt, is not an ethic for operating responsibly advanced economies. It is the instinct of perpetual countermovement. Yet to pursue and maintain a strong economy is a choice with inevitable consequences. It means that 'some things that are desirable must be subordinated to others that are more desirable'.[24] A positive facing up to the achievements and limitations of the social market economy is such an order of choice. For given the nature and importance of economics, existing alternatives do not allow any other.

2. Developing the market: promoting the least harmful economy

Affirming the market as the best available economy in the

contemporary context is now an essential part of Christian social witness. To do so is to reject the economic determinism of both libertarian and Marxist ideologies. It is to face up to economic necessities,[25] and to work for purposeful change in relation to those constraints.

And yet, beginning the development of Christian social thought with the market economy as senior partner in an interactive process with the great challenges, reveals, on closer inspection, two reasons why we cannot rest with a reaffirmation of that case on traditional economic and theological grounds. First, even the historical evolution of the market acknowledges that its effectiveness has depended on its response to the challenges of changing contexts. Facing up to its grave limitations will involve at least great change intrinsic to the market economy. Secondly, the challenges in the modern world are so substantial as to warrant recognition in their own right. International poverty and environmental issues, and the constant search for greater participation, are historical and continuing questions of such magnitude that they cannot be subsumed into the market or into any other economic system. They are a recognition of the constant need for external as well as internal checks and the resourcing of economic systems.[26]

The power and extent of intrinsic development and external challenges are sufficiently serious for us to be unable simply to reaffirm traditional arguments for the market economy as the preferable starting-point for the development of Christian social thought. Even on that basis, responsible living with the challenges will transform the social market economy. The shape of the task of developing Christian social thought therefore begins to clarify into a twofold form: how to establish a better and more realistic hold on the market economy; and, in the light of the challenges, at the same time to develop substantially our understanding of the market in an interactive framework and dynamic.

(a) A more realistic appraisal of the market

The need for greater clarity about the nature of the market in the interactive process is not suggested simply by the pressure of internal change and external challenges. Each of the Christian responses is also committed to changing it. Their programmes all recognize, in very inadequate ways, important defects concerned with *economic mechanisms*, *civic virtues*, and *the nature of economics*. Correcting them is essential for the development of a more realistic appraisal of the market economy.

Facing up to economic mechanisms: morality as more than social goals

So often, the Churches have given the impression that value can only be understood in terms of personal and social purposes. The significance of individuals can only be grasped in and through their relationships. Organizations, procedures and machineries only make sense in relation to the wider purposes of a society. It is as though individuals and mechanisms have no value in their own right. Value can only come from their incorporation into greater and essentially relational realities. Beyond this moral prioritizing lies an important perspective on human living which seeks to safeguard and promote the intrinsic worth of people in a variety of communities. So it was that F.D. Maurice vehemently opposed the erosion of relationships by a political economy which viewed people as atomistic individuals in a perpetual state of ruthless competition. Subordinating people to economic processes was a contradiction of human nature as created and intended by God's purposes. It was the promulgation of what a mid-twentieth-century theologian splendidly called 'the fearful assumption that man is there to be managed'.[27] It is that profound theological humanism which has dominated, and still does, the Christian view of the social order.

And yet, the rending asunder of that social order by the processes of industrialization and urbanization in the nineteenth and twentieth centuries has also, and indeed inevitably, reduced that important Christian perspective to a partial truth. And persistence in the advancement of partial truths soon becomes as damaging as deliberate untruths. For the nature of modern societies, and particularly their economic basis, depends to a great extent on an impersonal, organizational or collective reality. So significant and all-pervasive is that reality, that fundamentally pre-modern theological understandings are unable to grasp it. By deriving its value essentially from wider social purposes, they produce analyses and prescriptions that are inherently flawed. Any development of Christian social thought that is to have any serious chance of engaging the contemporary context has to address this problem. It can be described as the task of facing up to economic mechanisms for the sake of wordly purposes.

Engaging the market economy provides an ideal opportunity for such theological development. For if we are to build a more realistic appraisal of the market in an interactive process, we are driven to come to terms with the nature and contribution of economic mechanisms to the market, and thereby to wider concerns. Fortunately, even this general survey of modern economics and the market has revealed a recurring emphasis on the importance of such mechanisms in a variety of forms. These include the allocation function of the market, particularly as price mechanism; the self-regulating processes of the market; the growing importance of increasingly multinational corporations; the functions of economic growth; and the complex character of modern technologies. Running through all these manifestations of the collective reality are various characteristics, three of which are particularly important. Taken together, they suggest that economic mechanisms must be seen as purposeful in their own right; they should not be subordinated to wider social purposes, but rather develop an interactive relationship with them.

1. Economic mechanisms cannot be regarded simply or predominantly as means. Because of their strategic importance, they play a central role in the formation of social purposes. They are both ends and means. So technology is more than a tool: it helps to shape the very way we are.[28] So habits of consumption, in the broadest sense, are partly impressed on society 'by the requirements of the productive system itself'.[29]

2. It is therefore important to acknowledge the autonomous nature of economic mechanisms, however relativized by interaction with other realities. Without this freedom, the economy will not be able to do its job of economizing and maximizing scarce resources as efficiently and effectively as possible.[30]

3. Economic mechanisms have an intrinsic dynamism, particularly in the form of economic growth and technology; they contain 'their own inner logic, independent of individuals and groups'.[31] Often, these processes of change are also irreversible,

and to interfere unduly with them for external social purposes can result in what could be the much worse consequences of economic inefficiency. Benne partly understands this when he notes that, 'Higher values suffer in the demise of the instrumental value of efficiency.'[32]

Besides illustrating the nature of mechanisms, these characteristics also suggest the reasons why they should be taken so seriously in their own right. For example, without strong recognition of the relative autonomy of the economy, it will not deliver, with sufficient efficiency those goods and services essential for human living. Niebuhr talks of the need 'to preserve whatever self-regulating forces exist in the economic process'.[33] Without that, attempts to manage it result in inefficiency and authoritarianism. In this way, too, mechanisms provide a contribution to human well-being on which other values are heavily dependent. We therefore need to avoid talk of good economics being a 'pre-condition' for justice and other 'Christian' values; that is to play the old inadequate moral game. Finally, without this recognition of economic mechanisms, the balance between market and challenges is probably destroyed, with all its damaging consequences for human living; in Munby's words, it is a matter of being 'entirely realistic as to the functions of organisations and the actual historical situation'.[34]

The implications of these arguments for Christian social thought are important for what they reject and propose. In terms of rejection, they conflict with the three responses that subordinate economic mechanisms to wider social purposes and selected Christian values. The radical and conservative[35] responses, but particularly the former, do this quite blatantly. Yet even the liberal response regards the mechanism as a servile drudge, as a servant of greater objectives, including political ones. Running through them all is a Christian tradition, essentially pre-modern in origins and formation, that regards economics as a very subordinate secondary human task. Within that perspective is a related commitment to regarding economic life as fundamentally relational, not primarily about producing things.[36] The historic views of usury, regarding money only as a means of exchange and not in itself capable of productive activity, reflect this refusal to face up to the value of mechanisms in themselves.

However, the arguments about mechanisms also propose developments for Christian social thought by interpreting mechanisms through three perspectives. The first is an understanding that the collective reality is more than personal, is more than the sum total of the people involved.[37] The second is a recognition that relationships are improved by being translated into procedures. (The use in industrial relations of procedural agreements is a good illustration of this development.) The third accepts that economic mechanisms, including technology, generate a continuity with a tangible nature which, once created, by 'human wills, acquires a certain fixity' independent of people.[38] William Temple observed that it emerged as a 'product of various elementary needs of man; but having emerged it is found to possess a value far beyond the satisfaction of these needs'.[39] It is precisely that substantive autonomy which people regard as such a threat, and which led all three responses to talk of it in terms of idolatry.

It is the cumulative effect of these perspectives that enable economic mechanisms to be interpreted as of value in their own right. They can then play their part in the interactive process, on the basis of this greater realism and clarity, two essential prerequisites for effective human development.

Facing up to civic virtue: morality as more than Christian values

Christian tradition has always recognized the important contribution made by Christian values to the development of the market. The conservative and liberal responses clearly approved this function of Christian values. Without them, the market would not survive in an acceptable form. Indeed, they argue that the fundamental defects of the market often related to its erosion of these values. Any reform or development of the market would therefore require a greater contribution from Christianity. Some liberals argue that this would involve collaboration with morally concerned non-Christians. The radical response sees no such role for Christianity. Its task is to work for the replacement of the market economy. However, most Christian opinion in the West assumes that the market will continue to be an essential part of the interactive process, and that Christian values will have an indispensable role in that future. The market alone can never achieve such a goal.

And yet, in the same way that Christianity failed to understand the autonomous nature of the market, so it fails to recognize the contribution of the market to the development of necessary civic virtues in the modern context. It is unable to acknowledge the market as generator of social values as well as recipient. It is the old confusing Christian dichotomy of separating morality from the market-place.

Consequently, the argument is not about the essential role of civic virtues in economic life. It rather concerns the Christian interpretation of that role, and its traditional failure to recognize the contribution of the market to an ethos of civic responsibility. It is this wider understanding that needs to play a part with the challenges in the interactive process. To persist with the restrictive view of Christian values in the market-place is to continue with 'The inability of the old moral order effectively to encompass the new social developments.'[40] Facing up to the relationship between civic virtues and the market in the interactive process therefore involves developing an understanding of the contribution of the market to those virtues, as well as recognizing its critical relationship with contributions generated outside the market.

It is important to begin this task by clarifying the role of the market in the civic arena as producer of supportive values. In this, it shares in and becomes a 'requisite for prosperity',[41] and thereby gives new significance to economy-related virtues. It is the moral importance of the latter that is derived partly from an acknowledgement of efficient production as a 'primary moral demand on economic institutions'.[42] Yet it also relates to the judgement that, 'Civic virtue is not a matter of charity or ethics; it is the adhesive of social and economic life.'[43] It is that combination of the morality of effective production and pragmatic bonding that allows us, indeed requires us, to acknowledge the contribution of the market to civic virtues. That, in turn, leads to a major change in the understanding of values and market in Christian social thought.

There are four market-related values that are likely to play a part in this market promotion of civic virtue. The first is self-interest, 'the permanent treasure of a free society'. The survey of the market's evolution revealed the central role of self-interest in the operating of modern economics. What needs to be made equally clear is its moral priority in comparison with the traditional

Christian valuing of 'benevolence'. Reinhold Niebuhr supports the need to morally harness self-interest in the economic arena, and gives two reasons. On the one hand, it is not simply that it is too powerful a motivation to be suppressed. It is a far more reliable virtue than the traditional virtues of 'pure disinterestedness' which it is impossible for 'collective man' to achieve. On the other hand, self-interest must be given sufficient play because 'there is no one society good or wise enough finally to determine how the individual's capacities had best be used for the common good or how his labour is to be rewarded.'[44] It is the economic elaboration of the old biblical injunction to love your neighbour as you love yourself.

The second virtue is efficiency, including as the allocation of scarce resources. It is this that makes it the most characteristic economic value. It has been observed already how it competes necessarily with justice in the economic task, in that without it justice may be irreparably damaged.

The third virtue is the importance of freedom in competition, which is also closely connected to the development of liberal democracies. Without this, political criteria are used to measure 'each man's due' with the known consequences of inefficiency and authoritarianism. Niebuhr rightly prefers the solution of democratic market economies which allow 'a free competition of social forces' to make and resource claims on society.[45]

The fourth and final virtue is the importance of the individual and of individualism. This too conflicts with the traditional Christian assumption that the values on which the market depends for its survival are external to it, and essentially relational. Most, if not all, Christian proposals in this field stress communitarian solutions, relying on virtues like interdependence, persons-in-relationships, and the common good.[46] And yet, without the development of the individual, through self-help and independence, communitarian proposals would be valueless if not highly restrictive of personal development.

It is the coming to terms with these sharp challenges to traditional Christian virtues which constitutes one of the most important tasks for Christian social thought. For the contribution of market economies to the development of modern civic virtues, by promoting responsible economizing, flies in the face of much Christian tradition. So often the Church has assumed that the 'well-springs of cultural health reside in religious faith and life'.[47] Yet understanding the virtues of the market is but a recognition that God's purposes for human living, particularly in and through the economic order, are not restricted to proclaimed Christian virtues external to the market.

Of course, none of this detracts from acknowledging the central role of non-market values in the development of civic virtues, and indeed of the conflicts that will occur between them and market-oriented values. For example, no civic life worthy of the name can be sustained for long without the ordinary graces of life. A minimum of decency and civility is always required to sustain good public life, just as the former is also dependent on the latter. Such virtues do not arise from the market alone. And that is certainly the case with the all-embracing virtue of love which has always been resistant to the commercializing spirit of market economics. Indeed, fortunately in so many ways it works according to quite different laws. Unlike the material factors of production, 'the supply of love, benevolence and public spirit is not fixed or limited'.[48] It leads rightly into the concern for relationships and community without which civic life would not deserve to be regarded as civilized. It is important to recognize too, that the commercializing spirit has not replaced many stubborn social practices and commitments rooted in older views.[49] The family, religion and public life continue to exhibit a remarkable vitality, even as very traditional forms of relationship and moral discourse.

It is out of this interaction between market and non-market oriented values that our understanding of civic virtues should emerge. That will surely not be about reconstituting a communitarian ethic or an undiluted individualism. Neither reflect the complexities of the contemporary context and so both, when promoted, continue to generate the dissatisfaction synonymous with a real missing of the mark. The emerging habits of the heart will probably depend upon a realistic facing up to the relationship of market and non-market virtues, in such a way that private living will develop into public practice. It is in the exploration of the interactive process that such a way of life may be developed. It will certainly be about more than what we have traditionally called 'Christian values'. That is why the Bishop of Oxford's advocacy of Christian ethical criteria to determine church investment policies is so deficient in its understanding of both values and economics.

Facing up to economics: transcendence within limits

The relationship between modern economics and the market economy is historical and contemporary. Both began to evolve at the end of the eighteenth century. Both continue to be linked inextricably in that most economics relate to Western-type economies. Many textbooks are still concerned with a 'traditional preoccupation of economics with value and distribution, with how the prices of goods and services are determined and the resulting income is shared'.[50]

And yet, recent years have seen important questions raised about the way economics has been developing, just as great challenges now interact with the dominance of the market economy. But that has been the history of economics throughout the ages, the response of economic understandings to changing contexts. The development of the market from *laissez-faire* to social market, and economics from classical to neo-classical and beyond, exemplify this dynamic reality of economic life.

The increasing complexity and growth of advanced economies in this century has presented one such challenge to traditional market economics. Accelerating production on a world-wide scale has begun to put unprecedented pressure on the earth's resources in terms of their use and abuse. Yet the discipline of market-oriented economics regards that abuse as an externality because it is omitted from the price calculations of the market. So an externality like pollution is defined as 'when production or consumption by one firm or consumer directly affects the welfare of another firm or consumer, where "directly" means that the effect is not mediated through any market and is consequently unpriced'.[51]

In similar ways, there has been a deep-seated tendency in modern economics, going back to Ricardo in the early nineteenth century, of so developing it as an autonomous academic discipline with a scientific character, that it has become at times divorced from the realities of economic life. An emphasis on mathematics has symbolized this inclination. Present in the discipline for over a century, it reached a new level of intensity after the Second World

War with the development of mathematical economics. The value to the discipline was clear. It gave greater scientific certainty and precision, and reflected the ability of the discipline to be tested by an internal logic. Yet the cost was high, resulting in 'the removal of the subject several steps further from reality'.[52] The understanding of 'economic man' as it emerged in the nineteenth century likewise illustrated a tendency to work with abstractions divorced from historical reality.

All these developments exemplify the charge against economics of 'misplaced concreteness'.[53] All have been used to argue for the development of economics beyond the restrictions of these traditional boundaries and tendencies. Many now therefore struggle to find ways of connecting economics and externalities, and to break out of the compartmentalization of macro- and micro-economics. So with the latter, facing up to contemporary inflation and unemployment in the West increasingly requires a comprehensive view of economic sources, including price theory and overall economic policies. It is not surprising that such responses to the context are producing requests for a restoration of the larger discipline of political economy.[54] Life in modern societies does not distinguish so easily between economics and politics.

Some, however, have gone far beyond this in demanding change. Their concern is to replace modern economics and the market by a quite different understanding of economic life. In a moving interpretation of the parable of the prodigal son, Meeks regards the elder son as the established economy of the West, unable to change and enter into the necessary redemption of the younger son – that is, to recognize the new context set by Third World need. Thus:

> We stand between the economies. On the one hand is the old household in which each of us knows what we will inherit and are so intent upon it that we do not even question the old household rules. And on the other hand is the new household that God is building. The church in the developed world is standing in the position of the older son. The household rules are changing. Whether we shall work for the household of life and experience its joy is our question.[55]

Yet going beyond the market and modern economics so that they are transcended completely is not simply the economic dream of theologians. Even J.M. Keynes assumed a world of abundance for his grandchildren, a world when we shall

> once more value ends above means and prefer the good to the useful. . . . But beware! The time for all of this is not yet. For at least another hundred years, we must pretend to ourselves and to everyone that fair is foul and foul is fair; for foul is useful and fair is not. Avarice and usury and precaution must be our gods for a little longer still. For only they can lead us out of the tunnel of economic necessity into daylight.[56]

And yet, so often these dreams of delight go so beyond present realities as to lose all contact with the actual world. So often they communicate a desire to reformulate what is in effect pre-modern responses and understandings. For some theologians that has meant promoting an economics of sufficiency, based on household economies and use value.[57] There is no sense of recognizing an interaction between markets and challenges. Of course radical critics will argue that such a process is an accommodation to the status quo, with its unacceptable injustices. But that is not the case at all. Promoting the interaction between the dominant partner of the market economy and the great challenges is a recognition that the practice of economics and the question of modern economies reveals no serious alternative at this stage of human development. Yet given that understanding, the existing arrangement is never regarded as fixed economic laws for all time.[58] So significant are the challenges, so deep are the internal defects of the market, and so dynamic is the changing context, that the future shape and outcome of the interaction can never be prejudged. Out of it could emerge a new economics based on the needs of the environment and Third World, which could then become the dominant partner.

Our task, however, can only be to persist with the existing interaction. Hopefully that will also include reading the early signs of an emerging new consensus. Changing economies and economics is essential and inevitable because of the changing context. The way of interaction is but a recognition that facing such changes in the contemporary context is always about transcendence in relation to the limits of the interactive process. It is never about a transcendence into a blissful economic synthesis.

(b) Facing up to the market's limitations: developing the market as the least harmful alternative

> Government in general is the ordinance of God: the particular Form of Government is the ordinance of man. . . . The form of Government therefore has not an absolute, but only a relative, goodness (The Bishop of Oxford, 1767).[59]

In a period of rapid and extensive change, refusal to change to any significant degree is the way of eventual irrelevance. The future development of the market economy is no exception. Facing the contemporary context will certainly require its reforming progression as a social market economy. Life in the European Community after 1992 is likely to illustrate that trend as its defects are worked on with greater skill and commitment. Responding to the great challenges in our world will confirm these developments. Yet because of the entrenched and pervasive nature of poverty and environment, they will continue to demonstrate the grave inadequacies of such progress. That is the nature of the task that constitutes the agenda for the development of Christian social thought. How do you realistically hold on to market economies while responding to intransigent imperatives?

The more one ponders that challenge, the more one cannot continue simply to affirm the market as the best available economy, and leave it at that. It certainly was a necessary basis for argument in the early construction of the interactive process. After all, there are no alternatives operating with anything like the same economic effectiveness. Yet it can no longer be sufficient, knowing as we do both the market's intrinsic limitations, and the seriousness of the external challenges. It cannot be advanced as a means of 'secular redemption'.[60] The only way forward out of this predicament is to acknowledge the market economy as the least harmful way known to us of operating advanced economies. Of course, many will say that changing times demand new and appropriate languages, and the proposed concept is distinctly 'old hat'. It certainly has a long history, beginning with Adam Smith as founder of the market and modern economics. He regarded the free market as the least harmful economic system, a view shared by two of the three Christian responses: the conservative and the liberal. Yet none has supported the concept with the necessary detail, or, more importantly, within the dynamic and framework of an interactive market and challenges. That being so, it becomes essential to fill out the concept using that material. Once the distinctive thesis is thus grasped, others may find a more appropriate concept.

To so regard the market economy as the least harmful economic option reflects two affirmations about the market in the interactive process: the positive and the constraining.

It is important to begin by acknowledging the positive character of the concept. It is not simply about identifying the market as the 'best of a bad bunch'. Three features of the market substantiate this conclusion:

1. As we have seen, the market economy is the most effective way of operating a modern economy known to us. Given the basic economic problem of the allocation of scarce resources, and the problems which flow from that, the market appears to be best able to deal with them. To recognize the market economy as least harmful must therefore not be reduced to Yoder's reluctant acceptance of the state in terms of 'the minimal level of wrong'.[61]

2. The concept is a recognition of the positive value of the untidiness of reality: 'The nature of man is intricate; the objects of society are of the greatest possible complexity.'[62] It is this mood of reality that also highlights the significance of empiricism. Commenting on political democracy in ways appropriate to this understanding of the market, Niebuhr observes that, 'A high degree of empiricism is a basic requirement for democratic health. All sweeping generalizations and assumptions must be eschewed and the questions must constantly be asked.'[63] In many ways it is therefore a style reflecting the limits of life, and their close association with the understanding of economics as the allocation of scarce resources. It is these characteristics that lead into a recognition of the value of political skills, including compromise, and a preference that, 'It is better to be vaguely right than precisely wrong.'[64] It is this spirit that Tawney captured in his comments on the responsibilities of trade union officers: 'Trade union executives are often criticized for being cautious. They ought to be cautious. They are responsible for some hundreds of thousands of men

and women. They have no business to play fast and loose with them.'[65]

3. Affirming the market as least harmful is a rejection of any commitments to blueprints, whether of a Marxist, libertarian, Christian kind, or any other type. No human design or planning capacity has the 'degree of wisdom and foreknowledge' to meet the economic needs of large modern populations.[66] To pretend otherwise would be productive of gross economic inefficiency and political authoritarianism.

The other principal affirmation emphasizes the constraining character of the least harmful concept. It is best not to interpret this in negative terms, because of its constructive and realistic contribution to understanding the market. It includes two main aspects. On the one hand, it is a recognition that the market economy has harmful tendencies because of its intrinsic defects and its inability to deal completely with the great challenges. Both generate damaging consequences which have been vividly charted in the history of Christian socialism and the social gospel. However, the radical response, particularly as liberation theology, and official church statements in the West, continues to over-concentrate on these damaging implications of the market for people and communities, and neglects its greater advantages.

On the other hand, the concept is also an acknowledgement of the structural as well as personal nature of the deep strain of imperfection in reason and morality. Essentially, it represents what Christians have described traditionally as original sin. A reviewer of Reinhold Niebuhr's *Nature and Destiny of Man* commented that it was the most empirically verifiable Christian doctrine. Most importantly, it confirms the least harmful as a recognition that all economic arrangements, including the market, are essentially provisional, although some are to be clearly preferred to others.[67] There is no once-for-all system in politics or economics, but the underlying political and economic order continues to be indispensable for human living.

The understanding of the market as least harmful that is beginning to emerge from these insights is essentially constructive. Its empiricism and pragmatism contribute to this positive nature and, in doing so, warn against two misinterpretations. First, it stands against the use of theological realism, or original sin, to support conservative reaction rather than progressive justice. The relative autonomy of the economic order does not reduce the importance of the political order as democracy and modern state, and their obligation to contribute to the socialization of the market. The economics of imperfection[68] is not an excuse for supporting the libertarian Right. The concept of the least harmful is a realistic and hopeful force for change. Secondly, the understanding of the least harmful also questions the too-simple use of theological realism to deny the power of Christ to transform even the economic order.[69] It is true that the promotion of the market as least harmful rejects the view that faith in God will replace economic scarcity with abundance.[70] Yet it is an acknowledgement that we can co-operate with God's purposes as we discern them through the interaction of Christian tradition and economic realities. It consequently frees us to recognize that 'The politically (or economically) right is not unequivocally determined by the morally right'.[71]

The commitment not to throw down the ladder is therefore not about fighting for the status quo in order to exclude others or to perpetuate remediable injustices. It is about a positively realistic recognition of achievements in contrast to other alternatives. It is about the struggle to change, to press on up the ladder by facing up to internal defects and engaging with external challenges. It is an acknowledgement that the market economy is the least harmful way of operating an economy known to us at this moment in history. And to declare that that can only be done through involvement with the challenges. Indeed, it is as though market and challenges, together, become the least harmful way of responding to our contemporary context.

Notes

1 Quoted in D.L. Munby, *Christianity and Economic Problems* (Macmillan 1956), p. 238.
2 B. Hilton, *The Age of Atonement: The Influence of Evangelicalism on Social and Economic Thought*, 1785–1865 (Clarendon Press 1988), p. 46.
3 R. Bellah, ed., *Habits of the Heart* (New York, Harper & Row, 1986), p. 264.
4 D.L. Munby, *God and the Rich Society* (Oxford University Press 1961), pp. 55–6.
5 There is a helpful discussion of property in M.D. Meeks, *God the Economist: The Doctrine of God and Political Economy* (Philadelphia, Fortress 1989), pp. 101f.

6 J. Bennett, ed., in *Christian Values and Economic Life* (New York, Harper & Row 1954), p. 252.

7 P. Donaldson, *Economics of the Real World* (BBC and Penguin 1973), p. 73.

8 H. Daly and J. Cobb, *For the Common Good* (Merlin Press 1990), p. 53.

9 E. Mishan, *The Costs of Economic Growth* (Staples Press 1967).

10 D. Hay, *Economics Today* (Apollos 1989), p. 287.

11 F. Hirsch, *Social Limits to Growth* (Routledge & Kegan Paul 1977).

12 Quoted in R. Preston, *Religion and the Persistence of Capitalism* (SCM Press 1979), p. 34.

13 A. Buchanan, *Ethics, Efficiency and the Market* (Clarendon Press 1985), p. 101.

14 J. Le Grand and R. Robinson, *The Economics of Social Problems* (Macmillan 1976), pp. 230-1.

15 R. Benne, *The Ethic of Democratic Capitalism: A Moral Reassessment* (Philadelphia, Fortress, 1981), p. 127.

16 Munby, quoting Boulding, in *Christianity and Economic Problems*, p. 239.

17 Benne, p. 69.

18 Benne, p. 135.

19 Purchasing power is normally acquired by supplying resources to the processes of production for money as rent, wages, interest. Therefore, the distribution of purchasing power is related directly to the allocation of those resources to the production of commodities. Objectives for the distribution of purchasing power cannot be separated from society's objectives in production (Le Grand and Robinson, p. 171).

20 Munby's judgement on Niebuhr in *Christianity and Economic Problems*, p. 241.

21 Munby, *Christianity and Economic Problems*, p. 259.

22 A.M.C. Waterman, 'Denys Munby on Economics and Christianity', *Theology* (March–April 1990, no. 752), p. 112.

23 Benne, p. 135.

24 Bennett, ed., p. 163.

25 A.D. Lindsay, *Christianity and Economics* (Macmillan 1933), p. 106.

26 Bennett, ed., p. 245.

27 R.G. Smith, *The Free Man: Studies in Christian Anthropology* (Collins 1969), p. 36.

28 H. Cox in D.L. Munby, ed., *Economic Growth in World Perspective* (SCM Press 1966), p. 173.

29 Bennett, ed., p. 234.

30 Benne, pp. 128–9, partly sees this point in his discussion of 'provisional autonomy' in relation to the economy.

31 Munby, *God and the Rich Society*, p. 138.

32 Benne, p. 129.

33 Quoted in M. Novak, *The Spirit of Democratic Capitalism* (American Enterprise Institute/Simon & Schuster 1982), p. 328.

34 Munby, *God and the Rich Society*, p. 200.

35 Brian Griffiths quotes Ellul's rejection of technological autonomy, in B.

Griffiths, *Morality and the Market Place: Christian Alternatives to Capitalism and Socialism* (Hodder & Stoughton 1982 ed), p. 24.
36 See A. Storkey, *Transforming Economics* (SPCK 1986), p. 202.
37 J. Atherton, 'R.H. Tawney as a Christian Social Moralist', Ph.D. thesis (University of Manchester 1979), p. 167.
38 Atherton, p. 163.
39 W. Temple, *Church and Nation* (Macmillan 1915), p. 52.
40 Bellah, ed., p. 43.
41 C. Strain, ed., *Prophetic Visions and Economic Realities* (Grand Rapids, MI, Eerdmans, 1989), p. 201, quoting R. Reich.
42 Bennett, ed., p. 210.
43 C. Strain, ed., p. 201, quoting R. Reich.
44 Quoted in Novak, pp. 327–8.
45 Quoted in Novak, p. 324.
46 For example, the two recent major Church reports *Economic Justice For All* and *Not Just For The Poor*.
47 Benne, p. 260.
48 C. Wilber in Strain, ed., p. 238.
49 Bellah, p. 141.
50 J.K. Galbraith, *A History of Economics* (Penguin 1989), p. 289.
51 Daly and Cobb, p. 53.
52 Galbraith, p. 259.
53 Daly and Cobb, pp. 44f.
54 Galbraith, p. 299. 'The separation of economics from politics and political motivation is a sterile thing.'
55 M.D. Meeks, *God the Economist: The Doctrine of God and Political Economy* (Philadelphia, Fortress 1989), p. 183.
56 Quoted in E.F. Schumacher, *Small is Beautiful: A Study of Economics as if People Mattered* (Blond & Briggs 1973), p. 20.
57 See M. Meeks, *God the Economist*, and U. Duchrow, *Poverty and Polarisation: A Call to Commitment* (Report of the WEN Consultation, William Temple Foundation 1988).
58 As Meeks, p. 10, rightly argues.
59 Quoted in R. Hole, *Pulpits, Politics and Public Order in England*, 1760–1832 (CUP 1989), p. 15.
60 Used by Charles Elliott in connection with economic growth in Munby, ed., *Economic Growth in World Perspective*, p. 340.
61 J.P. Wogaman, *Christian Perspectives on Politics* (SCM Press 1988), p. 44.
62 Dahrendorf, p. 28.
63 Reinhold Niebuhr quoted in Novak, p. 323.
64 Quoted in Munby, *Christianity and Economic Problems*, p. 73.
65 Atherton, p. 387.
66 J.F. Sleeman, *Basic Economic Problems: A Christian Approach* (SCM Press 1953), p. 106.
67 A. Quinton, *The Politics of Imperfection: The Religious and Secular Traditions of Conservative Thought in England from Hooker to Oakeshott* (Faber & Faber 1978), p. 28.
68 I am aware that it therefore needs rescuing from the conservatives, as

appropriated by Quinton, and from the liberal tradition. (Preston uses the conservative interpretation in his attack on the New Right, in his 'The New Right: A Theological Appraisal', in *The New Right and Christian Values* (Occasional Paper 5, Edinburgh, 1985.)

69 McClendon condemns Reinhold Niebuhr's realism as 'a strategy for (discriminately) sinful living in an (indiscriminately) sinful world, rather than a strategy for transformed life in a world become new in Jesus Christ' (in Wogaman, p. 49).

70 Meeks argues this.

71 In Quinton, p. 61.

Eight

Promoting the Challenges:
The Role of Interrogation

We are inescapably bound to a perpetual life of protest and rebellion, that will continue until the Last Day (D.L. Munby).[1]

Raising questions is a well-established way of furthering our understanding of what lies behind our changing contexts. It can then become part of the process of change itself. So it was with Max Weber, a founding-father of sociology. In 1904 he published one of the great books of this century, *The Protestant Ethic and the Spirit of Capitalism*.[2] What is particularly impressive is that he began his studies by addressing an important contemporary question: Why were there far more Protestant technical college students and industrial apprentices than Catholic ones? He then began to enquire into the causes of this phenomenon. This investigation took him back to the sixteenth and seventeenth centuries, to the early and powerful connection between capitalism and Protestantism.

It was to stand against the damaging consequences of this relationship that the great counterproject of Christian socialism was formed. R.H. Tawney, with his development of Weber's thesis, *Religion and the Rise of Capitalism*, addressed the same question as Weber, followed by V.A. Demant and R.H. Preston.[3] As a result, they played an active part in the countermovements against capitalism.

Following this tradition of discerning great questions in our contemporary context, I turned to the newspaper headlines on the day I began writing this chapter: 14 July 1991. Many of the themes of the interaction between market and challenges were addressed. For example, at the economic summit of the Group of Seven leading industrial countries, the economic and political history of the last 150 years was encapsulated in the questions: How can the Soviet command economy be transformed into a market-oriented economy? Has the great socialist project, originating in the Soviet Union, run its course?

The papers were also full of the closure of the fifth largest private bank in the world, the Bank of Credit and Commerce International. Founded by an Islamic puritan, it had a sense of mission to help Third World governments, partly by beating Western banks at their own game. Strongly supported by Asian businessmen around the world, it was used by the central banks of Nigeria, Zimbabwe, Bangladesh and Kenya. Yet despite its good intentions, it has been overtaken by classic financial misdemeanours and malpractices. Can ethically motivated counterprojects, sensitive to Third World problems, really succeed in the struggle against the increasing domination of the market economy?

If moral conviction is anything to go by, the answer must still be 'yes'. For the five hundredth anniversary of the 'discovery' of America by Columbus has been appropriated by those who attribute the evils of the world to white-dominated capitalism. In the words of one commentator, 'Europe's poisoned gifts still stunt the New World's growth.'[4]

Environmental concerns appeared to be encountering even more difficulties, with the announcement that Britain's leading acid rain laboratory was to be closed by National Power. The pledges that environmental work would not suffer under privatization appear to have been discarded. Even more bizarre was the reported proposal to store the genetic information of the world's most threatened tribes in a 'frozen' museum of mankind!

The origins of so many of these issues have emerged in the analysis of the market economy and its main Christian responses. They are equally well illustrated in the story of Walter Rauschenbusch, the great American Baptist, and principal exponent of the Social Gospel movement. He identified some of the great questions facing his generation while serving in his first pastorate on the edge of the notorious New York slum nicknamed 'Hell's Kitchen'. The pervasiveness of poverty, the powerlessness of the masses of ordinary people, and the appalling social environment drove him to recognize that his traditional religious piety completely failed to engage contemporary society. Faced with 'men out of work, out of clothes, out of shoes, out of hope', he began to fashion a new social gospel which would seek to Christianize the social order as well as individual men and women.

It was over one hundred years ago, in the spring of 1891, that Rauschenbusch arrived in England on his way to Germany. Landing in Liverpool, he was greatly shocked by the poverty he saw. But then he went to Birmingham, where he discovered another world. As he later recorded: 'I have traversed the city in various directions to the outskirts, but have nowhere found that awful, loathsome poverty which flutters in rags and scowls in the faces of the people of Liverpool.' Instead he discovered a strong local government, education system and housing policy. Under its reforming Lord Mayor, Joseph Chamberlain, Birmingham had become a forerunner of what Rauschenbusch called 'municipal socialism', with the city government initiating 'an aggressive program of reform, taking over the water and gas systems, renovating a major slum district, building parks and libraries, giving the suffrage in local elections to women, and providing free meals to schoolchildren'.[5]

So many of these challenges to Christian social thought and practice still dominate our context. Questions concerning poverty, participation in decision-making, the international character of industrialization and urbanization, and the whole environment of human living, continue to exercise a profound influence over the human and Christian agenda. Yet although the questions may be similar, the context has changed so greatly as to present a quite different agenda. For Rauschenbusch, the answer was to promote a socialist alternative to the capitalist market economy. That would solve the problems, he believed, and thereby become the actual human project.

The challenge we now face is totally opposite to that Rauschenbusch faced. For the market economy now appears to be the only feasible way of operating an effective modern economy. So many of the challenges are now being incorporated into it, as the newspaper reports for 14 July 1991 indicated. It is as though the market economy is becoming the human project.

And yet, the interactive process includes both market and great challenges. A study of the market may have confirmed its position as the dominant partner in the process at this stage in human history; what it has not done is to remove the grave intrinsic defects of the market. Nor has it removed their connection to the challenges that possess a significance much greater than that derived from the relationship. There remains, in other words, a case to be made for the significance of the challenges for human living which is as strong as that for the market economy. That being so, it is important for the development of the interactive process in general, and of the market in particular, that the nature of the challenges is understood. After a discussion of these characteristics, it will be helpful to note the contribution to the process of four great contemporary challenges: poverty, environment, participation and international life. We can then return to the current problem facing the process: the threat to amalgamate the challenges into the market economy. The argument over the death of socialism poses this question in a dramatic way.

I. Raising the questions in the human project: characteristics of the challenges

> My reason for writing . . . is to urge a new generation of persons concerned about Christian ethics to press the socialistic questions even though they do not accept ready-made socialistic answers (John C. Bennett, 1975).[6]

Pursuing the questions characterizes the various strands of the Christian socialist tradition. So much of its history has been a reaction against the harmful effects of the capitalist market economy on people and their communities. Indeed, so influential has been this reactive character that the countermovements have always been much better at raising the questions than finding feasible answers. That is one decisive reason why the socialist project has run into insuperable difficulties when in competition with the market system. Modern societies cannot live for long on questions alone. Yet the contribution of the interrogative function none the less continues to be of great importance to human development and certainly to the interactive process. Its persistence can be explained by taking note of some of its more significant characteristics particularly relating to its extent, its ability to reflect the depths of human experience, and its function as a countermovement.

1. The great challenges facing the world and the market economy cover a broad spectrum. They cannot be restricted to one or two of the major questions confronting the human community. Those selected for this argument illustrate the interaction with the market, but are none the less of much wider significance. For example, poverty, within advanced economies as well as in the Third World, has presented traditionally the sharpest challenge to the established orderings. That is why the preferential option for the poor is so determinative of the explanations and solutions of economic and political problems, and of an appropriate form of the Church and theological reflection. The growing number and significance of environmental questions likewise reflect a broader and deeper agenda. They perform a particular role in crystallizing much more fundamental tensions in industrial societies, as the discussion of the social limits to growth has already revealed. Relating to poverty and environment is the increasing pressure for greater involvement in decision-making. The movement to liberal democracies and market economies has partly reflected this demand. Yet the challenge is wider and more radical, including arguments for extending democracy into the heart of the economic process and power structures. The fourth and final challenge again relates to the others as the all-pervasive reality of the international character of modern life. In the form, for example, of the multinational corporation, it brings market and challenges into sharp confrontation as well as dialogue.

The extent and variety of the challenges is of particular import- ance. It warns, above all, against the temptation to concentrate on any one question, however significant. For there is a tendency to so focus on a challenge that it is required to carry the weight of the other challenges and the productive contributions represented by the market. In effect, it begins to reflect an 'apocalyptic consciousness' so typical of a catastrophic reading of world problems and of the drift into revolutionary solutions. Its concern becomes 'precisely with the contrast between the ideal as they conceived it, and the actual as they saw it'. It is as though, in the undue concentration on one great challenge, 'all time-span' is 'foreshortened into a moment'.[7] It becomes the way of the millenarian and crisis theology.

Recognizing the breadth of the spectrum of the challenges reduces greatly this danger of an apocalyptically oriented single question zeal. At the same time, it is also much more representative of the complex and plural nature of reality itself. The framework and dynamic of the interactive process is a substantial contribution to that end. The economic enquiry by the American Churches, *Christian Values and Economic Life*, rightly recognized that no one economic goal should ever be regarded as absolute. Rather, 'the pursuit of each must be guided in part by its effect on the attainment of the others. The object is to achieve a good life, viewed as a whole, not to maximize some arbitrary sum of discrete parts viewed separately.'[8]

The interaction between challenges is as essential for the effectiveness of each as it is for their combined relationship with the market economy. Taken together, they produce a pressure for change that questions the effectiveness of the piecemeal, hybrid approach of the liberal response. 'Our present economic system – if it is not to destroy the environment, dehumanise the work-force and engender gross inequalities and public impoverishment – requires a good deal more than minor piecemeal adjustment.'[9]

2. The challenges are inspired and characterized by a commitment to the human project. Underlying each is a deep concern for human dignity and the whole created order. Consequently, their rejection of the market's harmful outcomes is far more than a reactive force; it is a powerful manifestation of a positive view of human value and potential. The way of interrogation is therefore partly a reflection of the continuing search for human dignity. Its radical questioning spirit projects 'historically something of the eschatological renewal of all things promised by God'.[10] And yet the challenges can never be reduced to a theological humanism or personalism in the way some theologians have been tempted to do. For they also include impersonal empirical data and the analysis of structures: what Munby called the 'growth of the body of accurate understanding about the economic order'.[11] It is this dimension that is heightened through interaction with the market mechanism.

The commitment to human dignity that pervades all the challenges is reinforced by an 'entrenched argumentativeness'.[12] It is this habit of persistent questioning that emphasizes the interpretation of the interactive process as a continuing series of challenges rather than the creation of syntheses. It is as though the interrogative spirit needs to be an intrinsic part of the human project. Its form as particular questions may change as contexts change, but it always stands distinct from the established orderings so exemplified by the market economy.

It is that spirit of persistent critique which lends the challenges the character of a perennial counterproject in the human endeavour. In particular, when conflicting with the market, it has represented the great moral questioning of the tendency to pragmatism and the so-called realities of life. The challenges have always been 'equity-laden' and in competition with the forces of efficiency. That is why they have dominated Christian social thought and practice, with damaging as well as positive consequences. For they can encourage Christians to mould the facts in accordance with their moral and theological imperatives in order to produce the illusory distinctively Christian solution to complex modern problems. Insights into the human predicament, which equity-laden challenges suggest, are assumed to 'provide answers to technical problems which experts have unaccountably failed to see'.[13] They can so easily be productive of the way of Christian utopias.

3. The challenges have generated countermovements on a regular basis in reaction to the all-pervasive nature of industrial capitalism. The growth of Christian socialist groups in Britain in the late nineteenth century illustrates the connection between the challenges and socialism as organized protests against the processes and consequences of the early market economy. Yet the development of countermovements has been a much broader force than the socialist project. As pressure groups campaigning on particular issues, they have always played a major part in the continuing importance of the great challenges. Poverty, the environment, democracy and internationalism have been especially appropriate issues for such developments.

In recent years, however, the countermovements have moved on a stage further. Still representing major means of protest against the colonization of the world by the spirit and forms of capitalism, they have acknowledged the domination of the market over socialist alternatives. Accordingly, they do not represent the older traditional reactions against the production and distribution system as much as particular campaigns against the market's intrusion into all areas of life. As new social movements[14] (Habermas's concept), they include the anti-nuclear and environmental movements; 'the alternative movement' with its urban squatters and rural communes; minority groups such as the elderly, homosexuals, black people, and the disabled; and finally, the women's movement. They are all characterized by collaboration to meet needs unmet by established orderings, and indeed, are often in conflict with them. Their organization is not simply for achieving particular goals; the form of the movement itself becomes a message, a symbolic challenge to dominant codes.[15] They become both organized criticism and practised alternative.

Interestingly and importantly, their history and character has been complemented by the development of new social movements in Christian social thought and practice. As liberation, black, feminist and minjung theologies, they represent a struggle against bureaucratic and organizational forms of capitalist societies, and their processes of marginalization. As Charles Elliott has observed,[16] they too incorporate the critique of the market and the promotion of alternatives. A Catholic sister and member of one such American group exemplified both strands:

> We try to envision an alternative system – and then we live out that vision. We think that this is one of the most creative things that is coming out of the women's movement here. It's a refusal to accept that the old ways – essentially the male ways – of exercising authority, of organising relationships, of understanding community, are the only ones or the best ones.[17]

It is as though the divine sparks[18] in a variety of liberationist perspectives are beginning to coalesce into a mosaic, into 'prefigurative pieces of an unrealized collective vision'.[19] It could represent a reformulation of the great challenges in ways appropriate to the context at the end of this century.

The impact of the new countermovements has spread way beyond the organization of the Church, into the heart of the theological establishment. The demand, again, is for new forms and, in this case, for new languages, as a sign of the break with dominant groupings. So, if conventional theology is 'transcendental and deductive', the theology of the new social movements is 'this-worldly and inductive', relying heavily on narratives.[20] 'The theological jargon is then exposed to the test of whether it can do justice to the experiences of those whose voices have not been heard.'[21]

As Churches and theologies of resistance, these countermovements are representative of so much of the nature of the challenges themselves. Taken as a whole, they manifest only part of the total context as framework and dynamic. By their very nature they tend never to become mainstream. The challenges may therefore have to be content to remain as countermovements, and never to become governing authorities. Yet because of their significance they should never be referred to as marginal. For this is precisely their strength and indispensability to the human project: to stand in constant criticism of, and alternative to, the established orderings and their abuses of power.

2. The challenges of poverty, environment, participation and the international

In the end we will not be safe or free unless people in all the villages and towns of the world are citizens (Ralf Dahrendorf).[22]

Life, and certainly economics, is about making choices. Those undertaking a research project are not exempt from that law of life. They always have the problem of what to leave out of a report as much as what to include. So it is with this programme and this book. Acknowledging the importance of challenges for the interactive process cannot be allowed to develop into their detailed elaboration. Space alone forbids that option, not to mention that this project is concerned to explore the market economy as a contribution to the development of Christian social thought. It is not about challenges in general, or any one in particular. Others have explored both in more detail and with greater competence.

Despite these warnings, the four issues chosen to represent the great challenges warrant clear recognition. The importance of the interactive process, and the relationship between the challenges, surely demand no less. However brief the consideration, it will at least confirm their right to be regarded as major challenges in our world and to the market. The justification for that claim has recurred throughout the book, with the challenges' continued prominence in the elaboration of the market and its Christian responses. What can be done now is to indicate examples of the effects of the interactive process on each issue.

The selection is not intended to be exhaustive. Others may have different lists, although it is difficult to envisage one without poverty and the environment. What has become clear is that no one issue can be given absolute priority over the others at this moment in history. There can be no preferential option for the poor as the exclusive arbiter of Christian discipleship, not least because of the highly significant series of interconnections between the issues and, in turn, with the market economy. It is this dynamic interaction that has to be acknowledged and promoted with all the provisionality of the least harmful way of engaging contemporary life at this moment in our history.

Poverty: arguably one of the most important facts in the world today[23]

Facing up to the contemporary context must include the recognition of poverty as a dominant world phenomenon. Although governed by its sheer extent and depth in the Third World, the growth of poverty in the First World is also causing widespread concern. Indeed, the more one considers the analysis of the market and its Christian responses, the more one is driven to reflect on the convergences between First and Third World poverty, without in any way detracting from their great differences. The following reflections have been selected to elaborate this complementarity.

First, most responsible commentators struggle to come to terms with the sheer size of the problem whether in absolute terms or as a growing gulf between rich and poor. However, all would agree with Donald Hay that: 'A very large proportion of mankind lives in conditions of great personal deprivation. By comparison the inhabitants of the industrial countries live in prosperity and luxury.'[24] The World Development Report (1986), and its survey for 1984, illustrates this catastrophe. It divides the world economy into three groups: the low-income group with 2,390 million people, the middle-income group with 1,888 million, and the high-income group with 733 million. In terms of annual per capita income, the difference between the first and last groups is $380 to $11,430, a ratio of 1:44. What this meant in 1991 was the threatened starvation of over 30 million people in Africa alone.

For some, the danger of such 'talk of catastrophe' is that it could all too easily become self-fulfilling.[25] Yet the stark threat of such large-scale poverty does possess an apocalyptic character that reasoning alone cannot engage adequately. When it comes to trying to understand the causes of poverty, the failure to agree is much more decisive. For example, the dependency theory clearly raises important questions about the explanation of the relationship between rich and poor. As so often the case with unitary theories, its answers are much less convincing. The tendency of conservatives to emphasize cultural and other causes internal to the Third World, to the exclusion of international structures and the market economy, is equally unsatisfying. Yet whatever the arguments over the causes and extent of poverty, few seek to avoid 'the simple fact that, whatever the moral obligations of each, both do live in the same world, and that the rich cannot permanently be happy in a world of poverty'.[26] Most therefore agree that the challenge is how to enable all to have a relevant and materially satisfactory life by breaking out of the cycle of precarious subsistence and starvation.[27] It is therefore much more than a matter of ethics.

Similarly, confronting poverty in the First World generates fundamental agreements beyond profound arguments. So, with over 33 million people living below the poverty line in the biggest market economy in the world, and homelessness as its fastest growing statistic,[28] the challenge of poverty is also intrinsically part of the market's agenda. Once again, arguments over definitions and explanations of poverty are seen as not detracting from the greater need to at least alleviate the problem. For most agree that one of the most urgent tasks facing advanced market economies is to discover ways to reduce the marginalization of significant minorities of populations, to ensure all members of a society are able to participate properly in it.[29]

Secondly, First and Third World poverty illustrate the contribution to the growth of poverty, as well as its amelioration, of a framework allowing considerable freedom to the market system. For example, what has become known as Ricardo's theory of comparative advantage recognizes that the best way to maximize economic output is for each country to contribute what it is best at producing, and to use it as a basis for trade with others.[30] The problem, of course, is that those who enter the free market with most resources obtain the best results, and vice versa. This penalizing of Third World countries is exacerbated by their overdependence on primary products, since the more affluent nations become, a reduced proportion of their income is spent on such goods. The task is always to develop into manufacturing industry, which is precisely what the rich world's club has dominated. In other words, people and nations with no or little access to resources to work with and produce lack the basic power to enter and use the market system.

Similarly in the First World, such understandings of poverty are interpreted through the problem of unequal power. As a positional goods, power can only be obtained from others, and so it is connected inescapably to the unequal distribution of resources, including income and wealth. It is the lack of access to these that excludes people from effective participation in the market, and accentuates the power of others. Both are related to 'a framework which is itself imperfect and inequitable'.[31] The dynamic of a free market operating in such a framework invariably tends to confirm and exacerbate unequal access to resources and power. Consequently, a principal means for amending such unfairness is through government intervention via tax and welfare systems. The continual socializing of the market illustrates the progress and the difficulties of moving towards more equitable frameworks.

Thirdly, the extent and depth of the challenge of poverty in First and Third Worlds is such that piecemeal reforms are unlikely to enable all to achieve a materially satisfactory life, or to reduce the growing gap between rich and poor. It is clear, too, that only a variety of strategies could engage effectively such a complex and comprehensive reality. No one strategy would ever be sufficient. And yet, the pressure for radical change is associated invariably with the increasing authority and involvement of the state in economic affairs, with all its implications for the erosion of the dynamic of the market economy. Undue interference with incentives, private property, enterprise and economic growth has a real tendency to produce disturbing economic, social and political consequences, often unforeseen. It so often seems to imply a return to a more static supervised society. A too unequivocal concentration on poverty can also destroy the delicate yet solid trade-offs between economic efficiency and equity, which appear to be intimately part of a prosperous democratic society. The alternatives appear to be more harmful, although the market should never be imposed on all societies irrespective of their stage of development. However, sooner or later some kind of market system will be needed, given its position in international life and basic economics. Yet the challenge of poverty can never be evaded, irrespective of (indeed, some would argue because of) the trend to market economies. The framework and dynamic of the interactive process can only suggest a way of facing up to such alarming polarities.

The environment: the challenge of limits

Threats to the environmental context have been observed and criticized for many centuries. Yet it was the accelerating pace of industrialization and urbanization that brought concern to the high pitch of anxiety and creativity of recent years. Threat and reaction were intimately connected to economic growth, but especially to its great increase in market economies since the Second World War. The desire of Third World countries to enter into the same economic processes in order to share in the prosperity has exacerbated these trends.

Like the other great challenges, concern over the environment is profoundly equity-laden, representing as it does the deep interrogation of the human use and abuse of resources as they menace the integrity of the created order. It is therefore centrally concerned with challenges and countermovements, and with the functioning of economics and markets. Illustrating all these trends, in 1972 the Club of Rome produced its first report, *The Limits to Growth*, and caused a major sensation. Based on the dynamic interaction between population, food production, pollution, the level of industrial activity and the use of non-renewable resources, it predicted the rapid acceleration of the world into deep crisis. Indeed, unless dramatic measures were taken to address these related problems, it foresaw the end of civilization by the year 2100. Much opinion has rightly indicated the deep flaws in this analysis, not least its failure to take account of technological responses to perceived threats. Yet the significance of the concern over the environment that the Club of Rome represents should not be downgraded by the importance of the justifiable criticisms of some parts of its argument. Whatever the pros and cons of the debate, none can escape the world's finitude.

From this paramount fact, transcending all reason and ethics, springs the environmental challenges and countermovements that have become so significant in this generation. Understandably, they represent counterprojects often fundamentally at odds with economic growth and the market system. Yet, as usual, the relationship between challenge and market is profoundly ambivalent. Most opinion agrees that the market system, and its increasing international dominance, represents one of the gravest threats to the environment: 'the pressure on resources which we witness in the world economy is largely a by-product of the demands arising from the high income countries of the OECD nations'.[32] Yet there is equal conviction that the market economy can be adapted to deal with many of the problems of pollution and resource over-use. The ambivalence should not surprise us. For economics and environment are concerned with the best use of limited resources. The former represents the drive to greater efficiency in their use, and the latter concerns the need to address them in a wider and more inclusive agenda.

The challenge to the market by the environment relates principally to pollution and the exhaustion of resources. They represent threats to its costing tradition, its access to factors of production, and its survival on the earth. Of course, pollution itself is not a new phenomenon, but the extraordinary increase in economic growth has resulted in an alarming acceleration in the volume of waste that now threatens whole environmental systems. The market's satisfaction of more immediate material needs has only exacerbated the problem by enabling more people to pursue environmentally oriented activities. As a result, there is a growing recognition that the market's concern with private costs and benefits (internal, that is, to the price-mechanism's operation) has to be amended so that the external costs of pollution can become internal to the polluters. The use of charges and fines are among the methods suggested to achieve this change.

The exhaustion of resources affects renewable and non-renewable, and the latter particularly presents a major challenge to the market economy. Again, there are suggestions that the processes of the market can be used to meet some of the challenge. For example, the pressure of demand could stimulate discoveries of further resources and, more importantly, of substitutes. The question is always whether too little is attempted too late in relation to finite environmental systems. Three issues express this tension and connect in turn to the interaction between market and challenges. They include suggestions for the development of Christian social thought in this field.

The *first* concerns the pressure to see industrial growth in terms of total social welfare rather than simply material goods and services. The very concept of externalities points up this predicament and need, providing that the broader more inclusive view of economics does not lose the central concern of economics. The allocation of scarce resources for the most efficient production of goods and services will continue to be fundamental to economic life for the foreseeable future.

Secondly, the growing importance of government and inter-governmental action in economic life also relates powerfully to attempts to meet the environmental challenge. Within market economies the presumption appears to be still in favour of using the market, suitably broadened to engage externalities, as against undue reliance on state regulations. Yet the threat, for example of pollution, now so transcends national boundaries that intergovernmental action and agendas are becoming essential parts of the total response to the environmental challenge.

Thirdly, the struggle to develop practical ways of responding to the threats of pollution and resource depletion continues to dominate political and economic policies. The Brundtland Report of 1987, *Our Common Future*, exemplifies the careful attempts to face up to problems like the greenhouse effect, the loss of the rain forests, and the flight to the cities. Always on the side of those who seek 'appropriate and possible'[33] ways of dealing with issues, it rejects the advocating of a halt to, or reversal of, economic and technological growth. Yet its laudable concern to promote sustainable growth is challenged by those who regard such responses as radically insufficient. For them, it is not simply that the challenge to the life-system is so fundamental as to be beyond the traditional measures of proven progressive change. Acknowledging the threat also provides an opportunity to develop quite different economic systems. It is in this sense that Wogaman is right to regard the conservationism of Schumacher and others as an economic type in its own right, to stand alongside market and command economies. Indeed, in many ways, environmental economics now provides the radical alternative to the dominant market economy, a position once occupied by the command economy. The danger, of course, is that of elevating one challenge into an all-embracing system, ignoring so many of the lessons of liberal democracies and market economies.

Locating the environment in the framework of market and challenges is another way of recognizing that dynamic which requires of the environment, as of all the challenges, 'the critical balance of decisive international action and the commitment to preserve elementary freedoms'. The alternative could be the propensity of every such system to degenerate into an all-embracing ideology. 'The benevolent dictatorship of ecologist-kings would be no better than any other dictatorship.'[34]

The pressure for participation: the ambiguities in extending democracy

The processes of modernization, in which the market economy plays such a prominent part, are characterized by complexity, the subdivision of labour, larger companies, and the separation of family, community and work. They present a continuing and increasing challenge to the desire of men and women to have some say in matters affecting their lives, to resist the fatalistic pressure to submit to external forces. The market contributes to the alienation and oppression, and yet also provides opportunities to increase participation and resist estrangement. The pressure to extend democracy into the economic arena sharpens and confuses this debate, as does its connection with the commitment to intermediate associations.

The concern to extend greater participation in economic decision-making has a long and important history in the story of Christian responses to the market. It is a narrative much influenced by the early attempts of Maurice and others to set up producer co-operatives, and the later full-blown worker-control schemes of guild socialism. Its contemporary advocates can be found among the American Roman Catholic Bishops in their report *Economic Justice For All*, with their appeal for a 'new experiment in economic democracy';[35] others, like Gary Dorrien, regard wider participation in at least investment decisions as essential for effective democratic socialism.[36]

The commitment to greater democracy has essentially two aspects relating to a view of human dignity and contemporary power structures. The first claims that participation in the economy affirms a high priority for human worth in the market economy. It is an acknowledgement that labour is a vital resource in economic functioning, and yet must not be reduced to a factor of production alone, subject only to the forces of supply and demand. From the early stages of industrialization, this concern has been influential in arguments for human rights and their support by regulations. It is a trend exemplified by the early Factory Acts to the current commitments to a Social Charter in the European Community. The second is a recognition that the reality of contemporary power is significantly about economic life. For Reinhold Niebuhr, 'Economic [power] rather than . . . political and military, has become the significant coercive force of modern society. . . . Political power has been made responsible, but economic power has become irresponsible in society. The net result is that political power has been made more responsible to economic power.'[37] For example, of the one hundred largest economic institutions in the world only fifty-nine are nations, the rest are multinationals. Confronted with such a concentration of power it is not surprising that many now argue that: 'Perhaps democracy now requires the same kind of popular accountability for large business institutions that it has always required for government institutions.'[38] Indeed, some are convinced that the future of the 'global household' depends on restoring 'many aspects of economy to community accountability'.[39]

The means to achieve such ends are varied, moving from full-blown worker control or command economies to more modest proposals like the reform of company law to allow consumer and employee involvement in the governing of enterprises. What most commentators are agreed on is that something must be done to increase participation in economic life. Unfortunately, the debate over how to achieve these ends is fraught with confusions and ambiguities. However, a possible resolution of some of these difficulties could begin to emerge from the interaction between market and challenges. Three matters then warrant serious consideration.

1. It is important to recognize that the operating of a market economy itself makes a vital contribution to citizen participation in economic affairs. By standing for, and enabling, the freedom of individuals and households to spend according to *their* own preferences, the market can be seen as a 'form of democracy, by which people express their wishes in many important fields of life'.[40] It can be seen, too, to provide a way of restraining economic power by competition and the encouragement of a multitude of centres of economic activity. However, many of these concerns and mechanisms are dependent upon extra-market activity, in the forms of ensuring *all* citizens have the resources to participate in the market, and of the effective policing of monopolistic tendencies in the market.

2. The commitment to extending participation in the economic arena immediately encounters the problem of the relative autonomy of politics and economics, on which the market economy and liberal democracy place such a high value. Although the market has a clear tendency to invade most areas of human living, including the political, there is at least an equal tendency for the political to impinge on the operating of the economy. It becomes an undue interference when it expands well beyond the accepted strong role for government in economic life in advanced economies. Many arguments for the extension of democracy into economic life do not appear to have taken into account sufficiently the likely damaging economic consequences of such developments. The promotion of forms of 'economic socialism' can so easily become 'a system of political thought and action that tends inevitably in a totalitarian direction by reason of its project of absorbing the economy within the state'.[41] The relative autonomy of the market system illustrates the value as well as problems of allowing the economy significant freedom of performance.

3. Whatever the value of the argument that the market enhances democracy, and there is much truth in it, it is also evident that 'unaccountable control and domination within market exchange deters democracy'.[42] For this reason alone, it is important to encourage greater participation in the market. Three ways of achieving this regularly surface in works of many of the Christian

commentators on economics. The first encourages employee involvement in decision-making internal to the operating of the enterprise – for example, over working conditions and practices. Yet this should not intrude on management decisions proceeding with the necessary authority in external areas like market operations, new products, relations with suppliers and competition. In other words, there are clear limits regarding information and time which constrain the extent of participation in relation to the need to maintain efficient production.[43] The second way relates to profit and capital-sharing schemes for employees, including the remarkable drift to 'pension fund socialism'.[44] The third way links up with the major arguments in favour of intermediate associations, those bodies which stand in between the state and the individual. These are generally acknowledged to be necessary for better participation because of their accountability to local involvement. It is interesting and significant that our generation has seen a great outburst of such local, community-inspired initiatives of an economic kind, both in the USA and Britain. They exemplify the well-known experience that, 'People will be most creative and productive under such conditions.'[45]

The danger of course is that Christian social thought has placed an undue emphasis on such necessary, but morally obvious, projects. And it has done this to the exclusion of a hard dialogue with the market's potential for participation, and the ways of reducing its harmful tendencies without an undue reduction of efficiency. Responding to the challenge of participation again indicates the importance of a combination of strategies for encouraging and restraining participation. It is this ambivalence that suggests an understanding of economics and market which is the equivalent of Niebuhr's judgement on democracy. While 'denouncing its sometimes exaggerated confidence in political reason', he affirmed democracy 'in the end as the form of government best suited to the ambiguous possibilities inherent in human nature'.[46] So it may well be with the market in its relationship with the great challenges.

The international order: taking account of wider alternatives

The early 1990s has begun to witness the attempt of what was the Soviet Union to enter the world economy. It will be a long tortuous road with immense suffering and dislocation inflicted along it. Yet what are the feasible alternatives facing any nation seeking to become a more effective and prosperous economy? At almost every point of its life, a country comes into economic contact with others. The challenges of poverty and the environment only reinforce that interdependence. It is now virtually impossible for one nation to go it alone.

The economic pressure for an international order comes from two main sources. On the one hand, the reality of a world economy is dominated by the international character of the market economy. The dynamic spirit of capitalism encourages the flow between nations of ideas, technology, labour, investment, production and trade. Pressure towards economic co-operation is intensified by the need to encourage a greater harmonization of economic policies; what can appear to be the solution of an internal problem may have 'international effects that are defensible neither on economic nor on moral grounds'.[47] It is a world over-influenced by the great market economies of the USA, Japan and Germany.

On the other hand, the pressure for an international order also arises from the Third World. Programmes like the New International Economic Order (NIEO) sought to achieve radical changes in international economic relations through the United Nations in the 1970s. By focusing mistakenly on international economic problems, and the contribution of the First World market systems to them, the principal advocates of the NIEO argued for a variety of objectives which powerfully evoked an international order – if not an international welfare state. Targets like full employment, low inflation, and a fair distribution of world income ignored the likely conflicts between them. Such misunderstandings of economic processes were only exacerbated by the fact that 'there is no guarantee at all that the interests of all countries coincide'.[48] Yet underlying all these concerns and inadequacies was the strong conviction that 'no automatic mechanism' would prevent the growth of poverty and of the gap between rich and poor.[49] The question was not whether to develop an international order, but how, because market systems and the Third World coincided in that wider priority, as both threat and challenge. Environmental concerns confirmed and extended it.

Given the growing recognition of the need for a more effective international dimension, supranational agencies emerged particularly after the Second World War. They began to cover many of the points of convergence of the international concerns of market economies and the Third World, even though they were often more representative of one than the other. Covering a whole series of fields, they ranged from trade agreements like GATT, and financial institutions like the International Monetary Fund and the World Bank, to much broader programmes like the NIEO. At all these functional levels, despite their serious inadequacies, 'It may be that this kind of activity is the real opportunity in the present era for laying the foundations for a new world order.'[50]

Yet such traditional Christian concern for the morally obvious can so easily collapse into the soft utopian hope that radically 'new possibilities will come into being as well'.[51] Internationalism and the ecumenical in contemporary life, and the brotherhood of man in the communities of memory, are not necessarily suitable tools for engaging the ambiguities of the international challenge. For that, the framework of market and challenges may be much more realistic, and therefore hopeful in relation to nationalism and multinationals.

For example, the former is a recognition that the inclination to internationalism of market and Third World cannot be allowed to subsume the continuing importance of the national economy. For the welfare of other countries cannot be made the primary objective of a state's policies and actions. Traditionally, this has meant that as far as 'the government of a sovereign state is concerned, the key to action, including action that promotes the welfare of other countries, is service to its own people'.[52] It is that use of national self-interest that the Brandt Report tried unsuccessfully to use to match First and Third World interests. For in the end, the management of national economies has to take into account more and more of the international character of economic life, and international issues like the environment. The key problem therefore remains how to find 'points of concurrence between the interests of the nation and the wider good',[53] which includes – but stretches beyond – self-interest. It is as though ways have to be found of enlarging national interests so that they coincide more with world interests. Facing up to the challenges in interactive relationship with the market offers such possibilities.

What of multinational corporations, for they too offer ways

of facing up to ambiguities? Given their economic power, most commentators acknowledge the threats they present, varying from using their internationalism to circumvent national attempts to regulate labour and taxes, to causing exchange rate instability by moving sums from one country to another in anticipation of devaluations and revaluations. Yet the advantages of multinationals are equally obvious. For example, unlike governments, they often see the real potential for profit and investment, and they continue to be a major source of jobs, training and infrastructures. It is as though multinationals exemplify both the necessity of the market economy and the inevitability of challenges. That predicament cannot be solved by throwing down the ladder. It relies rather on registering the pressures for the international by market and Third World, and thereby finding ways of organizing the commitment to efficiency and the need for equity. That can only be through the collaboration of nations through regional entities like the European Community, and world organizations like the United Nations; the future of multinationals can be located in such a context. It is out of these ambiguous struggles that 'decisions made well today in face of severely limited alternatives' could then develop into 'a much wider set of alternatives tomorrow'.[54]

3. The strange death of economic socialism:[55] the future of radical protest

Socialism is the great epitome of challenges and countermovements. Its struggles against the harmful consequences of market systems has inspired individuals, organizations and nations, and generated a long tradition of resistance. Yet it has been more than a reaction against the evils of capitalism. From its origins, it has sought to promote a feasible alternative to the market economy. It has been determined to become the human project.

In the commitment to become the focus of a new order through the rejection of the old, socialism displays important characteristics of all the great challenges to the market economy. It becomes a representative case study of the predicament, facing challenges of whether to remain a countermovement or to try to become the governing ethos of society. The story of the strange death of economic socialism questions the latter route, and clarifies the nature of the indispensable contribution of challenges to the interactive process.

The story of socialism has always included the pressures to be human project and counterproject. It is into the former concern, to replace capitalism with an alternative political economy, that the most substantial effort has been channelled. The results were inspiring, covering a great part of the inhabited world, and focused on the Soviet Union, Eastern Europe and China, with numerous protégés in the Third World. It was principally an economic project, based on the social ownership of the means of production, distribution and exchange, but systematically and comprehensively subordinated to the political authority of the socialist will. Despite early and substantial successes in the development of modern industrial states and in meeting basic human needs, command economies failed to meet the rising expectations of citizens for the goods and services and the basic civil and political liberties characteristic of advanced economies. For modern societies, the socialist command economy is being rejected 'as highly inefficient as well as inimical to individual liberty'.[56]

Given these failures, attempts have been made to rehabilitate the socialist project by the development of market socialism, by discovering ways of combining parts of the more successful market mechanism with socialist planning. From Oskar Lange[57] in the 1930s, to Gary Dorrien[58] in the late 1980s, various proposals have been debated that have revealed an increasing tendency to jettison most of the Marxist heritage with its commitment to man as rational planner and co-operator.[59] Only in the field of the political control of investment decisions does Dorrien still retain a substantive link with historic economic socialism. For the rest, the market mechanism replaces central planning as the principal means for organizing economic activity, with private property retaining a central but not exclusive role. Yet even this compromise fails to recognize the importance of market forces for investment decisions.[60] There is no evidence that any of these modifications to economic socialism, which persist in promoting the subordination of economic processes to central political decision-making, will emerge and survive as feasible alternatives to the market economy. Economic socialism does not appear able to overcome its central dilemmas which Kolakowski identified so clearly:

> We are *for* equality, but we realise that economic organization cannot be based on equality of wages, that cultural backwardness has a self-perpetuating mechanism . . . We are for economic democracy, but we do not know how to harmonize it with the competent running of production.[61]

As long as economic socialism is unable to solve these problems, it cannot be trusted to operate an advanced economy.

What has every chance of surviving and flourishing is the strand of socialism as counterproject. In economic life, the moral protest against market processes has a long history. Taking the form of small self-supporting projects, often of a co-operative kind, they have been invariably small scale. Sleeman has called them 'a kind of laboratory experiment',[62] but this is to underestimate their persistence in reappearing as communal responses to market defects like high unemployment, and their importance as self-help projects in alternative economics. So often they are attempts 'to put into practice, in a small-scale model, the principles and the spirit which it is felt should underlie economic relationships'.[63] And yet it is quite unlikely that they will ever become the dominant mode of operating an advanced prosperous economy. To that extent, they do so easily give the impression of being 'the failed children of capitalism'.[64]

What emerges from such history does amount to the strange death of economic socialism as the human project, even when attempts are made to reform it. In 1989, Dubček, the hero of the Czech revolt of 1968, tried thus to rehabilitate socialism by giving it a human face. Havel and the other leaders of the Czech uprising would have none of it. For them, even reformed communism was 'an idea whose time has gone'.[65] Yet in no way was that a plea for the return of libertarian capitalism or of a 'third way' between communism and capitalism. Essentially, it was instead an argument for social democracy of a more radical kind, based on liberal democracy and the market, with a strong commitment to social justice.

Some of course will say that this is a rather academic point. 'But actually a great deal of what is happening is precisely about words: about finding new, plain, true words rather than the old mendacious phrases with which people have lived for so long.'[66] New words I cannot identify, but what is emerging is the end of 'socialism' as we have known it. That word cannot continue to be used in the same way. Yet what we have to learn to describe are the consequences of that death for the great challenges. These are twofold, reinforcing and progressing the socializing of the market economy, and persistence as great counterprojects.

Regarding the development of the social market economy there is a sense in which we in the West are now 'all social democrats'.[67] Yet even to state that obvious truth is quite unsatisfactory, not least because it is so reminiscent of Westcott's vacuous claim in 1890 that we are all socialists now! Fortunately, we are able to give a more precise definition of what is meant by social democracy, and how it stands as an interim concept between the death of economic socialism and the triumph of the social market economy, and what will emerge out of the interaction between market and challenges.

With regard to its definition, the socializing of the market economy, partly through interaction with the socialist challenge, is exemplified by the commitment of the European Community to a Social Charter as much as to the free market. Edwards regards this not as socialism, but as the development of European civilization.[68] It reflects the commitment to a social market of a more radical kind, with a maximum amount of equal liberties for all to pursue their private ends and to participate in shaping the public realm.[69] Of course, achieving such a society requires the delivery of basic means for all citizens so that they can participate in it.[70] Yet it does not necessarily convey an overtly political notion of the common good which presses towards substantive ends. The commitment to the individual pursuit of self-chosen purposes through the public realm suggests rather that 'a plurality of ends must be allowed and perhaps even encouraged'.[71] The common good, with its overtness of undue political interference in economic life and private choices, may no longer be an appropriate concept for Christian social thought.

The development of what is understood by social democracy is also helped by a recognition of what it does not include. Thus it should not be confused with the continual search of the Left for a modified socialist project of, say, a democratic socialist kind to replace the collapse of centrally planned economies. To do so is to perpetuate confusion. For if democratic socialism then means accepting private property as the dominant mode of ownership, and if the market mechanism is the principal way of engaging the basic economic problem, then that is essentially a capitalist market economy. To call it democratic socialism or market socialism is 'not meaningful theoretically'.[72] Similarly, talk of 'third ways' between capitalism and communism are no longer convincing descriptions of what actually exists as operational reality or feasible alternatives. It really is not very helpful to use Sweden as such an example of democratic socialism, as though it represented somehow the mix of two great ideologies. As 'the accepted ideal for virtually everyone who styles themselves a Socialist from Britain to Vladivostok',[73] Sweden is actually a capitalist social market economy of a more liberal and progressive kind. The Sweden of so much of democratic socialism is essentially 'not Sweden; it is a dream with no base anywhere on the map of Europe'.[74]

To that extent, therefore, the agenda of radical reform that socialism used to represent has now to be the agenda of the continuing reform of the social market economy. Socialism as the human project no longer exists as a realistic radical alternative way for operating modern economies. Yet we should not be too surprised. For it was after the Second World War that the great shift in Western radical Christian opinion began. Believing that the argument of the 1930s was now defunct, that capitalism was in its final death throes, one or two leaders of Christian social thought began to recognize the death of socialism. Thus John Bennett changed his mind over the socialist project as the replacement for the market economy: 'I no longer believe that; because I believe that an experimental modification of capitalism to meet particular needs is better than change of the system at its centre.'[75]

What then remains of the socialist agenda, if it can no longer be promoted as a credible project for operating modern societies? What survives is the challenge of socialism as a persistent counterproject. It is as though it must always represent 'not so much a theory as a set of moral injunctions',[76] a constant reminder that we can 'never rest content' with the economic order as market economy.[77] It is this reflection of a central part of human experience that which has allowed Marx to continue to speak to people and communities around the world. In so many matters of everyday thought and expression, even in the non-socialist world, 'he is a major influence and force'.[78] It is this standing against oppression and standing for human dignity that has also resulted in the growing linkages between liberationist movements and socialism as countermovement. Some see the future of socialism in such a series of alliances and networks.[79] And it is here that any hope of challenges being able to generate a human project radically different from the social market economy is most likely to be found. For it is in the challenge of the environment, for example, that we can discover the possibilities of that radically different way of operating economies that socialism has traditionally represented. And yet, the story of the strange death of economic socialism can only suggest that the presumption is against such an eventuality. For when challenges seek to become the governing principle of a modern society, the tendency is for greater economic inefficiency and a greater political oppression. Yet the authenticity of the great challenges stand as a constant and necessary reminder that a market economy, however socialized, will never be more than the least harmful way of operating a society. For it is not at all clear that the human project in a finite world can ever be anything more than such an interaction at this stage of history between realities like the market economy and the great challenges. It is no mean achievement.

Notes

1 D.L. Munby, *God and the Rich Society* (Oxford University Press 1961), p. 190.
2 M. Weber, *The Protestant Ethic and the Spirit of Capitalism* (Unwin 1970).
3 V.A. Demant, *Religion and the Rise of Capitalism* (Faber & Faber 1952); R.H. Preston, *Religion and the Persistence of Capitalism* (SCM Press 1979).
4 *The Independent on Sunday* (14 July 1991).
5 P.M. Minus, *Walter Rauschenbusch: American Reformer* (Macmillan 1988), p. 72.
6 J.C. Bennett, *The Radical Imperative: From Theology to Social Ethics* (Philadelphia, Westminster, 1975), p. 156.
7 W. Temple, *Church and Nation* (Macmillan 1916), pp. 164–5, appendix 1, 'On The Apocalyptic Consciousness'.
8 J.C. Bennett, *Christian Values and Economic Life* (New York, Harper & Row, 1954), p. 63.

9 P. Donaldson, *Economics of the Real World* (BBC and Penguin 1973), p. 216.
10 B. Ward Jackson in D.L. Munby, ed., *World Development: Challenge to the Churches* (Washington D.C., Corpus Books, 1969), p. 185.
11 D.L. Munby, *Christianity and Economic Problems* (Macmillan 1956), p. 271.
12 D. Edwards, *Christians in a New Europe* (Collins 1990), pp. 102–3.
13 Munby, *Christianity and Economic Problems*, p. 270.
14 J. Habermas, *The Theory of Communicative Action*, vol. 2 (Boston, Beacon Press, 1987), pp. 391ff. I owe this, and the following references to Charles Elliott, to John Reader, and his unpublished essay entitled 'Contextual Theologies and the New Social Movements – A New Critique of Capitalism?' (1989.)
15 A. Melucci, *Nomads of the Present*, ed. J. Keane and P. Mier (Hutchinson Radius 1989).
16 C. Elliott, *Sword and Spirit* (BBC and Marshall Pickering 1989).
17 Elliott, p. 218.
18 Freda Kerna Furman writing on Arthur Waskow in C. Strain, ed., *Prophetic Visions and Economic Realities* (Grand Rapids, MI, Eerdmans, 1989), p. 114.
19 Gary Dorrien commenting on Rosemary Ruether, in G. Dorrien, *Reconstructing the Common Good* (New York, Orbis, 1990), p. 170.
20 Elliott, p. 53.
21 Reader, p. 18.
22 R. Dahrendorf, *Reflections on the Revolution in Europe* (Chatto & Windus 1990), p. 150.
23 Munby, in *God and the Rich Society*, p. 90, regards the struggles around poverty in the Third World as the most important fact in the world today.
24 D. Hay, *Economics Today* (Apollos 1989), p. 250. His chapter 8, 'Rich Nation, Poor Nation', is particularly helpful.
25 R. Fagley and A. McCormack (chapter 4) in D.L. Munby, ed., *World Development: Challenge to the Churches*.
26 Munby, *God and the Rich Society*, p. 94.
27 P. Berger, *The Capitalist Revolution: Fifty Propositions about Prosperity, Equality and Liberty* (Wildwood House 1987), p. 218.
28 M.D. Meeks, *God the Economist: The Doctrine of God and Political Economy* (Philadelphia, Fortress, 1989), p. 16.
29 See J. Atherton, *Faith in the Nation* (SPCK 1988), and the argument for a participating and reciprocal society, chapter 4.
30 Donaldson, pp. 232–3.
31 Donaldson, pp. 231.
32 Hay, p. 308.
33 R. Preston, 'Humanity, Nature and the Integrity of Creation', *Ecumenical Review* (October 1989).
34 Dahrendorf, p. 149.
35 D. McCann in Strain, ed., p. 204.
36 Dorrien, p. 3.
37 L. Rasmussen in Strain, ed., p. 139.
38 P. Camenisch, 'The Churches and the Corporations', in Strain, ed., p. 178.

39 Meeks, p. 182.
40 Munby, *God and the Rich Society*, p. 147.
41 A. Quinton, *The Politics of Imperfection: The Religious and Secular Traditions of Conservative Thought in England from Hooker to Oakeshott* (Faber & Faber 1978), p. 21.
42 Meeks, p. 63.
43 For example, see Munby, ed., *Economic Growth in World Perspective* (SCM Press 1966), pp. 57f.
44 R. Benne, *The Ethic of Democratic Capitalism* (Philadelphia, Fortress, 1981), p. 222.
45 Benne, p. 74.
46 R. Lovin in D. Ford, ed., *The Modern Theologians*, vol. 2 (Blackwell 1989), p. 78.
47 Bennett, ed., p. 101.
48 Munby, *Christianity and Economic Problems*, p. 218.
49 J. Tinbergen in Munby, *Economic Growth in World Perspective*, p. 281.
50 J.P. Wogaman, *Christian Perspectives on Politics* (SCM Press 1988), p. 274.
51 Wogaman, p. 275.
52 Bennett, ed., p. 110.
53 Bennett, ibid.
54 Wogaman, p. 275.
55 See G. Dangerfield, *The Strange Death of Liberal England* (Constable 1936).
56 A. Buchanan, *Ethics, Efficiency and the Market* (Clarendon Press 1985), p. 117.
57 See Buchanan, pp. 104f.
58 Dorrien.
59 Buchanan, pp. 104f.
60 See Buchanan, p. 111.
61 Quoted in M. Novak, *The Spirit of Democratic Capitalism* (American Enterprise Institute/Simon & Schuster 1982), p. 207.
62 J. Sleeman, *Economic Crisis: A Christian Perspective* (SCM Press 1976), p. 174.
63 J. Sleeman, *Basic Economic Problems: A Christian Approach* (SCM Press 1953), p. 178.
64 J.K. Galbraith, *A History of Economics* (Penguin 1989), p. 295.
65 T.G. Ash, *We the People* (Granta Books 1990), p. 115.
66 T. Ash, p. 113.
67 Dahrendorf, p. 50.
68 Edwards, p. 184.
69 See Robert Benne's use of John Rawls to this end, in Benne's *The Ethic of Democratic Capitalism*, p. 64.
70 See John Atherton, *Faith in the Nation* on a participating and reciprocal society. It can be compared to Karl Popper's Open Society, as developed in Ralf Dahrendorf, but there are differences.
71 Benne, ibid.
72 Berger, p. 174.
73 Ash, p. 152.

74 Dahrendorf, pp. 2–3.
75 Bennett, ed., p. 213.
76 S. Hampshire, in Novak, p. 197.
77 J. Sleeman, p. 182.
78 Galbraith, p. 139.
79 For example, Dorrien.

Nine

Encompassing Markets and Challenges: The Way of Interaction

A free society needs constantly to consider and discuss its present reality in the light of its past traditions and where it wants to go.[1]

Even in the midst of the heady days of 1989 in Eastern Europe, many of the leaders of the uprisings realized that the journey had only just begun. How do you replace totalitarian command economies, entrenched for nearly two generations, with liberal democracies and market economies? Would people cope with the inevitable drastic dislocation of economic and social life? How do you change the habits of a lifetime? Certainly the leaders of the Czech Forum, meeting in the Magic Lantern Theatre, had some understanding of the harsh realities and dilemmas that lay ahead:

> Taken all in all, however, the central assembly of the Forum in the Czech lands was an impressive body. It was as democratic as it could reasonably be, in the circumstances. It was remarkably good-humoured. It showed a genius for improvisation. Profound differences of political orientation, faith and attitudes were generally subordinated to the common good. A reasonable balance was struck between the political and the moral imperatives.[2]

Deprived of 'the most basic possibilities of political articulation' for many decades, they were able to come together and say 'This is what we want, this is how the face of the new Czechoslovakia should look.'[3]

It was this ability to recognize that the next stage of the journey would involve hard political decisions and skills that was so remarkably refreshing. It is so easy for radical reformers to assume that ideals are sufficient for the task of rebuilding society. Yet balancing moral and political pressures is the unchanging project of all who wish to take the realities of life seriously. Dahrendorf, commenting on the events of 1989, compared them to the American and French revolutions two centuries before. It was a perceptive way of highlighting the perennial pressure to balance seemingly opposing demands. Thus he noted that 'the two revolutions set in motion the creative modern conflict between those who seek more entitlements and those who want more provisions, advocates of citizenship and advocates of growth, who between them (and sometimes together) serve to enhance the life chances of all'.[4] The apparent novelty of the revolutions of 1989, after careful reflection, appear to be as much about the playing out of historic themes and tensions as the introduction of new ones.

In so many ways, the agenda for Christian social witness follows these developments. For the market economy now occupies the high ground for Christian social thought in facing the contemporary context. Even radicals like Ulrich Duchrow, when they paint a scenario dominated by the increasing gulf between First and Third Worlds, indicate the growing importance of the global economy, and within it the central role of the market economy. That significance is confirmed by all the major Christian responses to the market economy – as much by those who reject it, as by those who affirm it. It is the convergence of this opinion that suggests that the global market economy will continue to be the overriding issue on the agenda of Church and society for the foreseeable future.

Engaging the global market economy cannot, however, be restricted to issues intrinsic to the market. It was the earlier discussion of basic economics and the market that suggested that the effective operating of the market economy involved more than a price mechanism. The state, democratic politics and supportive institutions and values, while extrinsic to the market, were all related intimately to it, and contributed to the modern understanding of the market economy. It is these external factors that while being part of the formation of the market economy, lead naturally into wider concerns which also act as independent and major challenges to the market economy. Some of them, like poverty and democratic politics, have long been connected historically to the emergence of market economies. Others, like the international reality and the environment, have gained a new importance in recent times. All of them raise questions that the market economy alone cannot answer, and that demand a response if the market economy is to develop as an effective contributor to the resolution of world problems and as a meaningful option for Christian discipleship.

There is, in other words, a powerful interactive relationship between the market and its major challenges which is central to any consideration of the contemporary market economy and to any development of Christian social thought. It is the nature of that relationship that now needs to be explored.

The relationship of market economies and challenges: towards a framework and dynamic for Christian social thought

Changing one's mind can be a sign of weakness, if it means following fashionable trends. It can reveal a lack of independent judgement. Yet to ignore developments in the modern context, to refuse to listen and learn from the changing realities of life, is a mistake of equal gravity. It is to be condemned to the eventual side-lines of history.

Christians, of course, regularly fall into both camps, committing along the way the inevitable mistakes of what Tawney referred to as dilution by the world or petrifaction by the elect.[5] Yet even those bold spirits who do respond to change positively and discerningly often find it impossible to also divest themselves of the hope of progressive change towards a unity of beliefs, understandings and practices. Change, yes. The unlikelihood of ever arriving at a destination on earth when all will be one, no.

William Temple's later life expresses this dilemma in a powerful and illuminating way. For much of his career, he had followed the evolutionary gradualism of incarnational theology. By the late 1930s, under the impact of economic depression, secularization, and an approaching World War, he had begun to take serious account of the crisis theology of Karl Barth and Reinhold Niebuhr's theological realism. In a famous article in 1939, called 'Theology Today',[6] he reflected on this change of mind and called for the digging of deeper theological foundations, in the spirit of F.D. Maurice.[7] So great were the upheavals in society

264

and theology that he felt 'The world of to-day is one of which no Christian maps can be made.' Yet even in the midst of such a changing world and such changing minds, he still felt the need to argue that there would come a time when theology would once again be able to construct a 'Christian map' of the world.[8]

It is that tendency to map-making, to gathering disparate parts into a harmonious whole, that now needs to be questioned. For someone brought up in the mainstream liberal tradition, that is no easy decision. For even that fine 'gathering' concept of the common good must be forgone[9] if we are to do justice to the survey of the market economy and its Christian responses. It is too closely associated with the liberal and other responses, and is too suggestive of a Christian synthesis, a Christian overview of the world. Even a provisional framework appears too close to the concern for a Christian map, and its inability to reflect the changing complexities of an increasingly plural world. Even the recognition of this danger by emphasizing a dynamic framework does not seem a sufficient counterbalance to the propensity of the common good, the responsible society, and the Christian map, to a static representation of the contemporary context. The more I considered these problems and needs, the more important became the actual nature of *the relationship* between market economy and its challenges. I believe it is out of this interactive process of the market and its challenges that the provisional framework and dynamic has to emerge, and the focus of the Christian concern has to develop.

Understanding the nature of the relationship between the market economy and its challenges has to be built on a recognition of their relative autonomy: *autonomy*, because they are significant in their own right, since neither can be submerged into the other, as the radical and conservative responses try to do; *relative*, because of the inevitability and necessity of their interaction.

Within that relationship, the market economy, as described in Part One, is the starting-point for the consideration of economic life in most of the world, and is likely to be so for the foreseeable future. That description included the market as mechanism, but also as system, with an international character, and connected to certain values, institutions and political democracy. As we have seen in Chapter 7 an ethical dimension is inextricably part of *all* these aspects of the market economy, including the mechanisms. It can never be relegated to the function of the challenges.[10]

Because of the complex nature of the market economy it impinges inevitably on social and political affairs, and is central to an effective consideration of matters in these areas. In the modern world, problems in these areas cannot be solved without reference to economics.[11] Similarly, for the market economy to be effective, including its continued development and change, requires its involvement with the great challenges. That effectiveness includes breaking out of the isolationist tendency of modern economics to 'misplaced concreteness'. Keynes illustrates this potential of the market to develop in response to the needs and demands of the changing context. Stimulated by the great depression, he challenged some of the basic principles of classical economics. The result was a more accurate analysis of economic processes, and economic policies for growth and higher employment. It is this ability to change and develop in response to external pressures that has helped to make the market economy such a dominant force in the contemporary context. This is in stark contrast to the actual performance of command economies, and the likely performance of proposals for radically different economies, including ecologically based ones.[12] It justifies its description as the least harmful way of operating an advanced economy, as yet known to us.

The other part of the relationship consists of the great challenges to the market economy. Like the market economy, they exist in their own right, even though connected inextricably to the market economy and to one another. An important part of their character and function is to represent that dimension of human experience described as yearning for the ultimate or the desire to transcend self.[13] Taken to greater lengths, this can become, as we have seen in Chapter 8, a passionate commitment to human causes, born of 'indignation with oppression', often with an apocalyptic character.[14] Some have regarded this element of radical criticism as an argument for the challenges always to be in permanent opposition. It has certainly meant that they have been regarded as 'morally laden' in ways the market has never been. As observed already, the validity of this claim should never be allowed to detract from the intrinsic moral claims of the market economy.

It is important too to acknowledge that the challenges are

more than moral countermovements. They are, for example, a recognition that adequate living in contemporary society cannot be sustained, and certainly not developed, from the basis of the market economy alone. The latter is a necessary but not sufficient foundation for satisfactory modern living. It is the recognition, seen by Habermas, that civil society is always more than a market economy.[15] The European Community's commitment to a free market and a social charter is an acknowledgement of this wider reality.[16] What it does not mean is that only one challenge is needed to provide that sufficiency. No one challenge, whether Benne's use of justice or Novak's use of democracy can make the market into a 'morally defensible arrangement'.[17]

Without the market economy and its challenges, the question of their relationship would be obviously irrelevant. Yet it is the nature of that relationship that is so important in its own right, and for its creation of a framework and dynamic for Christian social thought. Accepting the relative autonomy of the market and the challenges is essential for an adequate understanding of this connection, if only to ensure that neither over-intrudes on the other. When this does occur the result is invariably disastrous, particularly if the market over-monopolizes the situation as libertarian extremism. No society has been able to tolerate such a fatal obsession. Yet the danger comes not simply from Hayek or Friedman. It is more likely to emerge from those who regard 'the unabashed victory of economic and political liberalism'[18] in the late twentieth century as overcoming all external challenges to the market. The only difficulties that would remain would be intrinsic to the market, and these would be reduced to endless technical problems. There is no understanding that the human dimensions and social realities, represented by the challenges, are so significant that they cannot be collapsed into the market. However, the results are equally harmful if the challenges collectively, or more likely individually, are used to dominate the market economy. Such a course almost invariably leads to an authoritarian utopianism. Both tendencies overemphasize by excluding the other, and are rightly regarded with deep suspicion in modern Europe.[19]

Even when the nature of the relationship between relative autonomies is accepted, it can lead to false understandings. For example, it resulted in Galbraith declaring that 'the greatest dialectic of modern life [is] that between morality and the market'.[20] Such a judgement now profoundly underestimates the complexity, including the ethical side, of the market economy in contemporary society and the great challenges to it. Morality impinges on both market and challenges. It is not an autonomous reality in the dialectical process. It is just such a conclusion that suggests a general unease with a too obvious and simple resort to the dialectical tool in the development of modern Christian social thought. Central to the crisis theology of Karl Barth and the theological realism of Reinhold Niebuhr, it has also been used recently by Alan Suggate in his work on Temple and theological method. Preston is right to warn against its overuse and misuse, preferring the less precise concept of the reciprocal.

At first sight such a judgement might appear inappropriate. The dialectical tool seems particularly fitted to denote the relationship between market as thesis and the challenges as antithesis, so that out of their interaction could emerge a new synthesis. Yet it should be apparent by now that such a use and such a conclusion is singularly inappropriate for the realities and relationships we are now confronting. The nature and function of market and challenges, and their relationships, have been seen to generate a variety and complexity that cannot be reduced to a dialectical model. To do so would be to impose restrictive patterns on very plural realities.

More importantly, there are strong arguments that market and challenges have always performed a mutually corrective function.[21] It is as though there is a general recognition of the need for perpetual dialogue and conversation between the kind of realities represented by market and challenges. To push them as arguments to their logical conclusion could so easily lead to the domination of either.[22] Maintaining the interaction between them appears to be essential for avoiding the dangers of a deified pragmatism, regarding economic principles as God's laws, or of an authoritarian utopianism, ignoring 'the empirical contours of human existence'.[23]

What therefore emerges at this stage is rather a symbiotic relationship which is continually bringing 'the two worlds into intimate conversation',[24] a truncated dialectic that persists in holding the tension between contradictory and complementary realities rather than seeking to deliver a fabricated synthesis. It describes a relationship between two realities which is profoundly contingent rather than essentially causal.[25] It leads to a complex of interactions, of perpetually unfinished achievements, of what can be described as 'the right kind of inconsistency'. It is but a firm recognition that 'one dimensional solutions to the dilemmas are not only wrong but impossible . . .'[26]

One of the important problems emerging from such understandings concerns their implications for the human and Christian concern for a common language to encompass them. Yet that can so easily be but another way of formulating the promotion of the common good, with all its attendant dangers of the Christian imperative for new paradigms.[27] Living in a perpetual interim is never the time to promote new unifying metaphysics,[28] but instead to recognize the profound inadequacy of traditional moral discourse. It is a time to recognize the contribution of various traditions, and not to seek to reformulate any one of them. They can no longer bear the weight of the complexity and plurality of the demands of the contemporary context. The task is rather to encourage provisional frameworks and dynamics to reflect this interaction. It is in relation to this that we can then bring the 'traditions, ideals and aspirations of society into juxtaposition with its present reality'.[29]

Given the thrust of the interaction between market and challenges, a framework and dynamic can only reflect these features and movement. Anything more would be too resonant of the simpler harmonies and unities so characteristic of pre-modern societies. The complexities and pluralities of the contemporary context, with its intrinsic conflicts of interest and fragmentation of culture and religion, make it too unrealistic to promote a common good in general, or as particularized versions like the responsible society, or the later just, participatory and sustainable society. 'The framework which binds us together in our complex world is much more subtle than to be comprehended in some simple principle.'[30]

With these warnings, a framework reflecting interactions has a legitimacy and value; a legitimacy because it relates more accurately to the actual realities of the contemporary context, and value because it enables people to express themselves in relation to it, without being dominated by it. The right sort of security is essential for enabling this to happen.[31] Indeed, this is but another way of acknowledging that the primary task is not about morality as traditionally pursued; it is rather about frameworks and dynamic, and the nature and contribution of morality within them. Such a framework, recognizing market and challenges, and ethics percolating both, is a way of preventing theologians from slipping too easily 'from the analytical to the moral, and from the contemporary to the eternal'.[32]

What is also difficult for theology to come to terms with is the requirement of provisionality as an essential part of the framework's character. The world is now too complex, plural and constantly changing for us to sustain universally valid overviews. They can never be regarded as permanent, especially as the basis for future action. What actually happens is never exactly what the reformer envisages. Unintended consequences, as Adam Smith realized, are often as important as the intended. Both have to be allowed for, by a provisional framework reflecting the interactive process. It enables a more purposeful living in between the times.

The character of interaction puts as high a premium, if not higher, on the dynamic of Christian social thought as on the framework. The entire process is essentially about institutions in constant transformation; it is not about an economics seeking eternal verities.[33] It is therefore a profoundly uncomfortable view to come to terms with for those Christians who, like Griffiths and Duchrow, have only accepted post-Renaissance and post-Enlightenment man in half-hearted ways.[34]

The commitment to a dynamic of Christian social thought is both a reflection of the contemporary context, and an attempt thereby to engage it more effectively. For that to be achieved requires, as Moltmann observes, the recognition that 'a thing is alive only when it contains contradiction in itself and is indeed the power of holding the contradiction in itself and enduring it'.[35] It is an acknowledgement that the market economy is in a process of constant change, never moving towards the perfection of final systems which are always formulae for disobedience and the accumulation of error. There is no place for a Hayek, Marx or a Temple. For because of this commitment to dynamic as well as framework, adjusting to both is never about developing a new equilibrium, so beloved of classical economics and Christian social thought. At most, it can only be about relating to essentially *moving* equilibriums. Yet through such involvements for change a profound sense of hope can be generated.[36] It becomes a journey into an uncertain future, where we often have to work by trial and error.[37]

A way of life?

A leading American Christian social thinker observed that the heirs of the social gospel were prepared 'to undertake the investigation even if it led them beyond the recognized boundaries of Christian truth and even if it called into question their own virtues and the virtues of the people they sought to help'.[38] It is such a view of Christian discipleship as going beyond traditional enclosures that is suggested by the interactive process. In itself, it relates to the mainstream liberal tradition and its development from the social gospel. It also resonates with the conservative and radical responses, since they too give a prominent place to the contribution of a way of life to their total schema. However, in so many other regards, it differs profoundly from all three responses.

What does the interactive process suggest for the life of Christian social witness? It is certainly about living in a likely permanent interim, given the rate of change in, and increasing complexity of, society. The dynamic of life is now such as to render redundant within only a few years even semi-permanent models of Christian overviews and lifestyles. It therefore suggests a way of living quite different from past traditions of moral and spiritual discourse, most of which are profoundly pre-modern in character. It indicates instead a way which is 'untidy, antagonistic, uncomfortable'[39] and always unfinished because always changing. It is a way of living that manifests the continuing interaction between market and challenges by being an integral part of it and so able to transcend it. It always has to be a way of compromise, and yet market and challenges contain perspectives that seek to question and move beyond contemporary realities. In consequence, it is a way of living that is well-suited to arise out of the struggle to live in and for liberal democracies and market economies in their involvement with the great challenges of our world.

Clearly, these insights represent only a restricted and unfinished view of Christian discipleship as traditionally understood. To do more is beyond the intention of this project and of my skills. More importantly, it would divert attention from the primary importance of the interactive process and its manifestation in frameworks and dynamics. It would begin to produce a way of life of substance, with all its propensity to develop independently rather than as part and parcel of the interactive processes in the contemporary context.

What can be done, however, is to elaborate a little further the nature of interactive discipleship by noting what becomes unacceptable. We can learn as much from negatives as positives in a period of rapid change, when improvization and therefore mistakes are inevitably and necessarily part of our involvements.

What then does such social discipleship not involve? Firstly, interim living cannot be derived from any one Christian tradition or response, however much attempts are made to reformulate them in the light of our changing context. It always draws from a variety of responses because none can capture the complexity and plurality of the contemporary. Secondly, living in the interim, in and through provisional frameworks and dynamics, removes the impetus for the traditional search for the distinctively Christian, the mythical holy grail of Christian social thought. Christian tradition contains much that is clearly relevant to economic affairs as the analysis of the responses has revealed, yet it does not offer 'answers that others have failed to see'.[40] Instead, it frees us to share fully in what is actually going on in the world from the perspective of Christian belief. Thirdly, facing the bleak realities of the contemporary challenges, including interaction with the market economy, can never condone the usual retreat into 'realpolitik and pietism'.[41] So much in all three Christian responses can produce variations of this in actual practice. It is one of the more fortunate consequences of the interactive process that it obliges us to focus our attention no longer on the division between morality and market, challenges and market, or whatever other dualism arises. For these invariably become diversions from entering into life with full commitment to faithful Christian living. Our concern is rather with the interaction between market and challenges, and then with the provisional framework and dynamics related to it. There should be no deviation from that task, and certainly not under the guise of spirituality, theology or Christian social ethics.

Addendum: Church and theology in the interactive process

As we have seen, engaging the contemporary context is significantly about understanding the relationship between market economy and challenges. It is into that whole process that the development of the Church and Christian social thought should be woven. The results would be far-reaching for the Church's social witness in the contemporary world, and for the interpretation of theological method.

The Church

There has been a tendency in the West, and certainly in Britain, for the Churches to be bound to the established orderings of society while retaining the freedom to be critical of harmful social tendencies and policies. It has been described as a relationship of critical solidarity.[42] This exploration of the market economy and its Christian responses suggests that such a concept is erroneous as a description of existing practice and as a preferred way of engaging the interactive process. It is illusory because for many generations the official Churches have not been in solidarity with the market economy as the heart of the contemporary social order. They have neither understood nor acknowledged it as the *positively* least harmful way of operating a modern economy. The criticisms of Thatcherite excesses by church governing bodies, social responsibility functions and church leaders in the last decade only accentuated an existing tendency. They never communicated a primary commitment to the market in relation to which criticisms clearly had a legitimate and necessary place. Of course, the established Churches have retained the illusion of being intimately part of the trappings of the established orderings. Yet, as society becomes more secular and plural (and particularly the latter, as a multi-faith and multi-cultural society), even that justification falls. The inability to engage the market economy constructively is at least as damaging for this case of being in supposed solidarity with the contemporary social orderings.

Much more disturbing is the challenge of the interactive process for what should be the form of the relationship between Church and governing authorities. For the combination of market economies and liberal democracies is invariably productive of at least a more open and secular society. The framework and dynamic emerging from the interaction of market and challenges emphasizes the purposeful yet provisional nature of tendencies and partial achievements. The commitment to liberal democracies and market economies as the least harmful ways as yet known to us for operating modern societies illustrates this dedication to a negativity inspired by positive deeds.[43] The promotion of basic civil, political and economic liberties is nothing less than that.

What such a commitment does not suggest, of course, is any understanding of an homogenous society expressed through concepts like the common good. Even more so, it rules out of court once and for all the pursuit of a distinctively Christian society: what T.S. Eliot called 'a Christian community . . . in which there is a unified religious-social code of behaviour.'[44] Both in the end assert the primacy of Christian values in the interactive process.

Interestingly, the early history of the established Churches and the persistence of the Christendom ethos overlap with the contemporary concern for the Church to rediscover a distinctive role in society. This has developed frequently into arguments for a more sectarian understanding of the Church, which is based, for example, on a confessional stance against the market on behalf of the poor. Moltmann therefore argues that, 'The more the church moves from being a church bound to the state to a free church, the clearer can become its witness to peace and the less ambiguous its initiative for peace'.[45] In reality, such convictions are more likely to result in the promoting of the Church as small groups with a prophetic function. Even though the Church will always have to relate to the state, with all the compromises that involves, such groups still 'demand that the whole Church shall act with them'.[46] Once again there is little understanding of the processes of the modern market and economics. There is little capacity for a public theology. In contrast to the official Churches, this distancing from the established economic order is much more clearly related to the great challenges. Both are joined in a commitment to the priority of Christian values over secular realities. Both seek 'to restore a sense of moral authority and an idea of moral obedience in a field from which the moral law as a guiding principle has been almost wholly dismissed'.[47]

It is precisely at this point that the way of interaction rejects the stances of both official Churches and the more radical ecclesiastical alternatives: on the one hand, it stands against the official Churches' commitment to Christian values which leads them to misunderstand and marginalize the nature of modern economics and markets. Consequently, it dismisses their retention of the form of establishment because it lacks the theological substance of an adequate understanding of the social order as market economy and liberal democracy. On the other hand, it conflicts with the radical Churches' promotion of the great challenges (especially the poor) as the Christian project, when they are manifestly incapable of operating a modern economy. Their way is the equivalent of persisting with economic socialism as the human project, and is equally doomed to failure.

What therefore emerges out of the interactive process is the requirement of Churches in the West to be able to take seriously the framework and dynamic of market and challenges. On this basis, it is increasingly unlikely that this can be developed by the existing mind-set of the established Churches. Churches may need to become more free-standing in order to begin to learn again what public theology and church witness in the public realm requires. Of course, such a form of disestablishment is not about becoming free in order to be radically critical of the economic order. The Free Churches and Roman Catholics in Britain suffer from exactly the same weaknesses of economic misunderstandings as the established Churches. It is rather about becoming free in order to engage the market and its challenges, holding the market, at the moment, as the principal partner in that process. It is about being open to whatever might emerge out of that dynamic interaction. It is about taking the contemporary context so seriously that we can engage the future with realism and therefore hope.

Such a free-standing Church will inevitably influence the character of Christian discipleship. Consistency itself requires it should reflect a commitment to free-standing men and women. For people need to be able to develop free-standing relationships to the Church as well as to the context. The way of interaction suggests one such framework and dynamic for supporting such necessary encounters. What it does not support, is the way of moving from the Church, from Christian beliefs, to the context. It is not a matter that: 'In order to repair the breach between faith and everyday life, we must act in the world of everyday life from within the world of faith.'[48] It is rather about Christian men and women inhabiting and engaging both communities of memory and context, and thereby engaging the interactive process itself. But that leads us to the nature of theological reflection in that process.

Theology

Just over fifty years after Walter Rauschenbusch commented so perceptively on the British scene, another American theologian repeated the exercise. Writing in 1943, Reinhold Niebuhr discussed what he called the curious inconsistency in British, as against American, Christian social thought. He observed how our social pronouncements seemed to be taken from the utopian pages of the American social gospel. In contrast, he judged our involvement in political realities to be far more effective and accurate. That inconsistency he also traced in our political life: the distinctive British 'political art has always been shrewder in weighing the realities of a given political situation than political science has been in stating the principles by which the realities must be interpreted'.[49]

Fifty years later the position has not changed in terms of theology. There is still a .'curious inconsistency' between the ordinary Christian experience of political and economic life and the statements of official Churches, leaders and theologians. Yet that inconsistency need not persist. In a fine introduction to *British Theology Through Philosophy*,[50] Daniel Hardy examines its distinctive character. He notes, with great sensitivity, its historic character as 'present organised practice', particularly as developed by Richard Hooker at the end of the sixteenth century. In the struggle to build a public theology for a comprehensive Church, theologians were unable to appeal to the Bible if they were to retain the support of the Roman Catholics, and unable to use natural law because of the Protestant constituency. Consequently, the task was to elaborate present organized practice in Church and society, as interpreted critically through corporate prayer, the Bible, Christian tradition and reason. Unfortunately, today's Church now interprets present organized practice as the religious life of religious people, and not also as the common life of the nation. The exciting possibility before us is therefore to establish once again Christian social thought as part of present organized practice by facing up to what Niebuhr called the curious inconsistency between British Christian thought and practice.

The entry point to that task is provided by the contemporary context, by our addressing the central importance of the market economy and its relationship with the great challenges. Facing the questions influencing all our lives means we may once again, in F.D. Maurice's words, 'be of much use to our generation'. It would contribute to building a common agenda with people and society. It could become the basis of Christian social thought as part of the present organized practice of Church and nation.

Working on the complexities of modern economics and market engenders a whole series of insights, constraints and possibilities. Appraising Christian responses to the market enriches these understandings, and begins to suggest ways of developing an appropriate framework and dynamic, built on market and challenges. It is the sum total of these experiences that suggests the pivotal importance of operative realities.

For doing what seems most practical affects theory and practice. Thus responding to economic problems has played an important part in the development of economic theories;[51] constructing modern social market economies means paying increasing attention to the trade-offs between efficiency and equity.[52] They all suggest the importance of coming to terms with pragmatism.

The first Professor of Economic History at Manchester University, George Unwin, and friend of R.H. Tawney, glimpsed this understanding of social thought. He argued that political and economic skills were in themselves part of the British moralist's craft. The problem was precisely how to relate moral theory and practice. For him this could only be done by 'the confidence acquired in long practice', not 'by logic. And the peculiarity of the English character is that it is based on a much longer continuous practice than that of any other people.'[53]

For Christian social thought, it becomes a way of facing up to Niebuhr's 'obvious inconsistency' between effective practical skill and ineffective theory. Interestingly, Cardinal Newman's understanding of the illative sense similarly emphasized the collective practical wisdom of tradition for the development of faith, rather than the narrow deductively logical attempts to prove God's existence.[54] It is also close to the Protestant

277

tradition of dissent, and a 'kind of empiricism, practicality, and respect for democratic compromise'.[55] Perhaps even more helpful is Richard Niebuhr's concept of the 'fitting act'. In contrast to traditional moral judgements, it emphasizes the primary importance of involvement informed by critical dialogue with Christian insights. Discovering the fitting act can therefore 'never be discerned without painstaking and rational analysis of the context in which it must fit, that is, of economics and politics . . .'[56] Tillich called it 'faithful realism', because it helps us to avoid the faithless realism of an exclusive focus on the market and the unrealistic idealism of a similar focus on the challenges.[57] Both fitting act and faithful realism support Christian social thought as addressing the contemporary context. They present more authentic and appropriate concepts than the ugly imposed use of praxis.

Of course, facing up to the present organized practice of market and challenges does more than suggest a way of developing Christian social thought and practice. It also reveals major defects in traditional Christian interpretations of realities like the market economy. For all three responses to the market, and particularly the radical and conservative ones, subordinate economic realities to Christian values. Even the liberal response reveals such a weakness with its commitment to Christian principles standing between great but vague Christian imperatives like justice, and the particular demands of a situation. For in the end the movement is always *from* the insights of faith *to* the realities of life. The market mechanism has no value in itself. It is always regarded ultimately as the servile drudge of wider social purposes; and these are always informed by Christian demands.

In contrast, the way of interaction recognizes the legitimate contribution of economics to the formation of Christian social thought, just as it acknowledges the contribution of Scripture and Christian tradition. Accepting the relative autonomy of economics and religion is an indispensable prerequisite for both engaging the contemporary economy, and developing Christian social thought in and through it. Most Christians accept the contribution of Christian tradition to that process. Few have really understood the equal importance of the contribution of secular realities and disciplines. Baron von Hugel, the great interpreter of modern spirituality, did precisely that. For he accepted that through the creative process, 'God has somehow alienated a certain amount of His own power and given it a relative independence of its own . . .' As a result, 'Creation will never be absorbed in the Creator, nor man, even the God-man, become (or become again) simply and purely God . . .'

The implication of these insights for our understanding of economics are immense. For never again will economics, science, morals or politics, 'be without each their own inside, their own true law of growth and existence *other than, in no wise a department or simple dependency of religion* . . .'[58] If God's purposes are mediated to us through such realities as well as through Christian tradition, it is surely out of the interaction between them that Christian social thought emerges.

The result is that we can be liberated from the impulsive desire to produce the distinctively Christian, when addressing such matters as the contemporary economy. We can reject with confidence those pre-modern attempts to impose, however decisively or subtly, religious understandings on secular life. Whether they take the form of Roman Catholic social encyclicals, biblically based systems, liberation theology, the confessional theology of the World Council of Churches, or even the social principles of the mainstream liberal tradition, we are freed to learn from them – and yet freed to move beyond them.

What we are left with is the contemporary context, and the continuing interaction between market and challenges. What we are left with is a Christian social thought that develops in and through that process. For that development also reflects the dynamic interaction between the understanding of God's purposes mediated through Christian tradition, but equally through the secular realities of life. What this argument has tried to do is to illustrate particularly the contribution of the latter to the development of Christian social thought. So many concentrate on the former that such a correction is long overdue. Indeed, some will believe it to be of greater importance if Christian social thought is to come to terms with modern thought and practice in the way other branches of theology have tried to do. The result may look and feel essentially reflective of the contemporary context. That is the intention. In so doing it will share in the ambiguities of Reinhold Niebuhr's much greater book, *Moral Man and Immoral Society*. For many years this book failed to find a British publisher. 'The Christian ones thought it not a Christian book and the secular ones would not take risks . . .'[59] That is a necessary and worthy price for taking the contemporary context seriously.

Notes

1 R. Bellah, ed., *Habits of the Heart* (New York, Harper & Row, 1986), p. 307.
2 T.G. Ash, *We The People: The Revolution of 89* (Granta Books 1990), p. 128.
3 Ash, ibid.
4 R. Dahrendorf, *Reflections on the Revolution in Europe* (Chatto & Windus 1991), p. 24.
5 Quoted in R.H. Preston, *Religion and the Persistence of Capitalism* (SCM Press 1979), p. 87.
6 In *Theology* (November 1939).
7 'My sole vocation is metaphysical and theological grubbing' (F. Maurice, *Life*, vol. ii, p. 295).
8 Quoted in A. Suggate, *William Temple* (T. & T. Clark 1987), p. 63.
9 This was a central concept in my *Faith in the Nation* (SPCK 1988).
10 The Christian engagement with the libertarians, in response to the latter's claims that the market is amoral because no moral claims are intended, can give support to this departmentalizing. The libertarian understanding of the market is essentially an aberration and should not divert Christian judgement from the much more plural nature of the contemporary market economy. Plant has perhaps fallen into this trap. See Plant in J.C.D. Clark, ed., *Ideas and Politics in Modern Britain* (Macmillan 1990).
11 H. Daly and J. Cobb, *For The Common Good* (Merlin Press 1990), p. 124.
12 For the latter, see Daly and Cobb.
13 D.L. Munby, like Reinhold Niebuhr, talks of the dual nature of man as 'firmly settled in his specific physical and historical environment, and at the same time filled with yearnings for an ultimate world beyond this', (*The Idea of a Secular Society and its Significance for Christians* (Oxford University Press 1963), p. 63).
14 A.D. Lindsay, *Christianity and Economics* (Macmillan 1933), p. 116.
15 In Dahrendorf, pp. 121f.
16 D. Edwards, *Christians in a New Europe* (Collins 1990), pp. 51f.
17 See R. Benne, *The Ethic of Democratic Capitalism: A Moral Reassessment* (Philadelphia, Fortress, 1981) and M. Novak, *The Spirit of Democratic Capitalism* (American Enterprise Institute/Simon & Schuster 1982).
18 Dahrendorf, pp. 33f, referring to Fukuyama's thesis, of the US state department, published in an article entitled 'The End of History' (1989).
19 'Nowadays no one in Europe really wants uniformity in politics or religion' (Edwards, p. 13).
20 Quoted in J.K. Galbraith, *A History of Economics: the Past as the Present* (Penguin 1989), p. 26.

21 J. Bennett, ed., *Christian Values and Economic Life* (New York, Harper, 1954), p. xiv. For example, 'The economist often provides a corrective for misguided idealism . . .'
22 See J. Sleeman, *Economic Crisis: A Christian Perspective* (SCM Press 1976), p. 17.
23 P. Berger, *The Capitalist Revolution: Fifty Propositions about Prosperity, Equality and Liberty* (Wildwood House 1987), p. 222.
24 C. Strain, ed., *Prophetic Visions and Economic Realities: Protestants, Jews and Catholics Confront the Bishops' Letter on the Economy* (Grand Rapids, MI, Eerdmans, 1989), p. 11.
25 This is Hole's interesting verdict on the relationship between theology and politics in the late eighteenth century, as against Clark's judgement that it was principally causal. The latter is more concerned to establish the distinctive contribution of Anglican theology to the political processes, in contrast to the liberal–Left historians who neglected it (R. Hole, *Pulpits, Politics and Public Order in England 1760-1832* (Cambridge University Press 1989) p. 268).
26 Wogaman, p. 271.
27 De Tocqueville talked of 'a new political science' for 'a world itself quite new', but in the early nineteenth century (R. Bellah, p. 297). Compare A. Storkey, *Transforming Economics: A Christian Way to Employment* (SPCK 1986), pp. 197f, and my own *Faith in the Nation*, p. 69.
28 Argued by M. Stackhouse in *Public Theology and Political Economy: Christian Stewardship in Modern Society* (Grand Rapids, MI, Eerdmans, 1987).
29 Bellah, p. 301.
30 Munby continues: 'Just as modern society does not cohere because of a common set of beliefs, and gains much from the richness of conflicting beliefs, so there is no one principle of organisation . . .' (D.L. Munby, *God and the Rich Society* (Oxford University Press 1961), p. 132).
31 D.L. Munby, *Christianity and Economic Problems* (Macmillan 1956), p. 255.
32 Munby's accusation against Coleridge in *The Idea of a Secular Society*, p. 39.
33 The early nineteenth-century German economist List (1789–1846) held such a view, in contrast to Smith's (Galbraith, pp. 93–4).
34 Munby, *Christianity and Economic Problems*, p. 257.
35 In G. Dorrien, *Reconstructing the Common Good: Theology and the Social Order* (New York, Orbis 1990) p. 85.
36 Supporting Coleridge, Munby stresses the importance of hope as 'the fact that a society which is aware of the reality of continuous economic and social change, as well as of the possibilities of democratic political action, gives discontented groups hope that they will be able to alter conditions to their liking' (Munby, *The Idea of a Secular Society*, p. 51).
37 Ralf Dahrendorf writes similarly of an open society, in *Reflections on the Revolution in Europe*, p. 37.
38 D. Ford, ed., *The Modern Theologians*, vol. 2 (Blackwell 1989), p. 87, chapter by Robin Lovin.
39 Dahrendorf, p. 25.
40 Munby, *Christianity and Economic Problems*, p. 268.
41 Munby, *God and the Rich Society*, p. 198.

42 G.S. Ecclestone, *The Church of England and Politics* (CIO Publishing 1981).

43 D.L. Munby talks similarly of a secular society: 'It has not escaped comment that descriptions such as mine are negative, in that they point more to the differences from previous societies and to the absence of traditional restraints than to anything positive. This is inevitably the case, given the nature of what is at stake. The positive aims of a sacred society, whether traditional or modern totalitarian, can be stated fairly simply. There are almost by definition no positive aims of a liberal secular society. But this is not to say that no positive ideals animate these rather negative aims' (D.L. Munby, *The Idea of a Secular Society and its Significance for Christians* (Oxford University Press 1963), p. 32).

44 Munby, *The Idea of a Secular Society*, p. 19.

45 Quoted in Dorrien, p. 95.

46 A.D. Lindsay, *Christianity and Economics* (Macmillan 1933), p. 145.

47 D.L. Munby criticizing the attempt of church leaders to reimpose moral rules on society. The position has not changed (see Munby, *God and the Rich Society*, p. 168).

48 L. Fein in Strain, ed., p. 122.

49 R. Niebuhr, editorial in *Christianity and Society* (1943, vol. 8, no. 3).

50 Ford, ed., vol. 2, pp. 30f.

51 Galbraith, p. 2.

52 See Buchanan.

53 G. Unwin, *A Note on English Character*, p. 450, cited in J. Atherton, 'R.H. Tawney as a Christian Social Moralist', Ph.D. thesis (University of Manchester 1979), p. 154.

54 See Quinton, p. 77.

55 Novak, p. 330.

56 Munby, ed., *World Development: Challenge to the Churches*, p. 98.

57 In Dorrien, p. 59.

58 Quoted in Lindsay, pp. 29–30.

59 Ronald Preston's 'note' in *Moral Man and Immoral Society*, in the first British edition (SCM Press 1963). It was published in the USA in 1932!

Postscript

Changing Minds

It is only the wisest and the stupidest who do not change
(Confucius).[1]

On what Karl Barth called 'a black day' in August 1914, ninety-three German intellectuals openly proclaimed their support for the Kaiser's war ambitions. To his horror, Barth discovered his former professors of theology were on the list. It was the final straw. If their theology led them to support such a manifestly unjust cause, then their liberal theology had to be jettisoned. So Barth changed his mind. A new chapter in the history of theology began, centred on the Bible as 'God's view of man' rather than as 'man's view of God'.[2]

Changing one's mind of course is often about facing up to one's mistakes.[3] The movement to the Right represented by some of the important apologists for the market economy exhibits all the signs of such a road to Damascus conversion.[4] Some regard the transformation as illustrative of a new commitment to the dynamic changing reality of the market. One of the most notable, Michael Novak, rightly observes how: 'The spirit of democratic capitalism is the spirit of development, risk, experiment, adventure.'[5]

Sadly, such conversions are so often a case of 'once bitten, forever smitten'. They rarely become a personal commitment to continual change. They invariably become the way of predictability. There is nothing sadder than knowing what a person is going to say before the book is even opened. And it is a deficiency existing in fields much wider than the Christian neo-conservative response. It is to be found equally in the radical and liberal responses. A simple personal story illustrates what the continuing change of mind can mean for the development of Christian social thought.

The place is 10 Downing Street. Gathered around the dining table in one of the splendid historic state rooms are a group of senior Conservatives, led by the Prime Minister Mrs Thatcher, church leaders and theologians. Most of them have been meeting for two years to promote a dialogue between the Established Church and the Conservative Party. Against a background of deep official hostility, it was important to form friendships across the divide of Church and state in the 1980s. Even more valuable was the opportunity to explore underlying differences. At the final dinner, members shared their judgement of the whole process. I ventured to describe how I had been helped greatly to understand market systems better. I regarded it as a significant contribution to a continuing 'personal intellectual pilgrimage'.[6] I waited for the conservative members of the group to share how they too had changed their minds as part of the rich process of dialogue. Sadly, not a glimmer of such change emerged in the presentation.

I went away from that meeting somewhat chastened, for my life has become increasingly a journey of openness to change. For example, by the end of the 1970s I had become more and more aware of the persistence and challenge of poverty in Britain. A series of articles and books, and the founding of the national pressure group, Church Action on Poverty, was the outcome of this growing awareness.[7]

Immersion in the Archbishop's Commission on Urban Priority Areas in the early 1980s began another stage of growth. Again, so much was learned, and so many friendships and collaborations were formed. Out of them all emerged *Faith in the Nation* in 1988, partly as an attempt to chart the weaknesses as well as the strengths of the official church responses to contemporary change. It represented the movement beyond an undue concentration on poverty by locating it in the wider framework of a Christian social vision for Britain. The next four years saw me driven to explore the nature of the market economy. For most of the 1980s I had become increasingly aware that economic processes lay at the heart of contemporary change, with all its disturbing as well as liberating consequences. It is out of such experience that this book has emerged.

In other words, responding to a changing context has become the catalyst for personal change and development. (Not, may I add, from socialism to conservatism, as many suspect!) Even the periods when the changes began can be easily identified. That is why the idea of continual change, and of a provisional framework and dynamic of market and challenges, is so personally convincing. They become both the expression of a changing response to a changing context, and the means for participating purposefully in it.

What will happen as a result I do not know. Neither do I know what the next change of mind will be. What I do know is that I could never write a book on 'How I Changed My Mind', as Barth did. For that is to suggest a once-for-all transformation. It would contradict the whole character of the way of interaction. Responding to contemporary change is always about changing minds. When that no longer happens, either mortal death or death as intellectual petrifaction will have occurred.

Notes

1 Quoted in P. Berger, *The Capitalist Revolution: Fifty Propositions about Prosperity, Equality and Liberty* (Wildwood House 1987), p. 167.
2 K. Barth, *How I Changed My Mind*, introduction and epilogue by J.D. Godsey (St Andrew Press 1966), p. 22.
3 J.F. Sleeman, *Economic Crisis: A Christian Perspective* (SCM Press 1976), p. 20.
4 For example, Paul Johnson, Michael Novak, Peter Berger and Robert Benne.
5 M. Novak, *The American Vision: An Essay on the Future of Democratic Capitalism* (The American Enterprise Institute for Public Policy Research 1978, 1982 edn), p. 48.
6 D. Hay, *Economics Today* (Apollos 1989), p. 8.
7 Reflected in my 'Religion and the Persistence of Poverty', in M. Taylor, ed., *Christians and the Future of Social Democracy* (Hesketh 1982); *The Scandal of Poverty: Priorities for the Emerging Church* (Mowbray 1983).

Select Bibliography

The principal sources used in this study will be found in the Notes at the end of each chapter. However, given the pressure of time on most people I have suggested a more concise and manageable way into this complex area of life.

Economics

This is a daunting issue for most people. By using different perspectives on the subject, their cumulative effect can begin to overcome this fear and ignorance.

Simple, clear introductions:

Gertrude Williams, *The Economics of Everyday Life*. Penguin 1951.
Peter Donaldson, *Economics of the Real World*. BBC and Penguin 1973.
John K. Galbraith, *A History of Economics: The Past as Present*. Penguin 1989.

Christian economists (noting their interpretation of economics rather than their theology):

Denys L. Munby, *Christianity and Economic Problems*. Macmillan 1956.
John F. Sleeman, *Basic Economic Problems: A Christian Approach*. SCM Press 1953.
Donald Hay, *Economics Today: A Christian Critique*. Apollos 1989.

More specialist books:

Allen Buchanan, *Ethics, Efficiency and the Market*. Clarendon Press 1985.
Julian Le Grand and Ray Robinson, *The Economics of Social Problems*. Macmillan 1976.

Christian Responses to Market Economics

These are built on a mixture of contemporary interpretations, and historical surveys. They also contribute to developing our understanding of economics.

Conservative Responses

Brian Griffiths, *Morality and the Market Place: Christian Alternatives to Capitalism and Socialism*. Hodder & Stoughton 1982.

Michael Novak, *The Spirit of Democratic Capitalism*. American Enterprise Institute/Simon and Schuster 1982.

Peter Berger, *The Capitalist Revolution: Fifty Propositions about Prosperity, Equality and Liberty*. Wildwood House 1987.

Alan M.C. Waterman, *Revolution, Economics and Religion: Christian Political Economy, 1798–1833*. Cambridge University Press 1991.

Boyd Hilton, *The Age of Atonement: The Influence of Evangelicalism on Social and Economic Thought, 1785–1865*. Clarendon Press 1988.

Radical Responses

Ulrich Duchrow, *Global Economy: A Confessional Issue for the Churches?* WCC Publications 1987.

Gary J. Dorrien, *Reconstructing the Common Good: Theology and the Social Order*. Orbis Books 1990. This includes good chapters on the leaders of European Christian Socialism (Tillich and Moltmann), the social gospel (Rauschenbusch) and liberation theology (Bonino and Gutierrez).

On the social gospel, Dorrien, above; also:

Max L. Stackhouse, *Public Theology and Political Economy*. Grand Rapids MI, Eerdmans, 1987.

C.H. Hopkins, *The Rise of the Social Gospel in American Protestantism*. 1865–1915, Yale 1940.

On Christian socialism:

E.R. Norman, *The Victorian Christian Socialists*. Cambridge University Press 1987.

Torben Christensen, *Origin and History of Christian Socialism, 1848–54*. Aarhus 1962.

Peter d'A. Jones, *The Christian Socialist Revival, 1877–1914*: Religion, Class and Social Conscience in Late-Victorian England. Princeton University Press 1968.

Liberal Responses

J.P. Wogaman, *Christian Perspectives on Politics*. SCM Press 1988.
J.P. Wogaman, *Christians and the Great Economic Debate*. SCM Press 1977.
Ronald H. Preston, *Religion and the Persistence of Capitalism*. SCM Press 1979.

General

There has been a spate of recent books in this field, written from a variety of perspectives. They include:

M. Alison and D. Edwards, eds., *Christianity and Conservatism: Are Christianity and Conservatism Compatible?*. Hodder & Stoughton 1990.
John Atherton, ed., *Social Christianity: A Reader*. SPCK 1993.
M. Douglas Meeks, *God the Economist: The Doctrine of God and Political Economy*. Philadelphia, Fortress, 1989. In the radical tradition.
Ronald H. Preston, *Religion and the Ambiguities of Capitalism*. SCM Press 1991.
Charles R. Strain, ed., *Prophetic Visions and Economic Realities: Protestants, Jews, and Catholics Confront the Bishops' Letter on the Economy*. Grand Rapids, MI, Eerdmans 1989.
Robert N. Bellah, ed., *Habits of the Heart: Individualism and Commitment in American Life*. New York, Harper and Row, 1986.
Herman Daly and John Cobb, *For the Common Good: Redirecting the Economy toward Community, the Environment, and a Sustainable Future*. Merlin Press 1990.

Index

conservative response: in general 20, ch. 4 *passim*, 217, 218, 225, 265, 271, 278, 283; characteristics 87–90; history as Christian political economy 99–109; as Church 109–10; as theology 111–12, 195; strengths and limitations 193–5

co-operation: in general 7, 58, 136, 144, 196, 255; producer co-operatives 7, 141, 142–3, 147, 151, 247

Copleston, Edward 101, 104

countermovements 8, 30, 33, 134, 213, 235, 238, 239, 240, 245, 253, 258, 267; *see also* new social movements

Darwin, Charles 48, 108

Demant, V. A. 46n, 56, 94, 107, 192n, 232, 258n

democracy, liberal 3, 10, 11, 12, 14, 16, 19, 59, 67, 69, 70, 72, 74, 87, 110, 151, 197, 209, 220, 236, 247, 249, 255, 271, 273, 275; political 6, 9, 19, 64, 79, 88, 121, 123, 133, 136, 139, 140, 143, 161, 169, 226, 265; social 64, 117, 118, 256; and the market 71–4, 96; extension of 247–50; industrial and economic 96, 119, 122–3, 140, 161, 254, 255; democratic capitalism 87, 88, 198, 283; democratic socialism 12, 118, 119, 123, 161, 167, 170, 177, 248, 256, 257

dependency theory 32, 123, 124, 129, 147

direct theology 111, 128, 173, 176, 188, 196–7, 199

Donaldson, Peter 2n, 57, 61, 62, 75n, 76nn, 229n, 259nn

Dorrien, Gary 26n, 119, 123, 152nn, 153nn, 190n, 248, 254, 259n, 260n, 261n, 281n, 282nn

Duchrow, Ulrich vii, 15, 32, 37, 39, 45, 82, 92, 119, 124–34, 135, 139, 148, 149, 150, 151,

153nn, 154n, 172, 177, 213, 263, 270

economic conservationism 81, 133, 247

economic growth 31, 32, 41, 44, 71, 93, 97, 131, 162, 182, 199, 210, 212, 216, 245

Economic Justice For All 32, 82, 89, 127, 148, 149, 157, 161, 162, 248

economics: definition 36, 52, 54, 108, 222; as scarcity 36, 48, 49, 50–2, 56, 58, 61, 103, 108, 162, 168, 176, 178, 197, 208, 226; as equilibrium 42, 43, 44, 54, 93; classical 42–4, 69, 107, 131, 183, 206, 222, 266, 270; neoclassical 43, 222, normative and positive 49–50, 101, 104, 105, 108, 206–7; as resources 51, 54, 59, 60, 66, 208, 229n, 248; as efficiency 58, 93, 96, 213, 217; as virtue 220, 238, 244, 245, 250; as household 36, 37, 38, 40, 45, 52, 69, 131, 223, 224

economy, command 11, 27, 28, 30, 33–5, 48, 50, 53, 57, 65, 66, 72, 73, 85, 87, 93, 133, 171, 176–7, 197, 199, 208, 233, 248, 254, 257, 262, 266

economy, market: definition 29, 64, 74; international 5, 28, 30–3, 35, 73, 82, 193, 199, 208, 263, 265; history 28, 35–46; defects 62–3, 71, 208–11, 234–5; ambiguously positive case for 212–13; as least harmful 225–8; participation in 249–50

economy, mixed 74, 163, 171, 177, 186, 187, 199, 257

Edwards, David 14, 25n, 26n, 201n, 256, 259n, 260n, 280n

Eliot, T. S. 94, 114n, 274

Engels, Frederick 8, 9, 12, 25n

Enlightenment 89, 94, 97, 194

environment 194, 195, 197, 204, 210, 214, 225, 233, 235, 236, 237, 238, 244–7, 251, 252, 258, 263
eschatology 6, 7, 175, 183, 237
European Community 14, 30, 64, 71, 209, 225, 248, 253, 256, 267
externalities 210, 211, 222, 223, 246

fitting acts 18, 26n, 278
'Four Little Dragons' 32, 73
Friedman, Milton 27, 73, 86, 87, 93, 158, 194, 209, 267

Galbraith, John K. 15, 26n, 43, 44, 47nn, 133, 172, 195, 230nn, 260n, 261n, 267–8, 280n, 281n
George, Henry (Single Tax) 146–7, 151, 180
Gladden, Washington 157
Godwin, William 102–3
Gore, Charles 5, 124, 136, 149, 154n, 157, 175, 179, 181, 184, 185
Griffiths, Brian viii, 15, 26n, 27, 36, 67, 69, 82, 85, 86, 90–9, 109, 110, 111, 112n, 113nn, 114nn, 115, 116, 120, 164, 195, 229n, 270
Guild of St Matthew 146, 180
guild socialism 140, 147, 151, 180, 247
Gutiérrez, Gustavo 32

Habermas, Jürgen 11, 238, 259n, 267
Harris, Lord vii, 27, 62, 70, 77n, 86, 87
Hauerwas, Stanley 20, 149
Havel, Vaclav 4, 10, 12, 27, 255
Hay, Donald viii, 22, 25n, 26n, 29, 33, 46n, 62, 75nn, 76nn, 77n, 83, 99, 111, 113n, 114nn, 152n, 229n, 241, 259nn, 285n

Hayek, Friedrich von 27, 62, 76n, 86, 87, 93, 158, 194, 209, 267, 270
Headlam, Stewart 141, 146–7, 151
Hesiod 36, 51, 58
Hinkelammert, Franz 124, 125, 153n
Hirsch, Fred 211, 229n
Hooker, Richard 276

impurity principle 64
individual 69, 93, 96, 97, 142, 162, 177, 183, 215, 216, 234; as value 220
Institute for Religion and Democracy 86, 112n, 129, 149
Institute of Economic Affairs vii, 86
interaction: of market and challenges 200, 208, 226, 234, 235, 237, 240–1, 252, 256, 258, ch. 9 passim; as framework and dynamic 264–71; as way of life 271–2; as Church 273–6; as theology 22–3, 175, 188, 195, 207, 214, 216, 218, 219, 221, 224, 228, 237, 265, 268–71, 276–80
intermediate associations 69, 86, 88, 95, 96, 247, 250
international order 250–3, 263
investment 34, 38, 51, 52, 55, 56, 60, 248, 251, 253, 254

Jenkins, David viii, 46, 95
Jevons, William 43

kairos 18, 26n, 32
Keynes, John M. 37, 42, 44, 50, 69, 90, 160, 195, 224, 266
Kingsley, Charles 5, 6, 9, 25n, 142, 155n
Kossuth, Lajos 3

laissez-faire 7, 36, 42, 63, 64, 74, 100, 104, 107, 110, 139, 141, 156, 158, 167, 176, 180,

182, 185, 186, 196, 198, 199, 206, 222

Lange, Oskar 254

Leech, Kenneth 112n, 118, 119, 122, 123, 152n

Lessius, Leonard 39, 40

liberal response: in general 20, 80, 100, ch. 6 *passim*, 217, 218, 225, 230n, 237, 265, 271, 278, 279, 283; characteristics 158–63; history 172–86; strengths and limitations 198–200; as Church 157–8, 163, 173–4, 181, 186–8, 198; as theology 163, 166–8, 188–9

liberation theology 16, 30, 32, 33, 66, 82, 92, 117, 118, 119, 121, 122, 123, 128, 146, 147, 150, 151, 157, 161, 227, 279

libertarianism 27, 63, 66, 67, 86, 94, 96, 158, 170, 194, 209, 214, 226, 228, 255, 267, 280n

Ludlow, John 6, 7, 145–6

Luther, Martin 40, 128, 129, 132, 148, 149

Lux Mundi 178–80, 183, 184

macroeconomics 44, 64, 70, 160, 209, 223

marginal utility 41, 43, 75n

Major, John 64, 85

Malthus, Thomas Robert 42, 99, 100, 101, 102–3, 104, 107, 108, 140

markets: factor 55, 56; capital 55; commodities 55, 56; labour 55

Marshall, Alfred 36, 43, 69, 182

Maurice, Frederick D. 1, 4, 6, 7, 9, 15, 17, 25n, 26n, 45, 47n, 48, 74n, 105, 122, 124, 135, 141–4, 145, 146, 148, 149, 155nn, 157, 174, 177, 179, 181, 183, 184, 190n, 197, 200, 206, 215, 247, 264, 277, 280n

Marx, Karl 8, 9, 12, 31, 35, 42, 43, 44, 60, 100, 131, 132, 197, 258, 270

mechanism: market 28, 48,

60–1, 63, 68, 81, 87, 118, 119, 121, 122, 131, 156, 162, 178, 186, 187, 189, 196, 199, 208, 215–18, 237, 254, 257, 265, 278; price 52–7, 59, 61, 66, 67, 71, 73, 93, 131, 162, 171, 194, 216, 245, 263

Medellin Conference 32, 148

Meeks, M. Douglas 23, 37, 45, 63, 75nn, 76nn, 79, 112n, 113n, 153n, 223, 230nn, 231n, 259n, 260nn

mercantilism 39, 40, 41, 66, 69, 72

microeconomics 38, 44, 223

middle axioms 176, 198

Mill, John S. 17, 144, 155n

Ministry of International Trade and Industry 32, 71

misplaced concreteness 43, 210, 223, 266

Moltmann, Jürgen 7, 15, 119, 123, 270, 274

multinationals 33, 90, 98, 123, 149, 164, 168, 216, 236, 248, 252–3

Munby, Denys L. 21, 26n, 29, 46n, 61, 75nn, 76nn, 77nn, 81, 83, 84n, 152n, 160, 162, 171, 189n, 190n, 207, 217, 228nn, 229nn, 230n, 232, 237, 258n, 259nn, 260nn, 280n, 281nn, 282nn

neo-Calvinism 92, 113n

New International Economic Order 33, 98, 251–2

New Right 27, 28, 85, 163, 176, 177, 188, 192n, 230n

new social movements 238–40

Newman, John H. 206, 277

Niebuhr, Reinhold 5, 67, 76n, 77n, 124, 157, 161, 162, 166, 178, 189n, 200, 212, 217, 220, 226, 227, 230n, 231n, 248, 250, 264, 268, 276, 277, 279–80, 282n

Niebuhr, Richard 26n, 278

economic socialism 235,
253–8, 275
Spencer, Herbert 62
Stackhouse, Max 80, 84n, 281n
state: in general 35, 67, 88–9, 96,
146, 175, 184, 185, 246, 263;
corporate 64, 95, 161, 163,
185, 187, 199; modern 70–1,
72, 74, 96, 121, 140, 143,
160–1, 170, 184, 209, 228
Storkey, Alan 29, 113n, 230n,
281n
subsidiarity 88
Sumner, John Bird 101, 103–4,
107
Sweden 64, 178, 199, 257

Tawney, R. H. 5, 7, 25n, 30, 31,
35, 36, 40, 46n, 76n, 81, 83,
100, 108, 115n, 117, 119, 120,
122, 123, 134, 135–41, 147,
150, 152n, 154nn, 175, 184,
191n, 192n, 226, 232, 264,
277, 282n
Temple, William 7, 55, 88, 134,
135, 136, 140, 157, 161, 164,
174, 179, 184–6, 193, 201n,
218, 230n, 258n, 264, 268,
270, 280n
Thatcher, Margaret 12, 13, 28,
31, 32, 64, 85, 86, 90, 107,
132, 163, 181, 273, 283
Tillich, Paul 18, 117, 119, 123,
152n, 165, 278
trade unions 24, 53, 87, 95, 134,
135, 136, 226

unemployment 44, 68, 94, 97,
171, 177, 209, 223, 255
Unwin, George 277, 282n
usury 37, 38, 39, 45, 60, 61, 96,
126, 131, 217, 224

utilitarianism 43, 105, 143

value: exchange 37, 39, 40, 43,
131, 132; use 37, 38, 39, 40,
60, 224
values: in market 68–9, 89, 93,
94, 97, 102, 107, 110, 144,
169, 187, 194, 197, 206, 211,
212, 263, 265; as civic virtue
218–21
von Hügel, Baron Friedrich 278-9

wages 37, 41, 43, 92
Waterman, Alan viii, 29, 100–1,
114–16nn, 189n,
190n, 229n
Webb, Beatrice 52, 75n, 142,
155nn
Weber, Max 232, 258n
Westcott, Brooke Foss 157, 179,
182–3, 185, 192n, 256
Whateley, Richard 101, 102,
104–6, 116n
Whitehead, A. N. 43
Wickham, Edward R. 18, 26n
Wogaman, J. P. 15, 46n, 70,
81, 82, 84nn, 86, 112nn,
113n, 152n, 153n, 157, 158,
159, 161, 162, 164–72, 177,
186, 187, 189nn, 190nn,
191nn, 198, 201n, 230n, 247,
260nn, 281n
Wordsworth, William 204
Working Men's College 7
World Council of Churches 13,
32, 37, 82, 119, 125, 130,
153n, 157, 167, 173, 174, 185,
186, 188, 213, 279

Yoder, John 226